How To Build Your Own PC

Save A Buck And Learn A Lot

Book cover design, artwork, and Ducker drawings by Jamon Walker of Mythic Design Studio (mythicstudio.com).

Printed in the United States of America

Library of Congress Control Number: 2004103360
ISBN 09671624-7-5

HCM Publishing
P.O. Box 18093
West Saint Paul, MN 55118

Table of Contents

All You Usually Need to Build Your Own PC is a Phillips Screwdriver

Purchasing Components

Assembling a PC is rather easy, but how do you choose which components to purchase and assemble? In particular, how do you decide upon a CPU and a mainboard? This advice will help you select components not just now, but far into the future.

Be Cheap

Most builders won't need and won't want to purchase the most expensive mainboards and CPUs currently available. If I were to give the first-time builder just one piece of advice, it would be to avoid the most expensive top-of-the-line components, such as the fastest CPU, the biggest hard drive, the most expensive video card, and the RAM type that is currently newest and still being innovated.

You pay dearly for the most current components. Real world performance is usually just as good if you purchase slightly less than the fastest or newest components. And, you'll save a bundle of money.

In choosing your mainboard, price and CPU type will probably be the key factors. Never purchase the fastest CPU because the prices rise rapidly with

CPU speed. Backing off just a bit from the fastest processor in a CPU family will save you considerable money. And, in a few short months, you'll probably be able to buy a much faster processor even more inexpensively!

To put the above into perspective, let's compare prices for Pentium 4 CPUs from the same source (www.insightcomponents.com). We see the following options:

3.2 GHz Intel Pentium 4 Socket 478 Processor @ 800 MHz FSB $758.99
2.4 GHz Intel Pentium 4 Socket 478 Processor @ 800 MHz FSB $221.99
1.8 GHz Intel Pentium 4 Socket 478 Processor @ 800 MHz FSB $161.99

and for the very budget conscious:

2.2 GHz Intel Celeron Socket 478 Processor @ 400 MHz FSB $88.99

For a modest 33% increase in CPU speed in going from a 2.4 GHz CPU to a 3.2 GHz CPU, you pay almost three and a half times more money! **The average builder could select the slightly slower CPU and pay for all the other PC components from the cost difference of $537!** And, for many purposes, selecting the lower-end Celeron for under $90 is even a better option.

If you really need a very powerful PC at a budget price, consider a two-processor mainboard. Two 2.4 GHz processors tag-teaming a 3.2 GHz processor will beat it. The mainboard and the operating system will both need to support two processors working together. For example, Windows XP Professional supports two processors, while Windows XP Home Edition doesn't. Linux will support dual processors. Most builders will only need one CPU on their mainboard.

In five years, the speeds and types of the CPUs will be completely different. But, the advice of not selecting the fastest CPU currently available is timeless.

If you know what kind of CPU you want, then you can examine mainboards that support that CPU. Usually, builders will select the type of CPU they desire and then find a mainboard to support it. Be sure that the mainboard also supports the CPU speed of your chip. For example, a board that supports a 2.4 GHz processor might not support a 3.2 GHz processor from the same family.

In practical terms, a PC you build for $600 might be just as useful to you as one that costs $1,000 or even $2,000 to build. And, an older system might work fine for you.

For example, I have many systems, but the one I'm writing this book on right now is a 200 MHz Pentium. (You can probably find such a PC on eBay.com for $100 or less.) Yet, if I type as fast as I possibly can, the computer easily keeps up! For writing using a word processor, I don't really need a faster system.

I have a very old 286 PC, which runs at about 20 MHz. I almost never use it, of course. But, occasionally, I'll be nostalgic and turn it on. It can only run DOS. (The earliest versions of Windows—Windows 3.x—are just too bloated for it.) Yet, the Chessmaster program on that PC can kick my butt just as easily as a much faster system. (Of course, that system can't browse the web or do things that are considered vital today. You won't be editing your home movies on it!)

The Chessmaster program brings up a good point about PC use in general. In particular, most CPU time is usually spent waiting for the slowest link—the human link—to do something. You make a move; the PC makes a move; and you need to stop and think. The PC just sits there waiting for you. It's all ready to move. We humans just aren't much of a challenge to it!

And, if you've only filled up 20 GB of drive space after a year of PC use, what's the big deal about having 30 GB remaining unused or 190 GB remaining unused? At the end of the year, if you desire, you'll be able to upgrade to a faster, bigger hard drive that will probably be cheaper than what you would have been able to purchase a year ago.

Spend the extra money somewhere where it will have more impact on your life. See a few more movies. Get a bigger TV. Save the money and invest it for the future. Whatever. Or, if you must put the money into your computer hunt around for a fairly-priced DVD burner or something else that will add value to your system.

Finally, the newest components are still being tested. A little increase in performance usually isn't worth the likelihood of more crashes and incompatibility problems. For example, many companies that have huge technology budgets measured in the millions of dollars won't run the most current operating system on their machines. They'd rather stick with what's worked in the past and what has been shown to be reliable. When the newer system is more debugged, then they'll adopt it. It's the software companies that want you to upgrade so they can earn more money.

As a rule, I probably wouldn't build a new PC or upgrade an older one unless I'm getting at least a factor of three or four more in performance at a reasonable cost. So, for example, a 600 MHz system wouldn't be changed until *reasonably-priced* systems could be made or purchased that ran at 1.8 GHz to 2.4 GHz or faster. A 2 GHz system wouldn't be replaced until a reasonably-priced system could be purchased that runs at 6 GHz or higher. Remember, the longer you can put off upgrading, the more you'll get for your money when you finally do upgrade!

I always shake my head when someone upgrades from a 1.7 GHz system to a 2 GHz system. Why do it? (The honest truth is they just love toying around with new PCs!)

The only exception is when software you want to run demands a better system. Maybe, you want to play a video-intensive shoot-em-up game, and your system just won't cut it. Or, maybe, you decide you want to study database development and you install Oracle 9i on your computer, but find you need a faster PC. Possibly, you decide to produce music videos on your PC, and you find that the best video editing software runs much better on a faster system. But, unless the software you desire to run demands a faster, better system, you'll probably do well to postpone an upgrade or building a new system until you can get a factor of three in better overall performance.

For editing the photos in this book, Adobe Photoshop was used on the 2000+ Athlon we built. The ultimate level of power your computer needs is determined by what you want to do.

Selecting Your CPU

It's usually good to select your CPU first. First, decide what "family" of CPU you want. In other words, decide if you want a Pentium or an AMD chip. (It usually doesn't matter which you choose! They're both fine CPUs.) If you really want to compare CPUs in detail, google.com is a great tool for finding information about CPUs. See what others have to say about the exact CPU you contemplate. For example, if you plan to run Linux, you might do a search of "Linux" and the CPU name. See if anyone has reviewed that particular combination.

In fact, google.com is a powerful tool for finding information about nearly anything. A family member had a car that kept stalling when it overheated. Garage after garage couldn't diagnose the problem properly. (Of course, some garages just want to keep you coming back and spending more money. Sometimes if you take a working car to a garage, it will come back not working!) I went to google.com, typed in the model of the car and tried various phrases such as "stalls overheats," "stalling at stops," etc.

In a few minutes, I learned that this was a common problem in that car model. The failure was due to the TCC solenoid which tends to stick when it overheats. I also learned that replacing the solenoid should cost about $200 and that diagnostic programs often fail to catch this problem. And, I learned that you can even disconnect the little sucker and the car will work fine, but it will have slightly lower gas mileage on the freeway. So, the next mechanic visit, I TOLD THEM what was wrong and the problem was corrected. And, yes, one website actually showed a do-it-yourself replacement of the part. Google.com is one of the consumer's best friends!

Now that you've selected a CPU family, purchase slightly less than the fastest chip in the family. Sure, you can get an AMD Athlon 2800+, but an Athlon 2000+ is far less expensive.

Selecting A Mainboard

Once you've chosen a CPU, it's time to select a mainboard. With experience, you might come to like or dislike certain mainboard manufacturers. Maybe you love Abit, but you hate Asus. Or, maybe, it's just the opposite. (I like both Abit and Asus boards). That's fine. Go with a name brand you like.

However, when evaluating mainboards, I think it's important to read some online reviews of the board and not rely totally upon past experience with the manufacturer. It's easy to over-rate the value of experience. For example, maybe you had a bad experience with an Asus mainboard. That doesn't mean that all Asus boards are bad. You might have just received one bad board. And, that could be the fault of someone other than Asus, as we discuss later.

When selecting a mainboard, examine how many PCI expansion slots the board has. See how much RAM the board supports. Does the board have the built-in features you want? For example, if you're running Linux, you might want as few built-in features as possible to prevent conflicts and unrecognized hardware. You might rather have PCI cards for sound, networking, and the like. Newer versions of Linux seem better at recognizing various on-board capabilities.

You might also find that you prefer certain vendors. For example, maybe, you've purchased components from www.insightcomponents.com and were happy with them in the past, so you go to their website and search for boards that support the CPU you've chosen. Shopping online will give you a good chance to compare mainboards and their prices. Select a mainboard that looks good to you and is in the price range you desire.

You can go to google.com and search for that particular mainboard to see what others have written about it. Usually, you'll read that it's a pretty good mainboard. If you read something that turns you off, you can select another board and try again.

You could also read about the chipset of the board. The chipset are the chips on the mainboard that support the CPU. The ultimate capabilities of the board are limited by the chipset of the board. For a first-time builder, I wouldn't worry too much about the chipset the board uses. If you want to learn more about a particular chipset, type the chipset name into google.com and see what's written about it. But, that's probably a step you don't really need to do.

Some more advanced builders might say, "How can you ignore the chipset? The chipset's the most important part of the mainboard! You can't ignore the chipset!" (Kind of like the nerdy kid in the movie *October Sky*). A first-time builder doesn't need to understand this level of detail. If the board has good reviews, supports the features you need or want, and is in your price range, you've made a good selection!

The point is that there are many technical details about the parts that you assemble that you really don't need to fully understand to successfully build a PC. How much you choose to learn about the inner workings of mainboards is entirely up to you. At the basic level, this book shows you all you really need.

For those who want to learn more about the inner workings of computers, you might want to take a college class that covers the topic. I also recommend *Upgrading and Repairing PCs* by Scott Mueller. You can learn about things like bus speeds and how data is actually transferred about on the board. Or, how RAM actually works. Maybe, someday, you'll decide to become a computer designer or an electrical engineer. But, that's a much higher level of knowledge than is covered here. And, if your goal is only to build a reliable and cost-effective system, you don't need a lot of extra knowledge.

One word you'll want to know is "bottleneck." The phrase "bottleneck" means the place where the speed of getting something done is slowed up. The expression comes from the neck of a glass bottle which limits how fast liquid can be poured out of the bottle.

For example, maybe you have a really fast CPU and something just isn't working as fast as you feel it should. What's slowing up the works? It's the bottleneck.

Finding the bottleneck isn't always easy. Maybe, it's the bus speed on the mainboard. (Bus speed is how fast data is transferred around on the mainboad, from the mainboard to RAM, etc. Different buses have different bus speeds. For example, there is a certain rate at which data can be transferred to and from a PCI card.) Maybe, you don't have enough RAM. Maybe, it's the speed and buffer of the hard drive.

For example, in backing up data to a CD, you might see that a slower CD-RW takes quite a bit of time. The CD-RW write speed might be the bottleneck. Getting a much faster mainboard won't help. You'd just need a faster CD-RW drive.

For browsing on the Internet, the bottleneck is usually the speed of your Internet connection. Going from a dial-up phone connection to a DSL or cable modem connection will speed up your Internet surfing far more than a faster CPU. In fact, the CPU speed will have very little effect.

So, before you jump to upgrade a mainboard, ask if the thing that's really slowing down your work (or fun!) might be some other bottleneck.

If you want to compare the speed of your system to other systems, consider the free tool SiSoft Sandra, available from download.com.

Video Cards And Other Parts

Now that you've seen how to select a CPU and mainboard, you can use a similar approach to select all of your other components, such as a video card and PCI sound card.

Start by seeing what your favorite vendors have in a price range you like. (I like the price range of low!). Then, just go ahead and buy the component, or if it's more important to you, see if you can find a review of the component on google.com.

Low cost parts like a floppy drive can just be purchased. Don't worry about which brand is better.

Some builders argue that you should avoid the ultra-cheap parts, because they're more likely to fail because they're often built with cheaper components. While this has some truth, if you purchase a 52x CD-RW for $20 and it lasts two years, that seems a pretty good deal. Sure, you could have purchased a $60 CD-RW that lasts ten years. But, so what? By then you'll have purchased a new system anyway! And, just because a component is more expensive doesn't mean it will last longer.

What happens if you wish to upgrade or repair a slightly older system? Consider the CD-RW drive. On my older 200 MHz Pentium, the Hewlett Packard CD-Writer recently failed. (Searching online I found many complained about failures of similarly-aged HP CD-RWs.)

Going online and to the store and reading the system requirements for newer CD-RW drives tells us that they all required 300 GHz systems or faster. So the solution would seem be to look for a component that would work in the older system. Many CD-RWs were on eBay.com, but I didn't see any that I felt were reasonably-priced. When purchasing smaller components on eBay.com, don't overlook the cost of the shipping.

A trip to a computer show might turn up some CD-RWs. But, I didn't really want to spend the time noodling around for parts either. I could also experiment with newer CD-RWs operating at slower write speeds or using older versions of the software that the CD-RWs came with. But, I didn't want to monkey around with that either, because I didn't want to spend the time.

Eventually, I just decided I'd backup that system over a home network using another PC I had with a fast CD-RW!

The lesson is that as you upgrade older systems, at a certain point, you might just decide that it no longer makes sense to upgrade the system. It's easier and more effective to just get a new system. Or, you might find other solutions, such as not using the CD-RW and backing up the system over a network. Just choose whichever upgrade, replacement, or workaround option seems best for you and you'll make the right choice!

Hint: Don't worry about making a wrong choice when selecting components. You'll do a great job! There seldom is a "wrong" choice.

Returning Faulty Parts And ESD

Static electricity (also called ESD, electrostatic discharge) is very harmful to mainboards and other sensitive computer parts. And, the shock from an electrostatic spark might wound a component. The component might seem to work initially, but as the system heats up, or maybe in a few weeks or even months, the component seems flaky or unreliable.

This might not mean that the component model is bad or that this brand is bad. It might mean that this particular part was mishandled by some other builder who unintentionally zapped the part. This is one reason I wouldn't purchase a mainboard that's on display and which other people are touching!

If your mainboard shows any signs of not being new (and you purchased it as new), don't hesitate to return it. For example, damaged pins or anything of that sort might indicate an inexperienced builder attempted to build a PC, wasn't happy, and returned the part. Missing parts or a missing manual is also a tip off that the board may have been sold before.

If the part has been wounded by ESD, you don't want to be the one who gets it! Also, I would avoid purchasing used mainboards and used RAM. A used PC is better because there's less chance it's been opened and the mainboard harmed by ESD. But, how do you know that a used mainboard or RAM hasn't already been critically wounded by ESD? You don't!

Be sure to get all your parts at about the same time and to build your PC as soon as you have your parts. Test your system thoroughly the first 30 days after you build it. Try to use the new system a lot to see if any flaky behavior develops. Most parts can be returned within 30 days of purchase, if necessary.

It's important to know that just because a part isn't Dead On Arrival (DOA) doesn't mean it hasn't been damaged by ESD. The part could work for two weeks and then fail. This is why you must test a new system intensively for the first few weeks.

One computer repair instructor told me that a new PC repairman was hired to update some systems at their college. The new repairman installed the cards and tested the systems and the systems worked. But, he mishandled the parts, and the parts received small electrostatic shocks wounding them. The damage wasn't immediately deadly, but it would greatly increase the chance the part would fail in the future.

Two weeks later, the components failed. And, the repairman was called back. The repairman said these parts seemed to be flaky and unreliable. He replaced the parts and tested the systems again. The systems worked.

A few weeks later, the systems failed again! This time, the experienced computer repair instructor was on hand to examine the repairs and immediately saw that no precautions were taken to protect the sensitive cards from ESD. The parts were carelessly handled. The instructor predicted that the parts would similarly fail in the next few weeks, and he was correct. Improper handling of sensitive computer parts destroys millions, if not billions, of dollars of computer parts annually.

This is more of a problem for parts that could easily have been used before, such as mainboards which usually come in boxes that aren't shrink wrapped, than it is for parts that are packaged for retail sale and which are shrink wrapped.

For example, it's impossible to purchase a returned retail box version of the AMD Athlon CPU. Those plastic boxes aren't going back together after being opened! So, you know your CPU hasn't been improperly handled. That's much better than purchasing a CPU that doesn't come in a sealed box. (It actually takes some builders more time to figure out how to open the AMD plastic CPU box than it does to install the CPU!)

Some builders have also been ripped off by companies who "overclock" CPU chips and pass them off as faster chips than they are rated. Purchasing your CPU as a sealed retail box version protects you here also.

You probably won't have any trouble returning faulty parts to a reputable mail-order vendor, but if you run into any hassles, it might be useful to know that the reason most vendors offer 30-day money back guarantees isn't the goodness of their hearts. The 30-day return period is mandated by the Federal Trade Commission's 30-day mail-order rule, which says that consumers have the right to return mail-order products they aren't happy with.

Mail-In Rebates: Good Deal Or Rip Off?

Many reliable companies, such as BestBuy.com, offer mail-in rebates for products. I've purchased many products with mail-in rebates and have usually received the rebate. However, I feel that you should effectively discount the value of a mail-in rebate by about half.

In other words, if a product is offered for $100 with a $60 mail-in rebate, don't assume the final cost to you is $40. If you get your rebate, that's true. But, if they won't honor your rebate, your real cost is the full $100. For deciding if you should purchase the item, give the rebate about half its value—$30 here. If you're willing to pay $70 for the item, go ahead and make the purchase. But, don't weigh the rebate as if it's as good as money in the bank!

For the PC built in this book, one rebate (ViewSonic monitor $40 rebate) was sent in and not received. Even though the paperwork was carefully prepared, the rebate fulfillment company claimed no receipt was included. A follow-up letter was sent with a copy of the receipt included and the rebate was then received.

The company retailing the product, Best Buy, is reliable, and I've received many rebates for products purchased through them. (BestBuy.com is one of my favorite places to purchase hard drives, RAM, DVD drives, and other components.) The retailer benefits if the rebate encourages the customer to purchase a product he or she otherwise wouldn't have.

However, the rebate processing is sometimes done by a third party, and the actual refund is issued by the product's manufacturer. This can lead to nastiness in getting your rebate.

For example, wouldn't it be desirable for a manufacturer not to have to pay a rebate? That puts more money in their pocket! So, a less-than-ethical third party rebate fulfillment company might have a motivation to deny as many rebates as possible. For example, they could claim that you didn't include a copy of your receipt, even if you did. This makes it look like they're saving the manufacturer money. Most consumers don't aggressively follow up to protect their rights and some rebate companies prey on this.

Because of negative possibilities like this, I only give mail-in rebates half their value when deciding to make a purchase.

Another point to keep in mind is that some of the rebate fulfillment companies are diversified telemarketing companies. Unless mandatory, don't enter your e-mail address or you might wind up getting spam. Because of this, I'm tending to avoid smaller mail-in rebates. Or create a yahoo.com e-mail account and use that for rebate purposes, so you don't get your primary e-mail account spammed.

Fill in your rebate form carefully and include all requested documentation of your purchase. If you don't, your rebate will certainly be rejected. It's also important to keep copies of your rebate form and your receipt. If a rebate isn't received within the time period expected, you should contact the retailer or the rebate center and ask what the problem is. If worst comes to worst, threaten to contact the Federal Trade Commission. Remember, it's your money they're trying to keep!

I hope this chapter hasn't scared you about buying computer parts. Most of the time, everything will go smoothly. Your parts will be great and will work fine. And, if they don't, the seller will gladly accept the return and get you a working part.

How To Build Your Own PC: Save A Buck And Learn A Lot!

Component Overview

This book will teach you how to build your own PC. Building a PC is simple. If you can plug a power cord into a wall socket and you can turn a screwdriver, you have all the skills you need to build your own PC. If you can turn the screwdriver the right way half of the time, you can become a certified PC repair technician.

Once you've built your first PC, building others will be easy for you. Plus, you'll have all the skills and experience necessary to install any future upgrades you may wish to make to your system.

For example, if you later decide to add a second hard drive to your computer or you decide to add a PCI Firewire card to capture and edit camcorder video, you'll know what to do. Learning to build your own PC will give you maximum future flexibility in upgrading and repairing your PC. Plus, you'll be able to brag to your friends and family about building your own computer. They'll probably ask you to help them with their computer upgrades!

Building your own PC involves selecting and buying a few key components (Figure 2.1) and then connecting them together with ribbon cables (Figure 2.2) and other standard connectors that are usually provided with the

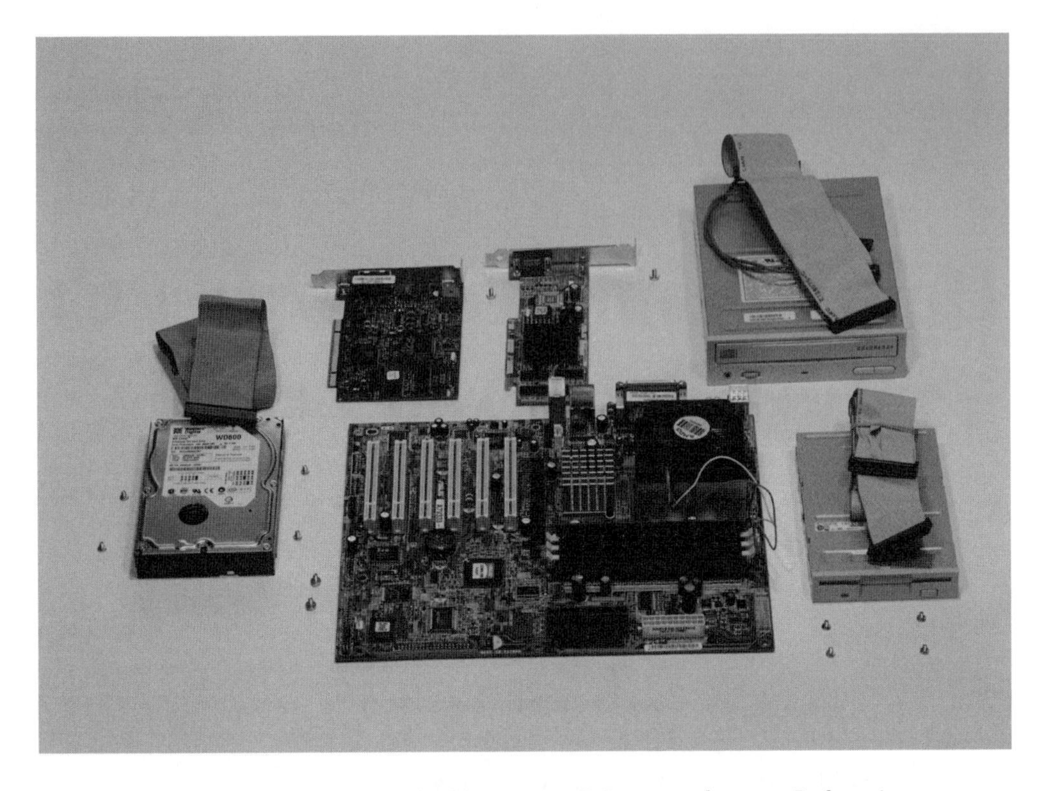

Figure 2.1. All the parts you need to build your own PC, except the case. In front is a mainboard with RAM, CPU, and heatsink installed. Above the mainboard are an AGP video card and a PCI modem card. To the left is the hard drive with its ribbon cable. To the right is the CD-RW drive and floppy drive.

components. For example, most power connectors come permanently attached to the power supply which itself usually comes with your computer case.

Some components, such as PCI expansion cards and the mainboard, will also require using a Phillips screwdriver to secure them properly. A Phillips screwdriver is probably the only tool you'll need. A small flat-nosed screwdriver is sometimes useful for prying out PCI expansion slot covers or the case's I/O shield. If you have short fingernails and you need to change jumpers, a needlenose pliers is sometimes handy.

After assembling your computer, you'll need to install an operating system, which is really just a software procedure. It's common to talk about "installing" software, even though it only involves inserting CDs into the CD drive as required.

Figure 2.2. Ribbon cables. On the left is a hard drive ribbon cable. On the right is a floppy drive ribbon cable. Notice the twist in the floppy cable. The end with the twist plugs into the floppy drive. The other end plugs into the mainboard.

Your PC will be fully assembled before we install software. We'll take you through installing an operating system step-by-step in detail in another chapter.

You may also want to examine and/or modify your system's BIOS, which we'll discuss later. Many times, you'll be able to get your PC up and running adequately without tinkering with the mainboard's BIOS at all. But, tweaking the BIOS may enhance your system's performance. Make changes to BIOS very carefully. For example, if you update your mainboard's BIOS with Flash BIOS and your computer hangs, it's possible your PC will no longer boot at all.

We'll also discuss partitioning and formatting a hard drive. But, first, we need to get our parts together.

Figure 2.3. A new PC case.

The key components you'll need to purchase are:

- Case and Power Supply
- Mainboard
- CPU With Heatsink and Fan
- RAM (Memory Chip)
- Video Card
- Hard Drive
- CD-RW and/or DVD Drive
- Other Removable Media Drives (optional)
- Sound Card (If your mainboard doesn't have onboard sound)
- Modem
- Network Interface Card (NIC) and Other PCI Cards (optional)
- Operating System
- Monitor
- Keyboard and Mouse

The above components are all you need. Most of the physical components connect together easily with standardized connections. Figure 2.1 shows all the parts you need.

Case And Power Supply

1) Case and Power Supply. (Figure 2.3). The computer case holds all the internal parts of your PC. Many case variations are available including tower cases, mid-tower cases, and desktop models. The case pictured is an Enlight mid-tower ATX case that comes with an AMD Athlon approved 360 watt power supply.

Most do-it-yourselfers choose tower or mid-tower cases. Most builders also prefer the ATX form factor. Smaller cases are said to have a smaller footprint and they save space. However, larger cases offer more room for expansion options. And, working inside a larger case is somewhat easier.

I'd recommend choosing a quality mid-tower or full-tower ATX case for your first PC build. These cases are designed to be paired with any ATX mainboard.

Most cases will cost between $40 and $100. Unless mainboard manufacturers change the basic ATX case style in the future, your case should last a long time and serve you through several years of mainboard upgrades. Choosing a quality case is a good investment.

Many quality PC manufacturers, such as Gateway and Dell, use proprietary mainboards and case designs that have unique drilling patterns that connect the mainboard to the case. This means that many cases from big-name PC manufacturers are not as easily upgraded.

For example, if you have a Dell computer case, you won't be able to replace an older mainboard with a newer mainboard from another manufacturer. You'll need to upgrade with Dell boards only. From a consumer's standpoint, this is somewhat undesirable because it means you can't upgrade by just adding a standard, but newer and better, ATX mainboard in the future. If you find a really great deal on a standard ATX mainboard, you can't just add it to your Dell case.

Figure 2.4. Inside of a new PC case. Here, the power supply sits at the top left of the case. Notice the many power connectors dangling from the power supply.

Building your own PC and using standard components will give you maximum upgrade potential. Choose the ATX form factor for your case.

With a standard ATX case, you'll have the fullest range of upgrade options to newer, more powerful mainboards. This standardization of components, which allows easy upgrades, is one big advantage of building your own PC rather than buying one.

Power supplies come with most cases today (Figure 2.4). The power supply has many power connectors to power the mainboard, hard drives, CD-RW drives, and other components.

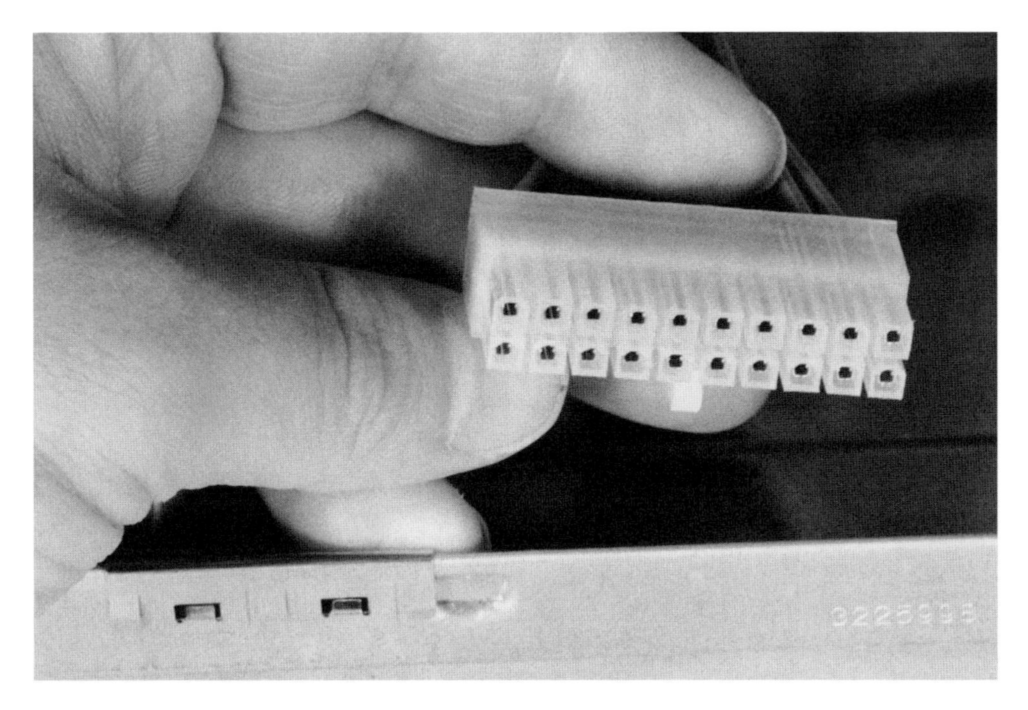

Figure 2.5. The ATX power connector. Most power connectors today are made so that they can only be plugged in one way. This connector provides power to the ATX mainboard.

Be sure that your case and power supply match the type of mainboard you want to install. This usually means purchasing an ATX style mainboard and case. Be sure your case supports a full ATX mainboard. I'd avoid micro-ATX and cases designed to hold only smaller boards.

Most mainboards today are ATX style. You can identify an ATX power supply and case by looking for an ATX power connection. See Figure 2.5. **Most important power connectors, such as the twenty-pin ATX power connection, are designed so that they can only be plugged in one way.** This prevents plugging the connector in the wrong way and causing damage to components by putting too high a voltage on a pin that isn't designed to take it.

Newer ATX power supplies also have a special four-pin power connector (Figure 2.6), which is used with Pentium 4 mainboards. If you're installing an AMD Athlon, you won't need this special four-pin connector. Just leave it disconnected.

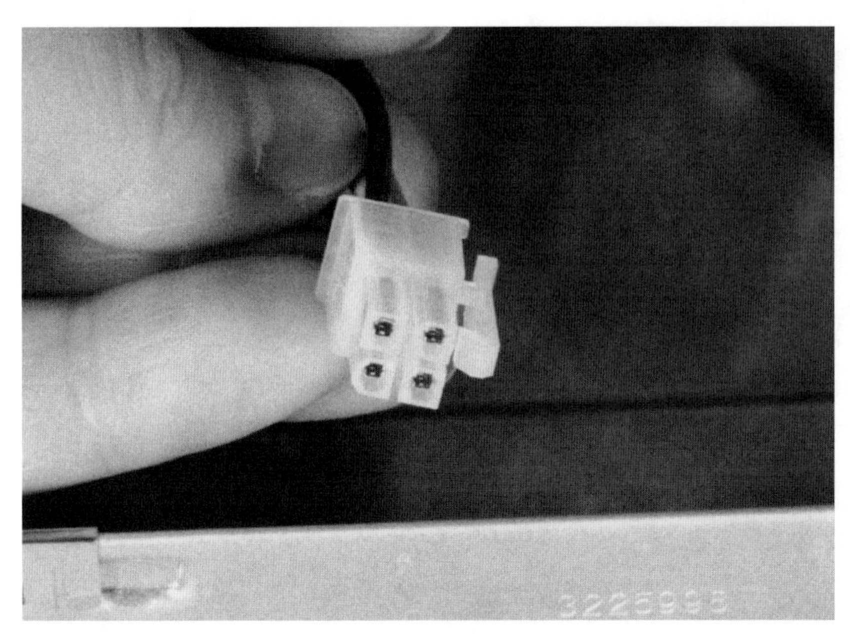

Figure 2.6. The special 4-pin Pentium 4 power header. If you're building an AMD system, just leave this power connector unconnected.

If you're building a Pentium 4 system, be sure your power supply has the necessary 4-pin power supply connector in addition to the standard ATX power supply connector. All newer cases will have it. When in doubt, ask if the ATX case is approved for the Pentium 4.

If your power supply ever needs replacement, you can keep the case and just purchase a new ATX power supply. Replacing the power supply only requires your trusty Phillips screwdriver.

As a general rule, most cases will have several extra power connectors which will remain unused when your system is built. Just tuck the unneeded power connectors out of the way when you close up your PC case. They don't all need to be connected to something. If you later add another hard drive or a DVD player, for example, you'll use one of the remaining power connectors to supply power to it.

If you run out of power connectors (unlikely), you can purchase Y Splitters which are small cables designed to give you more than one power connector from one existing power supply connection. It's just like purchasing a power strip that plugs into your wall outlet and provides six or eight new outlet sockets. Cyberguys.com is one source of different types of Y adapters.

Similarly, if you find some component needs a unique power connection that isn't provided for from your existing power supply connections, you can purchase a Y splitter or an adapter which will give you the specific connector you need. This is relatively rare as most modern power supplies offer a cornucopia of power connectors. There are also extension adapters which give power supply cables more length. You probably won't need these either, unless you install a new power supply in a large case.

Choose an adequate power supply. Today, that probably means at least 300 watts. Too large a power supply will make more noise than necessary and will consume more electricity.

If you're building your PC with an AMD Duron or Athlon CPU, be sure that your power supply is AMD Athlon approved. In particular, the AMD Athlon requires a more stable source of power than a Pentium CPU. If you're uncertain whether a particular case and its power supply is AMD Athlon approved, visit AMD.com.

Other connectors from the case don't supply power, but they connect the front panel of the computer case to the mainboard. These connectors are thin wires with little connectors on the ends that plug into pins on the mainboard (Figure 2.7).

For example, to turn the computer on and off, there is an on-off switch on the case. The small Power SW wire connects the power button on the case to the mainboard to let the mainboard know when you want the PC to turn on or off. This small two-pin connector may be plugged-in in either direction on the mainboard.

Basic switches can usually be installed in either direction, because they are designed to either open or close a circuit. So, the orientation of the two pins doesn't usually matter.

Figure 2.7. Thin-wire connectors connect the front of the PC case to the mainboard. Even though these connectors can be plugged in backward, don't fear, because doing so won't harm your system. Try to get them onto the right pins on the mainboard.

Most of these other small, thin-wire connectors are also ambidextrous. The thin-wire connectors typically include:

• Power Switch (P SW). This can be connected in either direction to the proper two pins on the mainboard. It turns the computer on and off.

• Reset Switch (Reset). This can be connected in either direction to the proper two pins on the mainboard. If Ctrl+Alt+Del doesn't work to reboot your hung-up PC, you can always use the reset switch to restart your computer. There should be a small reset button on the front of your case. Using the reset switch is more desirable than turning a PC on and off again rapidly. Always wait a couple of minutes after turning a PC completely off before turning it on again. This prevents a surge of current and charge from hitting components that may not have drained their existing charge yet.

• Power LED. LED stands for Light-Emitting Diode. These are the little blinky things on the front of your computer case. LEDs light up when a small current passes through them in the correct direction. The power LED goes on when the system is powered up. The small current to light the LED is provided by the mainboard.

• HD LED. This front case panel LED blinks when the hard drive is active. If this connector is installed in the wrong direction, your computer will work fine except your hard drive LED probably won't light up or it will remain on rather than blinking with activity. If you notice that it isn't working, just reorient the connector.

• Speaker connection. This connects the small case speaker to the mainboard.

Those front panel connectors that aren't ambidextrous (such as the hard drive LED, which lights up on the front panel to show activity on the hard drive) won't damage your system if they are hooked up backward. These thin-wire connectors to the mainboard aren't supplying power to the mainboard.

Examine your mainboard manual carefully to determine the proper pins to connect these thin-wire case panel connectors to. Also examine your mainboard carefully before installing it in the case, because you'll often have

Figure 2.8. Corner of the mainboard. The thin-wire connectors from the case will connect here. It's easy to plug them in wrong.

a better view of the pins when the mainboard is out of the case. Usually, a row of many pins will be provided on the mainboard (Figure 2.8). It's easy to plug the little fellers on the wrong pins if you don't pay attention to the mainboard manual.

The ATX power supply also typically provides a small current to the mainboard even when the computer is off. So you should always disconnect the power supply cord before upgrading your PC or working on its internals. Or, turn off your power strip or uninterruptible power supply (UPS) that your computer is attached to before working on it. The ATX power supply also usually provides a power switch at the back of the PC, labeled "O" for off and "1" for on. But, it's best if the power is off before reaching the PC power cord.

ATX mainboards often have an LED on the mainboard which will remain lighted all the time, even when the PC is turned off. This lets you know there is power to the mainboard. And, hopefully, reminds you to unplug the power cord before proceeding further! Inserting and removing parts on an ATX mainboard that has power can damage components.

Plugging your PC into the wall outlet or UPS will be the last step in building your PC. I recommend your purchase a UPS to protect your new PC from electrical surges. At today's prices, a UPS is a great purchase. If power fails, the UPS will give you time to shut down your system properly.

Do not plug in your power supply cord to an outlet until you have assembled your PC.

The older AT case style is outdated. Connections from the power supply differ between the ATX and AT style. Older AT cases will not work with a newer ATX mainboard. (You can buy adapters to convert AT power to ATX power. But, I'd recommend against this, because with your newer components, you'll probably want a bigger and more stable power supply anyway.)

Your case and mainboard will probably be based upon the ATX style. But, if you ever need to repair or upgrade an older AT style, it's very important to be sure that the two AT power connectors are connected with the black wires toward the middle of the two connectors. This is one of the few power connectors than can be assembled incorrectly causing damage. You don't need to worry about this with the ATX style cases. If you're working with new PCs, you'll probably never use the older AT style power connectors.

Figure 2.9. Standoffs inside the case hold the bottom of the mainboard above the case. Each standoff (whether plastic or metal) should line up with a hole in the mainboard.

If you disassemble an existing system, you might want to make yourself a drawing showing how things were connected, so you'll be able to reconnect them exactly the same way.

Many builders purchase a new notebook and they keep a diary of their build, recording the steps they take, the components used, and the settings. This helps knowing what was done to the PC and the components and how things were connected. For example, how is the jumper set on your hard drive?

One side of your case will contain an inner panel to which you'll attach the mainboard with standoffs and a couple of screws (Figure 2.9). The panel is predrilled and the drilling patterns for an ATX and an AT mainboard differ.

The standoffs and screws will come with the case. The drilling patterns for an ATX case are designed to match up with any ATX mainboard. That's the theory, anyway.

If you examine your mainboard, you'll notice holes (Figure 2.10). These holes are meant to line up with the standoffs in the case. The standoffs that don't

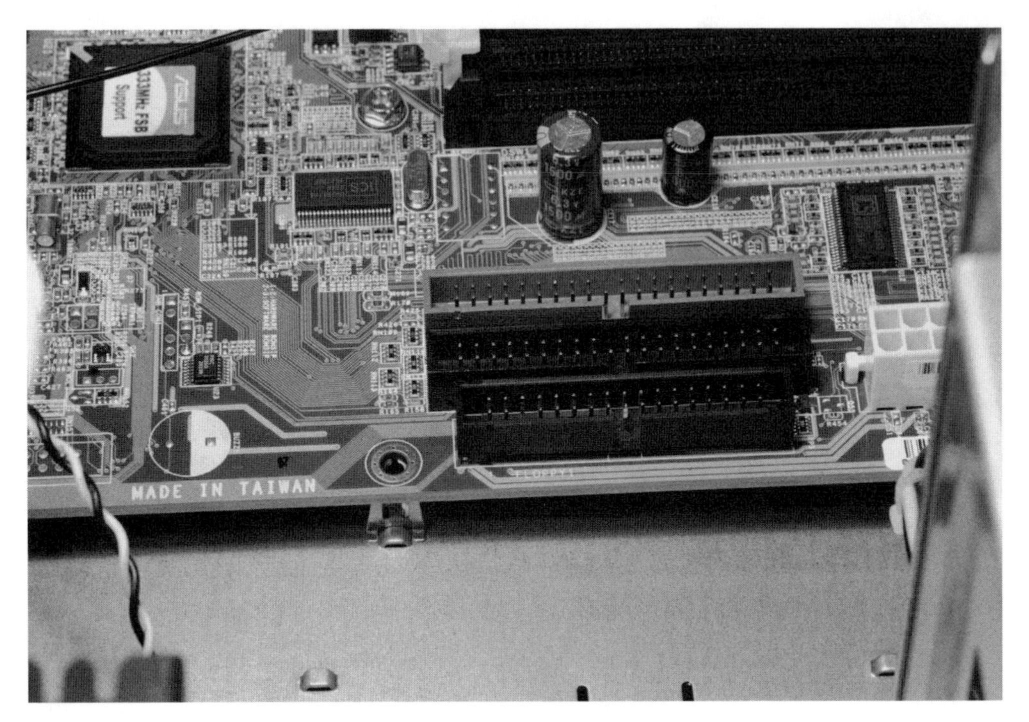

Figure 2.10. The mainboard sits on top of standoffs. Notice the standoff sits below a hole in the mainboard. All standoffs must line up with holes in the mainboard. Be sure to remove any standoffs that don't line up with holes.

line up with holes can be removed. The purpose of the standoffs is to hold the bottom of the mainboard above the metal of the case. If the bottom of the mainboard were allowed to rest on the metal case directly, it's possible the mainboard would short out and be damaged.

You'll learn about static electricity in another section, but all sensitive electronic parts such as mainboards, PCI cards, and CPUs should be carefully handled to avoid damage from static electricity. Touch your hands to something metal to ground yourself before picking up your mainboard or CPU. This draws away any small charge that might remain on your hands so that it doesn't zap a sensitive component.

Be sure to remove any extra standoffs that don't match up with any holes in the mainboard. It's possible that an extra and unnecessary standoff that doesn't match up with any hole would improperly sit on the bottom of the mainboard shorting it out.

I'd count the number of holes in your mainboard and count the number of standoffs on the case and be sure the numbers are equal. Or, at least, have the number of holes *exceed* the number of standoffs. Then be certain that every standoff is visible through one of the holes in the mainboard. For example, if you've counted eight standoffs, your mainboard should have eight holes and all eight standoffs should be visible through the holes when the mainboard is seated.

You don't need to place a standoff below every mainboard hole. But, be sure to place all the standoffs near where the ATX power supply, hard drive, and floppy drive cables will plug into the board. Figure 2.10 shows a standoff near the IDE and floppy connectors on the mainboard. It takes a bit of pressure to insert these cables, and you want the bottom of the mainboard supported in this region. You don't want the mainboard to flex as you push in cables.

Some cheap cases and mainboards don't match up as well as they should. But, usually, matching an ATX mainboard with an ATX case will work. If it doesn't, it isn't your fault. Blame the manufacturers for poor tolerances! And, you can always omit an offending standoff that just won't line up with a mainboard hole. Your mainboard should attach to your case easily, as long as you're matching an ATX case with an ATX mainboard.

If you examine the edge of one of the holes in the mainboard, you'll notice a ring of metal around the hole. If a metal standoff is below and if a screw is used to secure the board to the standoff, that will properly ground the board to the case.

I/O, I/O, It's Into Or Out Of The Computer We Go

When placing the mainboard inside the case, it will be necessary to push the mainboard toward what's called the I/O shield (input/output shield) of the case (Figure 2.11).

The I/O shield usually has several metal fins sticking out toward the mainboard. Various connectors that are permanently attached to the mainboard will protrude from the I/O shield. The serial ports, parallel port, PS/2 keyboard connector, and PS/2 mouse connector are among these I/O devices that protrude from the I/O shield. USB ports and Firewire IEEE 1394 connectors are other connectors that might protrude from the I/O shield. (If

Figure 2.11. The mainboard sits behind the I/O shield. The keyboard and other devices will attach through this I/O shield at the back of the case.

you're big into video editing, you might want to select a mainboard with a Firewire port. Otherwise, you can purchase a PCI card that gives your system a Firewire connection.)

The metal fins on the I/O shield ground the I/O connectors to the case and they will offer some resistance to the mainboard when it is placed. This is natural. Just manipulate and push the mainboard toward the I/O shield until the I/O device connectors protrude and the mainboard holes line up with the case standoffs.

If all the mainboard holes appear to be off just a bit, you probably need to push the mainboard more toward the I/O shield for it to sit properly. The I/O shield might provide some resistance and push the mainboard away from the shield. Just hold the mainboard in place as you secure it with a screw to the case.

We should note that the I/O shields are easily removable, and an I/O shield should come with your mainboard. Just replace the I/O shield that is part of the case with the one that comes with your mainboard. This might be necessary, for example, if your mainboard offers several USB connections through the I/O shield and the I/O shield that comes with the case won't accommodate them. Or your mainboard might have connectors for built-in sound or a network connection that wouldn't be accommodated by the standard I/O shield.

Some newer mainboards are using USB connectors in place of "legacy" keyboard and mouse connectors. If you purchase one of these boards, you'll need to use USB keyboards and mice or purchase adapters to use your older keyboard and mouse components.

Usually, when you open a PC case by taking off one side, you want to take off the side of the case *opposite* the mainboard. This allows you to easily install the mainboard and other components.

To see which side of the case must come off, examine the back of the case and find the side that contains the I/O shield. The side with the I/O shield is the side on which the mainboard sits. Take off the panel *on the other side* to get easy access to everything. There is usually little reason to remove the side of the case that secures the mainboard. And, if the PC is already built, PCI and other expansion cards will usually prevent the side with the mainboard from coming off conveniently. You'd need to remove all the PCI cards before you could take that side off.

Some cases have a removable panel to which you first attach the mainboard. Then, the panel is replaced and attached to the case. Other cases just have the mainboard attach directly to the side of the case.

Choose a quality case. It can be used for years and have many upgrades.

2) A mainboard and CPU (Figure 2.12 and 2.13). The mainboard and CPU are the key components of your computer. Your mainboard provides connections to all other components that must attach to it. The mainboard and CPU serve as the main computational and processing source of your PC.

Your mainboard will determine the maximum number of expansion PCI cards and the amount of memory (RAM, random access memory) which can be installed. The mainboard will also determine the type of CPU you can use because each mainboard is designed to seat a particular CPU. For example, a mainboard designed to seat a Pentium 4 CPU won't seat an AMD Athlon CPU.

Figure 2.12. Mainboard. Notice the white square socket toward the left. The CPU will sit there. Above the CPU socket are three banks for RAM. The mainboard will determine the type of CPU you must use. To the right are six PCI expansion slots (white).

Figure 2.13 shows an AMD Athlon 2000+ XP processor. AMD processors are solid and slightly less expensive alternatives to Intel Pentiums. Either an Intel or an AMD CPU is a great choice.

Notice the plus sign (+) after the 2000 for the AMD. This means that the AMD processor clock speed isn't actually 2 GHz (Giga Hertz). Rather, the effective speed of the AMD is comparable to a 2 GHz Pentium 4. The actual clock speed of the AMD Athlon 2000+ is 1.67 GHz. However, the Athlon is more efficient in that each clock cycle processes more instructions. This makes an Athlon running at an actual clock speed of 1.67 GHz comparable to a Pentium running at 2 GHz as far as getting things done goes.

Figure 2.13. CPU chip. The other side of the chip contains pins which will insert into the pin holes of the CPU socket in the mainboard.

Figure 2.14. Heatsink. The heatsink sits on top of the CPU and keeps it cool.

All CPUs will need a heatsink and a fan (Figure 2.14). The heatsink draws heat away from the CPU. The fins of the heatsink and the fan then dissipate this heat into the case. If an Intel Pentium overheats, it will stop working and your system will freeze up.

The AMD CPUs can actually burn themselves up. They aren't designed to shut down if they overheat. This isn't usually a problem as long as you

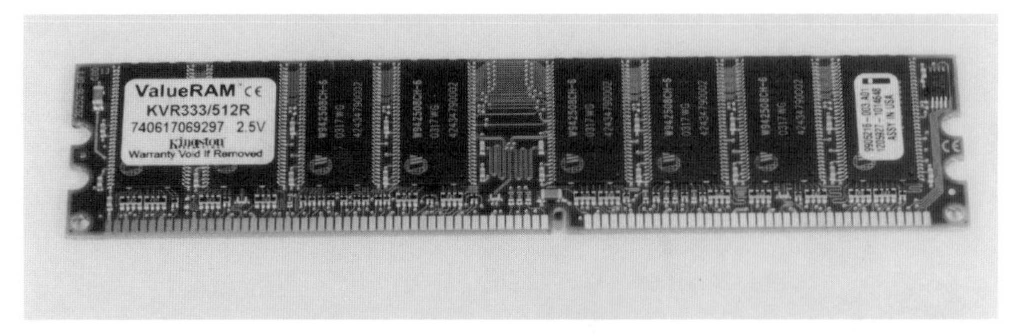

Figure 2.15. RAM memory chip. This chip is a 512 MB DDR chip. Like CPUs, memory chips are designed so that they can only be plugged in one way. This prevents installing the chip wrong. There is a hole between the row of metal leads. Because each side has a different length, the RAM chip can only be installed in one orientation.

properly install a top quality heatsink/fan combination with your AMD Athlon. If you purchase a retail box version of your CPU, it will include a quality heatsink and fan.

For the system built in this book, the Athlon 2000+ XP was purchased in its retail box version which includes a heatsink and a fan. The package also has detailed and excellent instructions about installing the CPU and the heatsink/fan. We'll show the installation of the Athlon XP CPU and heatsink/fan later.

CPUs are designed to fit into their socket in the mainboard in only one way. For example, with the Athlon, two sides have triangle corners, where the pins at the corner of the CPU end in a triangular formation rather than a square (i.e., the pin in the corner is missing for two corners). Thus, when you put the CPU in its socket, it will sit there naturally if placed in the proper orientation. But, it won't fit in at all if the orientation isn't right. There is also a small triangle drawing on the CPU to show the proper orientation.

The two most common CPUs for today's builders are the AMD Athlon XP (Socket A) and the Intel Pentium 4 Socket 478 CPU. I'd recommend using one of these CPUs and certainly nothing older.

Be sure your mainboard has a 4x AGP video slot or better. Once you've selected a mainboard, follow the advice in the chapter about purchasing components. Search for reviews of that mainboard on google.com. You can also visit the manufacturer's website and download a full mainboard manual to read about its capabilities.

3) RAM (random access memory). (Figure 2.15). DDR-RAM. RAM is comparable to short-term human memory. It holds what the computer is thinking about now. When the computer is turned off, the information in RAM is lost. This is why it's important to save important files regularly as you work on them, especially if you don't have a UPS providing emergency power. In general, the more RAM, the better.

Today, 256 MB of RAM is considered a minimum. You might want to purchase 512 MB. If you plan to do video editing or other memory intensive activities, you might purchase several Gigs of RAM. The mainboard will determine the number of memory slots and how much total RAM can be installed.

For the computer built in this book, we purchased one 512 MB Kingston Value Ram DDR memory chip for $40 after mail-in rebates from Best Buy (BestBuy.com).

To learn what kind of memory your mainboard requires, see your mainboard's manual. If you examine the connectors on a memory chip, they should be a golden color. Similarly, if you examine the connectors inside a memory socket on the mainboard, they should also be a golden color. Gold connectors are the best. It's relatively rare, but you might find a tin connector on either a memory chip or on a memory socket. These connectors will be silvery in color and not gold. It's recommended that you don't mix gold and tin connectors, because when dissimilar metals come in contact the result is often corrosion of one of the metals. The odds are great that you don't have to worry about this at all. Both connectors will be gold.

4) Video Card (Figure 2.16). You'll want to purchase an AGP video card, which is better than a PCI video card. Be sure your mainboard has an AGP slot for an AGP video card.

The video card will have a connector into which you'll plug your monitor. The video connector will be visible from the back of the PC. Most video monitors use the older analog connector that is common with CRT computer monitors.

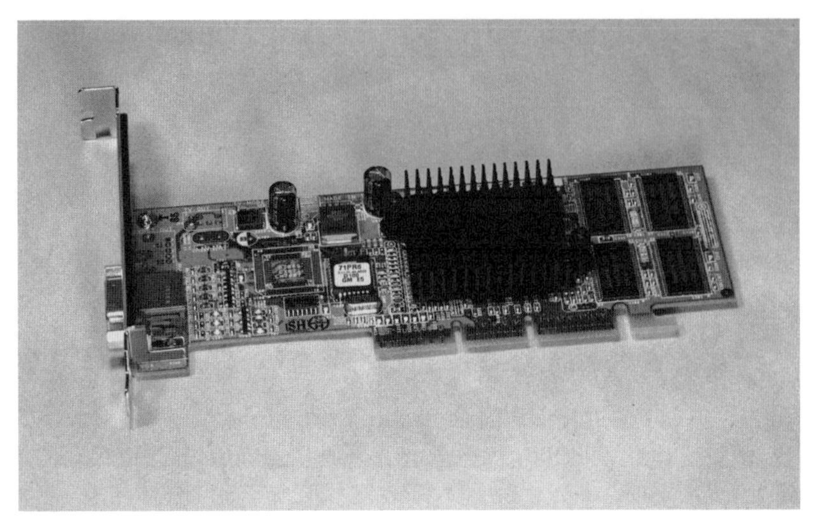

Figure 2.16. AGP video card. Notice the black blob of spikes. That's a heatsink to help draw heat away from the card. Some video cards will have their own fan which gets power from the AGP slot. You can identify AGP cards because the back of the card has a little notch to help secure it.

Newer video cards often have two monitor connectors—one for use with CRT monitors and the other a digital connector for use with LCD monitors. While many LCD monitors support the older analog connection, if you plan to use an LCD monitor, it's best to choose a video card with a digital connector.

I'd recommend avoiding mainboards with built-in video connectors. It's better to use a video card.

5) Hard Drive (Figure 2.17). The hard drive is like long-term human memory. Whatever's saved on the hard drive will remain after the computer is turned off.

The main factor in selecting a hard drive is its size, which is measured in gigabytes. Today, you'll probably want at least a 40 GB drive. For this build, an 80 GB Western Digital hard drive was purchased from Best Buy for $60.

A hard drive has platters which spin around (think of how a CD works). The faster the platter spins, the faster the hard drive can find, read, and write information. The speed of a hard drive is usually measured in RPM or revolutions per minute.

Figure 2.17. Hard Drive. A ribbon cable will plug into the back of the hard drive (left side) to send signals between the drive and the mainboard. A 4-pin Molex power connector from the PC case's power supply will provide power to the hard drive (right side). Usually four screws provided with the drive will attach the hard drive to the PC case.

The drive purchased for the build spins at 7,200 RPM, which means the platter spins around 7,200 times every minute. That's considered a good speed. If you're doing something that requires fast access from the hard drive, such as playing videos, you'll want the fastest drive you can afford.

The final hard drive performance factor you'll want to examine is the buffer size, which is usually measured in Megabytes (MB), with 2 MB to 4 MB being common. This western digital drive has an 8 MB buffer.

Buffers are like waiting areas where information can be accessed more quickly than if the information must be read from the hard drive.

The drives you'll use are referred to as IDE drives. Another type of drive, SCSI hard drives, are also available. A new builder should stick with IDE drives.

Figure 2.18. A CD-RW drive. CD-RW and DVD drives are called 5.25" drives.

Some people suggest purchasing the largest drive you can afford because you'll fill it up, especially if you download many webpages, photos, videos, or songs. However, if you don't intensively download from the Internet, a more modest-sized drive will probably work great.

6) CD-ROM, DVD, floppy drive, CD-RW, and other removable media drives (Figure 2.18).

You'll certainly want a CD-RW drive. This will let you play music CDs, install software which comes on CDs, and back up your important information to CDs.

Because hard drives do occasionally fail, it's important to back up all your important information to some other media. Your information can be backed up to another hard drive, a tape drive, or, most commonly for consumers, a CD.

DVD drives are discussed in more detail in another chapter. If you plan to produce videos, you'll want a DVD burner which will allow you to create your own DVD movies.

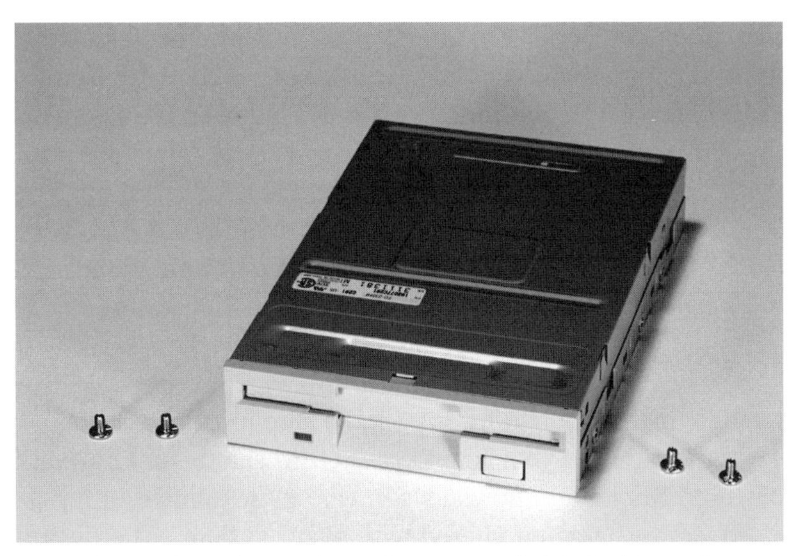

Figure 2.19. Floppy drive. Floppy drives are called 3.5" drives. Floppy drives and hard drives usually attach to the PC case with four screws.

Most CD-RW and DVD drives are also called IDE devices. They are also called internal devices, which means they go inside the PC case. That's the kind you'll probably want for a PC. If you plan to share a device between multiple PCs, you could use an external drive and move it between the PCs. Otherwise, you could install a home network and allow all your PCs to access the device while it remained attached to a single PC.

A floppy drive (Figure 2.19) isn't called an IDE device, but it's a standard component that's readily available for about $15. Nobody uses them anymore.

7) A Sound Card. Some mainboards have build-in support for sound. Highest quality sound is achieved by using a quality PCI sound card. Many PCs for business use don't even need sound. But, sound is good for multimedia, action games, and listening to commentary or music over the Internet. So, we'll consider a quality sound card or sound built into the mainboard a necessity.

If you plan to use Linux as your operating system, you might want to avoid extra functionality, such as sound, built into the mainboard. This is because Linux is sometimes less capable of recognizing extra mainboard features, such as built-in sound. This is less true today than it was in the past. Linux 9 immediately recognized our system's built-in sound.

8) Operating System. The most popular operating system is Microsoft Windows. The newest version is Windows XP. We'll show you how to install Windows XP on your system. And, we'll demonstrate installing Linux, a free operating system available over the Internet. Boxed versions of Linux are also available for purchase. If your connection to the Internet is a slow dial-up connection, you'll probably want to purchase Linux in a retail box. Or else have a friend with a faster DSL or cable modem connection download the Linux CDs for you. We'll also show how to install a dual boot operating system.

When purchasing your Windows operating system, be sure to purchase it as OEM software when you purchase your mainboard. OEM stands for Original Equipment Manufacturer. Microsoft allows its software to be purchased for slightly less if the software is being purchased with a new system or hardware components.

When buying main components for your new system, such as a mainboard, you'll have the opportunity to purchase OEM software. (This is why if you purchase Microsoft software on eBay, for example, the seller might send along an old hard drive. Microsoft's licensing agreement demands that the software only be sold with original equipment to build a system.)

When you purchase your mainboard, be sure to examine the vendor's selection of OEM software and determine if there is anything you wish to purchase.

If you forget to purchase some OEM software that you want, just purchase some low-priced component, such as a small hard drive, and you'll be able to buy the OEM software then.

OEM software is usually better than upgrade software. For example, Windows 98 OEM CDs will boot from the CD, while Windows 98 upgrade CDs won't. Plus, upgrade CDs will inspect your system for a prior version of Windows. Or, you'll need to insert your disk from your previous operating system to perform the install. So, if you upgraded from Windows 95 to Windows 98, don't throw out your Windows 95 CD! In the near future, Microsoft plans to stop supporting Windows 98. I'd recommend Windows XP or Windows XP Professional for your new system.

9) Monitor. A monitor is necessary to display the output from the PC. Most new monitors today are slim LCD (Liquid Crystal Display) models. But, older, more bulky CRT (Cathode Ray Tube) monitors are just as serviceable, if you're looking to save money, rather than be stylish. CRT monitors also have a faster response, if you need to battle aliens or such.

It's important to buy your CRT monitor locally or get it with free shipping. You might pay $90 for a 17" .28 dot pitch monitor. But, to ship that sucker across the USA might cost $50!

For this build, we purchased a 17" ViewSonic A70f+ Flat Screen Monitor online from Best Buy (BestBuy.com). Shipping was free, and the monitor should have cost $150 after a mail-in rebate. However, the rebate was initially denied, so the monitor could cost us $190. We followed up aggressively to get the rebate and received the rebate. See the chapter about purchasing components for more about the dangers of mail-in rebates.

The key parameters for a CRT monitor are refresh rate, resolution, and dot pitch. You want at least a 75 Hz or greater refresh rate. 85 Hz is even better. Lower refresh rates might cause eye strain. Refresh rates tell us how often the monitor screen is redrawn by the beam which displays it.

The dot pitch should be .28 mm or less. About .25 is ideal. Resolution should allow at least 1024 by 768 pixels for a 17" monitor. Most 17" CRT monitors support 1280 x 1024 pixel resolution.

If you purchase an LCD monitor, resolution is determined by the actual matrix of the display. For example, most LCD 15" monitors are designed to show 1024 x 768 pixels. Think of the monitor as actually having this many dots across the physical screen. Most 17" LCD monitors will allow 1280 x1024.

It's important to know that a 15" LCD display has about the same viewable area as a 17" CRT.

One important parameter of an LCD display is the contrast ratio which expresses the ability of the monitor to distinguish between lighter and darker colors. A contrast ratio of 400:1 or more is good. Another important parameter is the brightness of the screen which is measured in nits or $cd/m.^2$ 300 cd/m^2 (nits) or more is considered good.

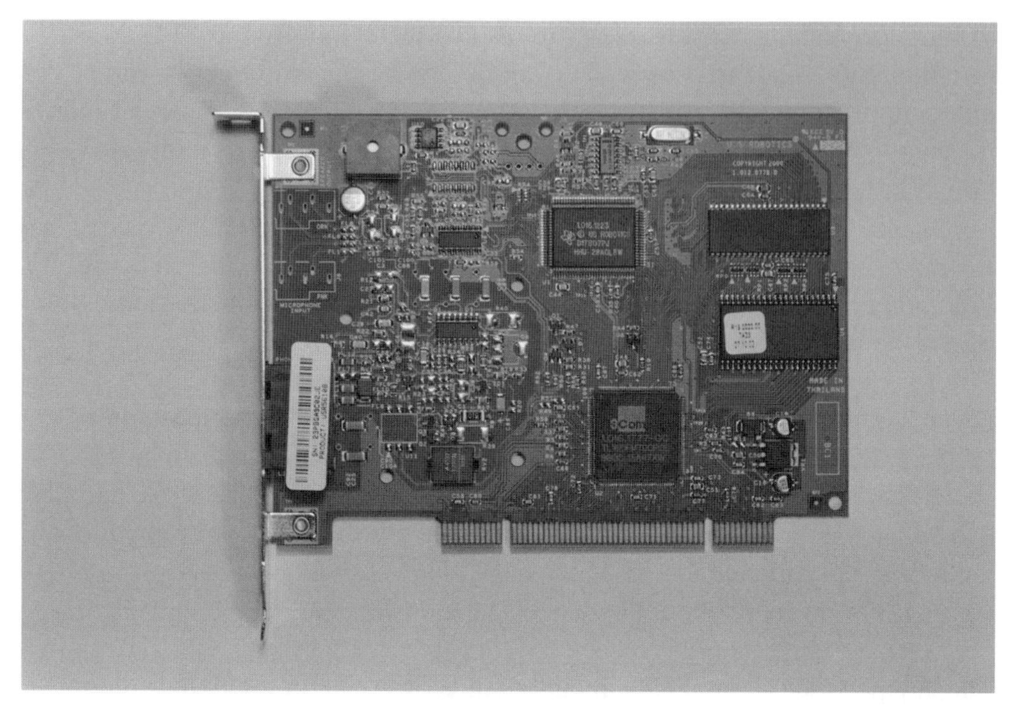

Figure 2.20. Modem card. This is a PCI modem card. The most common type of expansion cards are PCI cards. They plug into PCI slots in the mainboard. All PCI cards are installed in the same manner. Once you've installed one, you've installed them all!

If you plan to use an LCD monitor, also be sure your video card supports a DVI (Digital Video Interface) connector. LCD monitors can use analog VGA connectors, but doing so makes little sense. The video signal from the computer is converted from digital to analog and then back to digital! Analog signals were necessary for CRT monitors, but not for LCD monitors.

If you plan to purchase an LCD monitor, it might be a good idea to visit your local computer store and examine some models to be sure you're happy with the display.

10) Modem (Figure 2.20). Today, modems and an Internet connection are nearly essential. You have many options for modems and Internet service providers ranging from DSL Internet connections, cable modems and cable access to the Internet, slow 56k dial-up modems, and satellite Internet connections. The modem and other equipment you need will depend upon the type of Internet connection you decide to use.

Many people today will choose cable modems or DSL modems because of their much faster download speed.

Modems can also be internal or external. Internal modems usually plug into a PCI slot in your mainboard. Some internal modems are called Win Modems, because they rely upon the mainboard's processing power to help them do their job. Win Modems are less expensive and are affectionately known as lobotomized modems.

Unless you plan to do intensive computing while also online, a Win Modem should be fine if you plan to use a Windows operating system. If you plan to use Linux, you might want to avoid Win Modems, because they're sometimes more difficult to configure properly with Linux. Non-Win-Modems are called controller-based modems.

I like external modems (all of which are controller-based), because I like to see all the lights (LEDs) showing modem activity. And, if the modem disconnects, a glance at the external modem's LEDs will show it's disconnected.

Some operating systems are notorious for showing a dial-up modem as connected even if the connection has been lost. I also like to turn off the modem when it's not in use. That physically prevents a hacker from gaining access to your computer.

Some internal modems have lights showing similar activity. These lights sit at the back end of the PC where nobody can see them. I don't know what genius decided that modem lights on an internal modem was a good idea.

Most controller-based modems, whether external or internal, should work with Linux.

11) Network Interface Card (NIC) and other PCI controller cards giving your PC added capability. If you decide to connect your home or business computers together to form your own mini-network, you'll need to install network interface cards on each PC you plan to connect together (unless your mainboards include built-in LAN connections).

Adding a controller card to your PC is easy. These cards are designed to plug into existing slots in your PC mainboard. These slots are called expansion

Figure 2.21. Full System, includes a keyboard, mouse, and monitor.

slots. Today, PCI slots are the most common. The older ISA slots are now outdated.

10) Keyboard and Mouse. You probably have an older computer from which you can scavenge a quality keyboard and mouse. Otherwise, you can find cheaper ones free after mail-in rebates. However, most experienced PC users suggest purchasing high-quality keyboards and mice, because a quality keyboard and mouse make using your PC much more enjoyable. I like Microsoft keyboards and mice. Figure 2.21 shows the complete system with a monitor, keyboard, and mouse.

By building your own PC, you'll also learn how to upgrade your PC. You'll have the skills and confidence to install a larger hard drive, add more RAM, or install a DVD drive.

Will I Save Money By Building My Own System?

A big question new PC builders ask is: Will I save money building my own system? The answer is that it depends. Larger PC manufacturers purchase parts in quantity and will usually acquire parts at less cost than a typical builder.

OEM software, including an operating system and basic software, such as Word, will often come bundled with a new system. The manufacturers receive a far better price on this software than we do as builders. At the time of this writing, OEM Windows XP Home Edition was purchased for about $93 for our demonstration system.

Due to the value of this bundled software, the cost of building a PC usually isn't significantly less expensive than buying an off-the-shelf PC. If you plan to use Linux as your operating system, you can save more money, because the operating system and many useful programs, such as word processors, are free.

One disadvantage of purchasing a ready-made PC from a manufacturer is that sometimes the manufacturer will skimp on the cost of small parts. Doing so allows the computer company to make more profit. For example, some manufacturers might used relatively low-powered power supplies. Others might use cheaper fans that are more likely to fail. When building your own system, you can select better components. A good fan, for example, is crucial, because if your system overheats, it could damage the CPU or mainboard.

Many companies, such as Best Buy, offer come-on advertisements to get people into their stores. For example, you'll find deals, such as 256 MB DDR memory for free after a mail-in rebate, or a free or very low cost CD-RW after a mail-in rebate. If you shop around and purchase these special deals for your RAM, hard drive, CD-RW, etc., you'll probably save considerable money.

But, overall, you usually get a great deal of valuable commercial software when you purchase a ready made PC.

Total System Cost

The total cost of the system built in this book is:

From Insight Components:

Enlight en-7255 mid-tower case with ATX 360w power supply	$74.28
Asus a7v333-x socket A mainboard with audio & LAN	$89.99
AMD 2000+ Athlon XP CPU	$79.99
Asus v7100 Pro Geforce2 64mb 4x AGP video card	$44.99
Floppy Drive	$10.99
Windows XP Home Edition OEM	$92.99

From Best Buy:

Creative Labs Speakers	$19.99
Kingston Value RAM 512 MB PC2700 DDR RAM (after $30 in mail-in rebates)	$39.99
80 GB 7200 RPM Western Digital Hard Drive (after $40 in mail-in rebates)	$59.99
Verbatim 52x24x52 CD-RW Drive (after $55 in mail-in rebates)	$14.99
ViewSonic A70f+ CRT Monitor (after $40 mail-in rebate. Rebate was approved after follow up.)	$149.99
U.S. Robotics 56K V.92 Internal Modem	$79.99

From Amazon.com:

Red Hat Linux 9.0 Personal	$36.99

Upgrades (BestBuy.com):

Hewlett-Packard 300I Internal DVD+RW Drive	$179.99

Scrounged From Existing PC's:
Keyboard & Mouse

Total System Cost: $975.15

Static Electricity

It's estimated that every year as much as a billion dollars of otherwise good computer equipment is destroyed by static electricity, also known as electrostatic discharge (ESD). Careful component handling and a few basic precautions can help assure that you don't contribute to the pile of destroyed hardware!

Components sensitive to ESD include mainboards, memory chips, PCI and AGP plug-in cards, and the bottoms of hard drives. Any time you see a circuit board, you should take precautions to protect the board from ESD.

You're familiar with static electricity. If you've ever touched a door knob and gotten a shock or if you've ever pulled a sweater over your head and saw your hair standing up like you're in a horror movie, that's static electricity. If you've ever crawled into bed on a winter night and saw a spark, that's static electricity.

ESD is worst when it's dry. Winter months are generally the worst for static electricity, because it tends to be drier in winter. Moisture dissipates the build up of charge. If you live in a dry climate or if it's winter, you might want to purchase a misting spray bottle, the sort that's used to spray house plants, and mist the room where you'll build your PC right before you assemble your PC. Mind you, I'm not saying spray the mainboard and other components. Computers don't need watering! But, go to the other end of the room and spray some water into the air. This will increase the humidity and decrease the likelihood that static electricity will build up.

Carpet floors are bad because the process of feet rubbing against the carpet tends to generate electricity. If possible, work in a room with hardwood or linoleum flooring. Otherwise, try not to move around a lot as you install components. For example, after picking up a component, install it into the computer without walking around. Have your components laid out so you don't have to move around a lot. And, always touch the metal of the case before picking up a sensitive component. I've upgraded PCs on carpeted floors without a problem, but hardwood floors are better.

Professional builders have mats that have grounding straps that ground the mat. Then, they can set all the PC components on the grounded mat. As a non-professional PC repair person, you probably won't have a grounded mat. And, it's not really necessary. Just place your components on a flat, clean table. Or, you can set the components, like the mainboard, on the boxes in which they came.

The key points to handling components safely are:

1) Be sure to draw off any static electricity that may be built up on your hands before you touch a sensitive part. You should touch the metal PC case before touching the components. Metal will draw off any built-up charge. Even if you wear a grounding wrist strap, touch the PC case anyway as an extra precaution. Touching the case's power supply is usually recommended, because some say that touching a heavily painted case will sometimes fail to draw off the charge. The power supply is unpainted metal that is always grounded.

2) Touch the parts where they're the least sensitive to being harmed by ESD. Pick up mainboards by the edges (Figure 3.1). Pick up PCI cards by the metal part that attaches them to the back of the case and then handle them by the edges (Figure 3.2). Try to handle all sensitive parts by the edges. Pick up RAM by the edges (Figure 3.3). You can push RAM into place from the top.

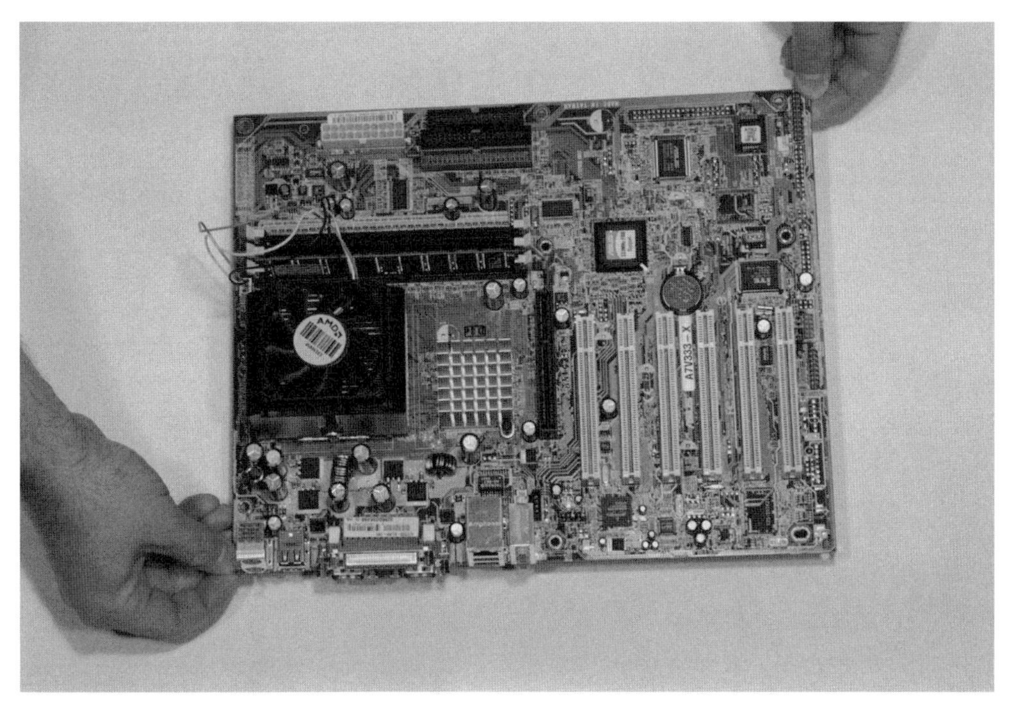

Figure 3.1. Holding a mainboard properly. Hold it by the corners.

Figure 3.2. Holding a PCI card properly. Hold it by the metal and the edges.

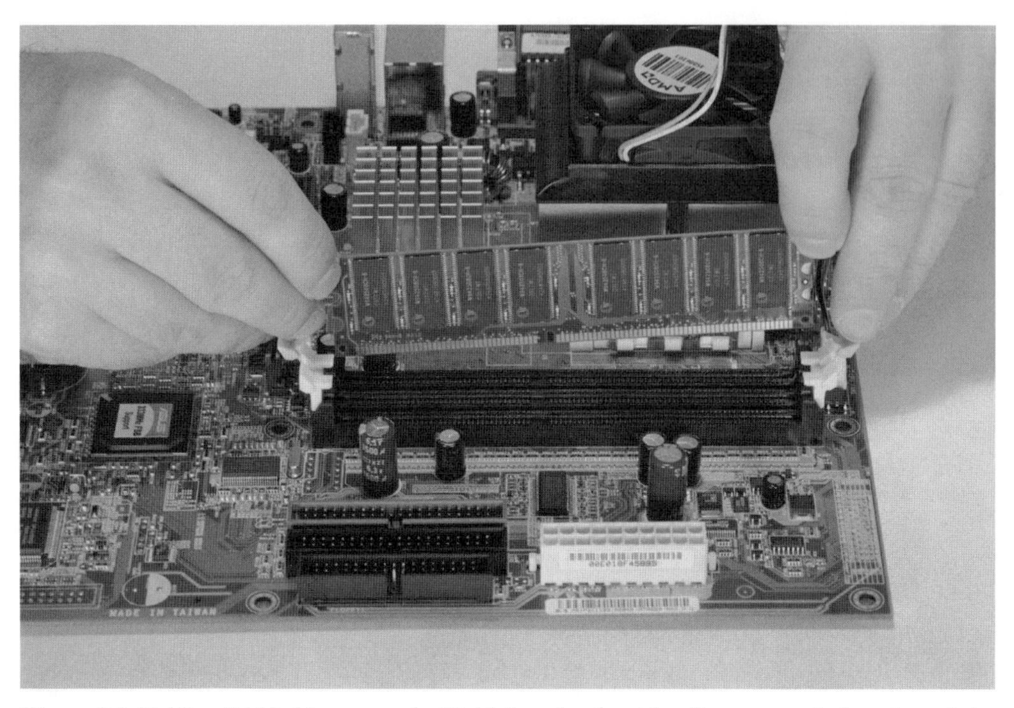

Figure 3.3 Holding RAM chips properly. Hold them by the sides. You can push them into their sockets from the top. Always prepare your work area in advance. For example, have your mainboard out and ready before removing the RAM chips from their packaging.

3) Always plan where you'll set a component before removing it from its electrostatic protection pouch. For example, after removing a RAM chip, you probably want to be near the mainboard, so that you can place the chip in the mainboard immediately. If you plan to place a mainboard in the PC case, it's good to have a preplanned place to set the board, such as on top of the box the mainboard came in. Try to remove components from their protective pouches only right before you're ready to install them.

Installing The CPU, Heatsink, And RAM On The Mainboard

Installing The CPU Into Its Socket

Placing the CPU into its socket is easy. Remove the mainboard from its box and static-proof bag. **Before touching the mainboard touch both of your hands to a piece of metal (the PC case) to draw off any static electricity that might be present on your hands.**

In addition, you might want to wear a wrist grounding strap, with its clip attached to a grounded metal object. Keep the strap tight to your wrist and clip it to a metal ground. Usually, the metal ground is the power supply attached to the PC case. Some argue that the heavy paint on a PC case can prevent proper grounding, so clipping it to the power supply is usually recommended. This should keep any static charge from accumulating on your hands.

As with all circuit boards, try to handle the mainboard only by the corners to minimize the chances of undesirable static shock being transferred to the components. Try to avoid touching components on the mainboard, unless necessary. Also, try to avoid touching the bottom of the mainboard. You can usually handle a mainboard by its edges and corners.

Place the mainboard on a sturdy, clean surface. Don't place the mainboard on a dirty surface or on a surface that will encourage the mainboard to pick up

Figure 4.1. Raising the lift lever on the CPU socket. There is a notch at the side of the lever. Pull the lever gently away from the socket to clear the notch. Notice that the pin holes at the top on each side lack a hole for the corner pin. This configuration prevents the CPU from being inserted in the wrong orientation.

lint, such as a towel or bedsheet. Plus, those surfaces are very bad, because they encourage the build-up of static electricity. Either a clean table or the top of the box the mainboard came in should work well. The mainboard pictured is sitting on a large sheet of clean paper.

Those who build many PCs can purchase grounded mats. As with everything else, it's good to prepare your work surface before you begin. Some builders suggest using a plant sprayer to mist some water into the room before you start working, because humidity reduces the chances of static discharge. If you do this, don't mist the mainboard itself or any PC parts!

First, raise the CPU socket lock lever on the mainboard (Figure 4.1 and 4.2) until the lever is fully opened. For the Athlon Socket A, this means lifting the lever so it points straight up into the air. A small notch locks the lever into place when it's closed, so you'll need to pull the lever very gently away from the socket to clear the closing notch when you first lift it.

Figure 4.2. The socket lever is fully raised. You can now place the CPU into the socket. You just need to set the CPU into the socket and close the lever.

Examine the pin holes of the socket (Socket Pins). You'll see that the pattern of the holes will only allow insertion of a CPU in one orientation.

For the Athlon, you'll see that two of the corners have pin socket holes that end in a triangular formation, i.e., they don't use the pins at the very corners. Thus, if you have the orientation of the CPU incorrect, a corner pin of the CPU won't have a hole to go into, and the CPU won't seat into the socket. This is designed to prevent people from inserting the CPU incorrectly and damaging the CPU. Rest assured, it's nearly impossible to insert a CPU incorrectly.

Figure 4.3. Place the CPU into the socket. Hold the CPU only by the edges. Due to the pin configuration, the CPU will only insert in the correct orientation.

Figure 4.4. CPU sits in its socket. Close the lever to secure it.

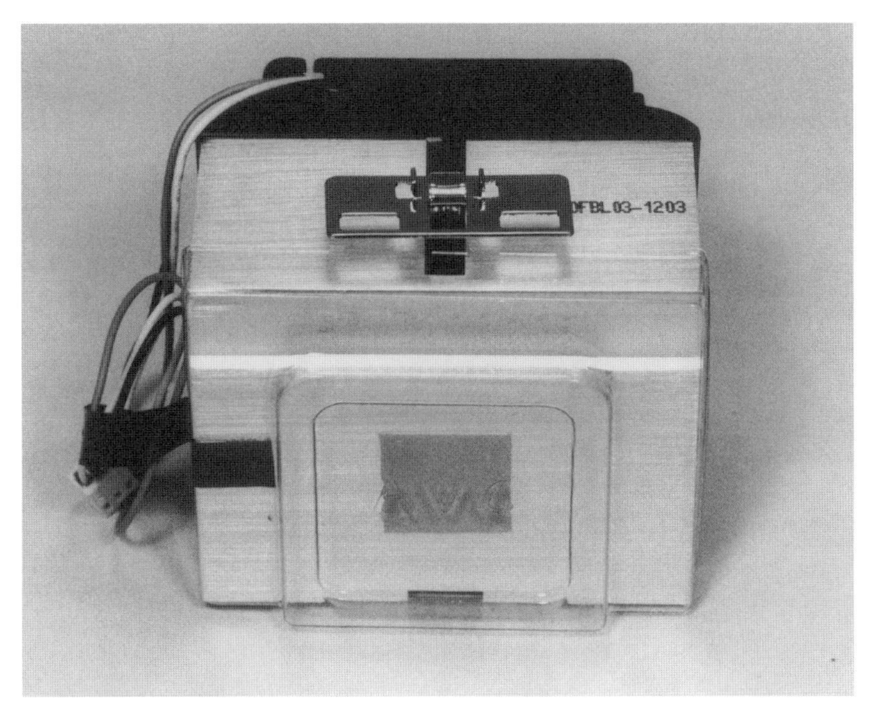

Figure 4.5. Heatsink and fan. Notice the thermal material at the bottom of the heatsink. This thermal material will touch the die of the CPU.

The Athlon also has a small triangle on the top of the chip to indicate its proper orientation.

Open the box the CPU came in and remove the CPU chip. **Before touching the CPU chip, touch your hands to a grounded piece of metal. Touch the CPU chip only by its edges to protect it from static electricity.**

Place the CPU into the socket holes (Figure 4.3 and 4.4). Don't force it down. Just set it in place. Then, push the lift lever down. It takes a little bit of force to push the lever down. This is normal, because the process of pushing the lever down locks the CPU pins in place and secures the CPU. As you continue to push, the force will subside. This is also normal.

Continue to push the lock lever down. When it gets to the close (fully down) position, gently pull the lever slightly away from the socket to clear the notch that locks it into place. Then, allow the natural springiness of the lever to move the lever back toward the socket so it's held in place by the notch.

You now have the CPU properly inserted into the socket.

Figure 4.6. CPU chip. One of the four feet is circled. The heatsink sits on these feet which compress slightly.

Notice the small square at the center. That's the CPU die. When the heatsink pushes down on the CPU feet, it will contact the die allowing heat to be effectivly conducted to the heatsink.

This figure shows the top of the CPU chip. The bottom of the chip has many little pins which will insert into the CPU socket shown in Figure 4.1 to Figure 4.4.

Installing The Heatsink/Fan

The next step is to install the heatsink/fan (Figure 4.5 shows a heatsink and fan). Examine the top of the Athlon CPU (Figure 4.6). You'll see four feet. These feet are designed so that the heatsink/fan can be placed on top of them. You need all four feet for proper seating of the heatsink. The feet should already be in place and ready to go. When the heatsink is secured, these feet will compress slightly, allowing the heatsink to contact the CPU die.

Examine the center of the CPU (inside the four feet). You'll see a small square, which is called the die. The die is important, because it will get really hot and heat will need to be drawn away from it. This will occur by allowing the die to thermally contact the metal of the heatsink. This effectively increases the thermal mass of the die and allows heat to be dissipated into the PC case. A CPU fan will blow air through the heatsink. Other fans will circulate air in the PC case and remove the heat from the PC.

Consider heating a pin until it's red hot and dropping it onto your hand (Don't do this!). It will hurt. But, imagine if the same amount of heat had been added to a much larger metal object, such as an iron bar. The temperature of the larger object will increase far less, and you could comfortably hold it. The installation of the heatsink will allow the CPU die to dissipate heat by providing thermal contact between the CPU and the heatsink. Heat will be *conducted* from the die to the heatsink.

Cooling of the CPU is absolutely crucial, especially for the Athlon CPUs which aren't designed to shut off if they overheat. They'll just fry. This isn't a criticism of the Athlon. Dollar for dollar, I think it's one of the best choices for a CPU.

It's considered almost impossible to fry a Pentium 4 processor, because they're designed to shut down if uncooled. I've been told that you can even remove the heatsink from a Pentium 4 while it's running and it will shut down in time to prevent damage to the chip. **Don't try this yourself! Even short periods of excess temperature greatly reduce the length of a CPU's life. More effective case cooling can significantly increase the life of your CPU.**

Ideally, it's good if a CPU can run at 100^0 F or less. Higher temperatures shorten the CPU's life. If you install the heatsink properly, your PC will probably be fine. But, if you're interested, there are PC monitoring programs that will tell you the actual temperature of your CPU when it's running. For example, a utility, called PC probe, which provides a temperature monitor, came with the Asus mainboard (Figure 4.7 shows Asus PC Probe). Similar programs are available from download.com.

To allow the most effective conduction between the heatsink and the CPU, a thermal conducting compound is used between the CPU die and the heatsink. This is because the more contact between the die and the heatsink, the better the transfer of heat will be.

Even flat objects that appear to be in full contact might have limited points of contact, due to the roughness of the surfaces at a microscopic level. It's estimated that only 1% of the surfaces may actually be in contact when two flat metal parts touch each another! The remaining space is filled with air, which is a poor thermal conductor. **Thermal compound fills in these gaps of contact and greatly increases the efficiency of the heatsink.**

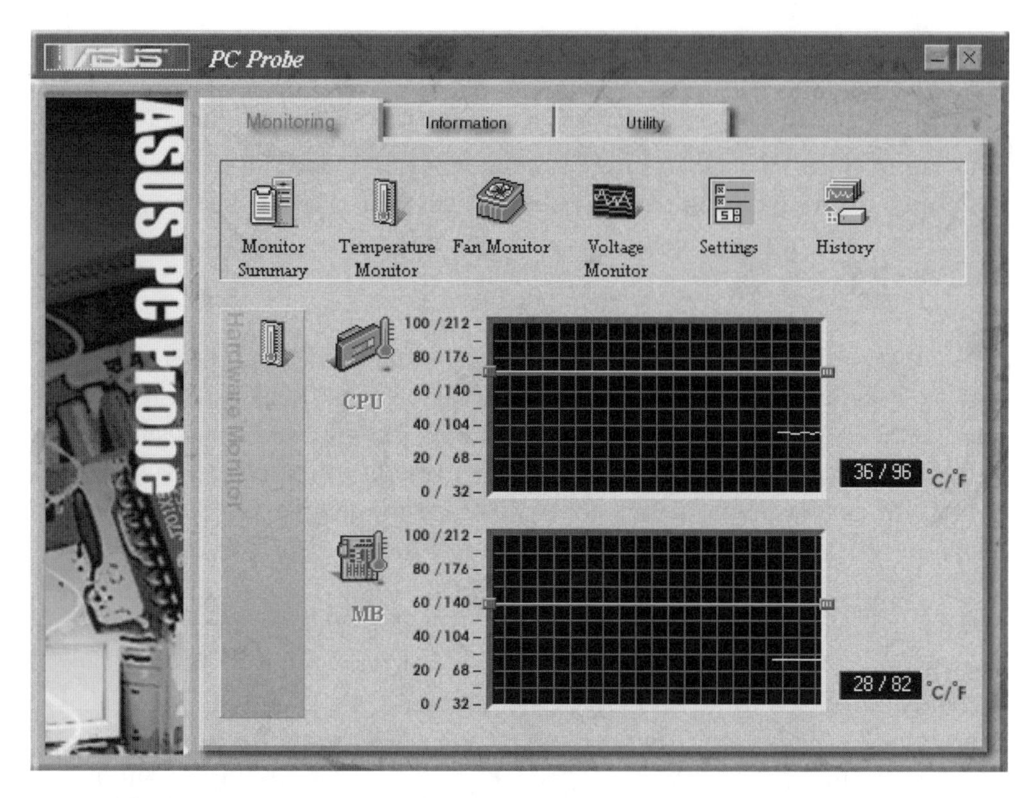

Figure 4.7. The program Asus PC Probe came with the mainboard. This program allows you to monitor your CPU's temperature and other conditions. It's useful to have such a program if you plan to install extra case fans, so you can see if the extra case fans are actually helping.

Proper use of a thermal compound between the CPU and heatsink is absolutely necessary for proper cooling of the CPU. If your CPU and heatsink instructions tell you to use a thermal compound, do not omit this step.

Thermal compound comes in two forms. First is thermal grease, which looks just like any other thick liquid. If thermal grease is used, you simply place a drop of thermal grease on the die before installing the heatsink. Use a drop just about the size of a small pea and place it at the center of the die. As the heatsink is installed, it is pressed down and the thermal grease will compress and flatten out.

Second, and a better, less messy method, is a thermal tape applied to the heatsink that comes with the heatsink (Figure 4.5 shows the thermal compound on the bottom of the heatsink). Examine your heatsink and your heatsink instructions to see which method is used. If your heatsink has a strip of thermal tape on it, you don't need to use thermal grease. The tape is used instead of the grease.

If your heatsink has a thermal tape applied to it, remove the cover of the tape just before you install the heatsink. Don't allow the thermal tape to be exposed for a long period of time before doing the installation. You don't want it to attract dirt.

If you ever need to remove the heatsink from the CPU, which originally had thermal tape and then reinstall the same CPU and heatsink (you probably will never need to do this), you'll need to scrape off all of the thermal compound from the heatsink. Because the material will fill in the pores at the microscopic level, you'll never remove *all* of the old material. But, try to remove *all visible material*. Then, you'll apply new thermal material. For the Athlon, AMD.com has a list of approved thermal materials, including Bergquist HF225UT (See AMD's Builder's Guide For Desktop/Tower Systems, Document 26003A for other thermal materials).

Incidentally, AMD only approves phase-change thermal material. So, don't use ordinary thermal grease of an unapproved type. If you purchase your CPU in a retail-box version, it will come with a proper heatsink and an appropriate thermal compound inside the retail box.

Examining the heatsink, you might guess that it can be installed in any direction. You might guess that you can just set it on top of the CPU in any orientation (Figure 4.8). This isn't so. Examine the bottom of the heatsink (Figure 4.9) and you'll see that one edge of the heatsink is slightly indented or cut away. This allows that edge of the heatsink to clear the top of the CPU socket (the part of the socket from which the lever pivots from, which is a bit higher than the rest of the socket). So, you'll need to pay attention to orientation.

Also, if you look through the fins of the heatsink (Figure 4.10), you'll see that the metal clip that will be used to secure the heatsink to the CPU socket isn't symmetrical. One side of the clip is shorter than the other. When the heatsink is seated properly, the clip is designed so that it will push the heatsink down onto the CPU, and the force from the clip will be directly above the CPU die.

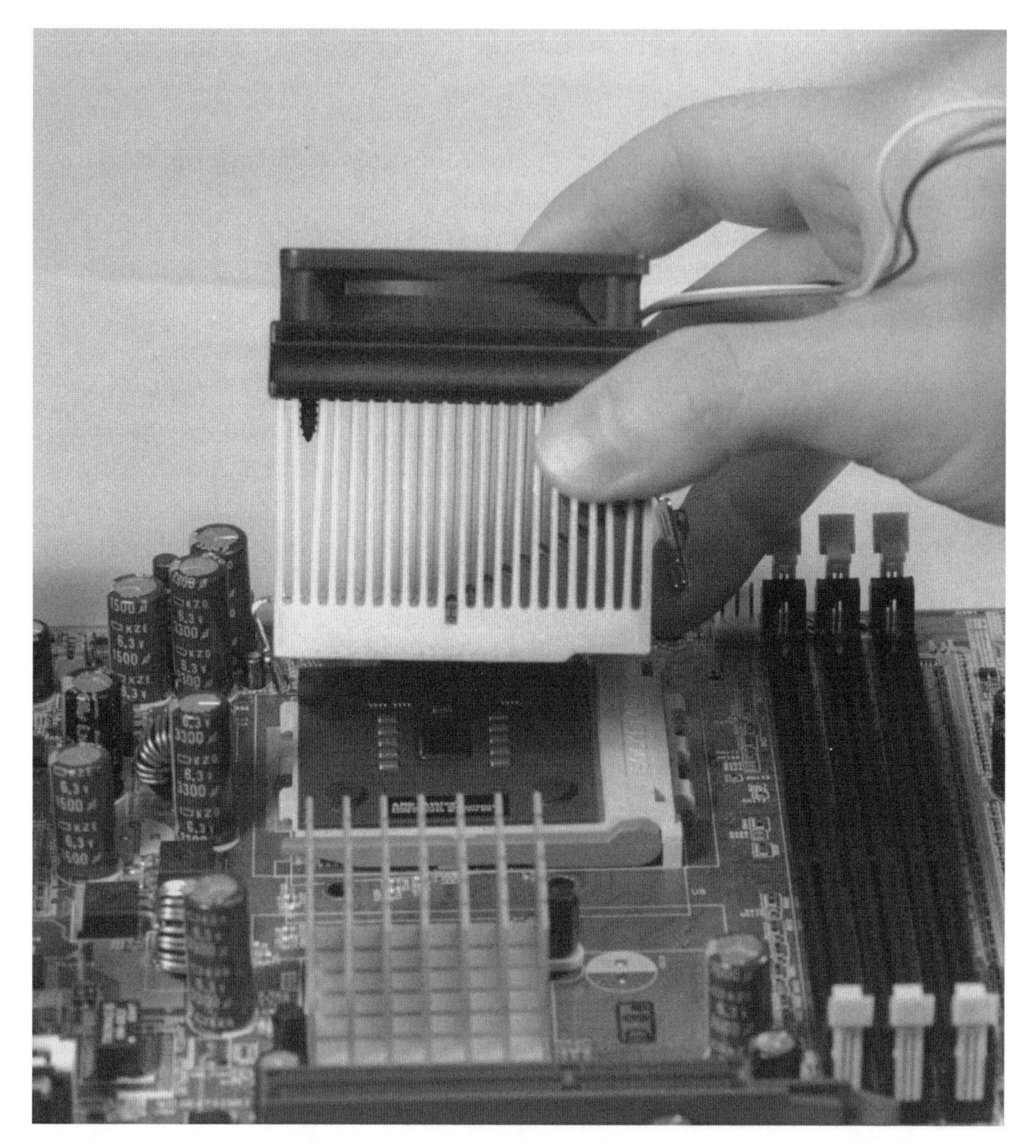

Figure 4.8. Placing the heatsink. Notice the cut-out notch on the bottom of the heatsink that matches up with the high end of the CPU socket. Be sure to install the heatsink in the proper orientation.

Seat the heatsink on top of the CPU, manipulating the shorter end of the clip so that the three holes of the clip engage the bottom of the three notches of the CPU socket. Don't push the heatsink down. That's done naturally by the heatsink clip as the clip is secured. Do examine the edges of the heatsink to be sure the heatsink isn't hitting anything besides the four feet it's supposed to rest on.

Figure 4.9. Heatsink sitting on CPU. Notice the notch at the left.

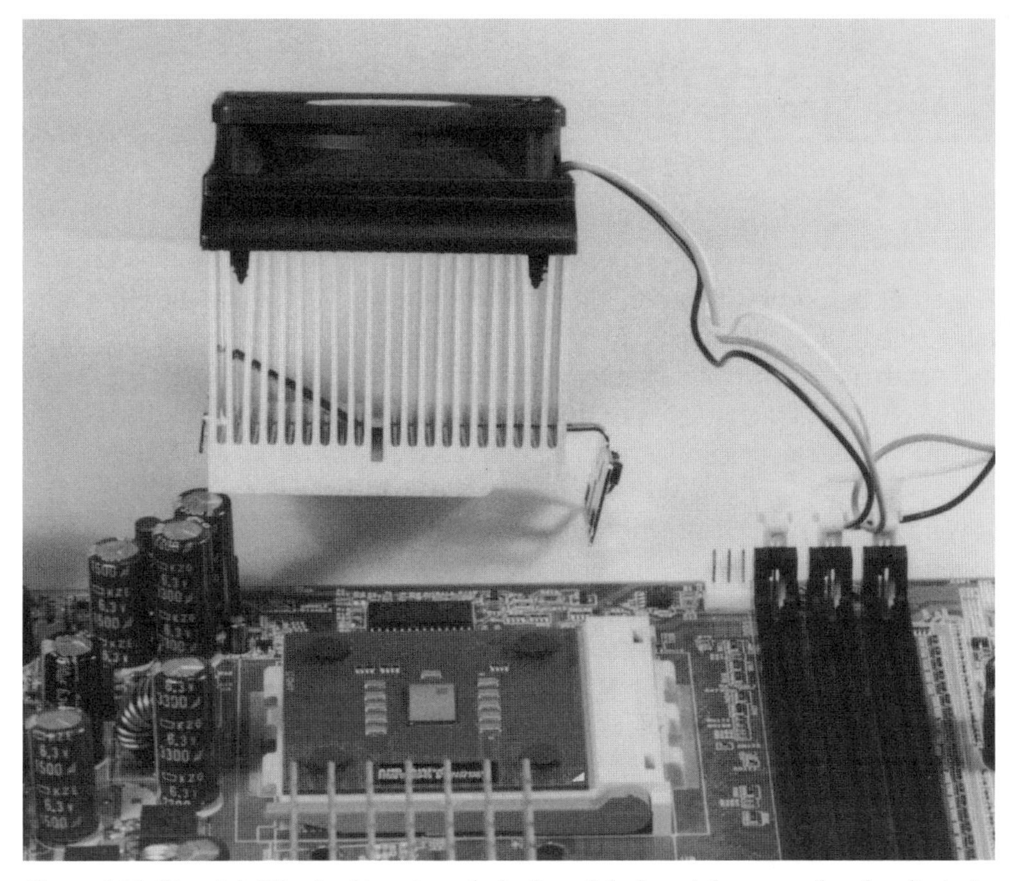

Figure 4.10. Heatsink Clip. Looking through the fins of the heatsink, we see that the clip isn't symmetrical. The point of the clip will push down on the CPU die when properly installed.

Figure 4.11. Secure the heatsink. Be gentle and avoid putting unnecessary force on the clip and the CPU socket.

Use a flat-head screwdriver or “other appropriate tool” to secure the clip to the other side of the CPU socket. Place the screwdriver into the clip opening for it and gently push down and slightly away from the CPU socket, allowing the clip to clear the three notches of the CPU socket. Then, push the clip back toward the socket, engaging the three notches (Figure 4.11 and 4.12).

If you read the AMD instructions for installing the Athlon, they say to use the “appropriate tool” to secure the clip, but they give absolutely no clue as to what that tool is. Pliers? Hammer? Power Drill? Weed Eater?

The heatsink here seems to have a natural affinity for a flat-head screwdriver, and that tool works well here, so it’s the one we’ll use. Be careful so that the tool doesn’t slip and damage the mainboard. Don’t use an “inappropriate” tool which you think might slip.

The AMD heatsink puts considerable force on the notches that the heatsink locks into. Because of this, be gentle when using the screwdriver to push

Figure 4.12 shows a flat-head screwdriver ("Appropriate Tool") engaging the clip of the heatsink. This allows you to push the clip down and lock it into place. The other end of the clip is already engaged to the notches of the CPU socket on the other side of the heatsink. Be sure to select a tool that won't slip and damage the mainboard. Do not push down on the heatsink itself. The clip will push the heatsink down naturally and allow it to contact the die of the CPU.

down and lock in the heatsink. Don't push the lever much farther down than necessary to secure the heatsink.

The installation instructions say you should examine the seating of the heatsink to be sure it's resting properly on the die. In practice, it's difficult if not impossible to do this (See Figure 4.9). But, if you have a good light handy, you can peek between the heatsink and the CPU if you want. (Incidentally, a Mini-Mag AA flashlight is a great tool to have handy here.)

Finally, examine the mainboard manual and see where the three-pin CPU fan power connection pins are. They're usually clearly marked (Figure 4.13). Then, plug in the heatsink fan. **Don't forget to plug in the heatsink/CPU fan! Do this immediately after the heatsink is installed!** If the heatsink fan isn't plugged in, it won't work and your CPU will overheat. When your system is fully assembled, it's a good idea to leave the side of the case off and examine all of the fans to be sure they're operating properly.

While the thermal grease and the connection between the CPU die and the heatsink allow heat to be *conducted* away from the CPU, the heat builds up on the fins of the heatsink where the fan dissipates it from there. The fins spread this heat over a large area, and the fan helps blow the heat away.

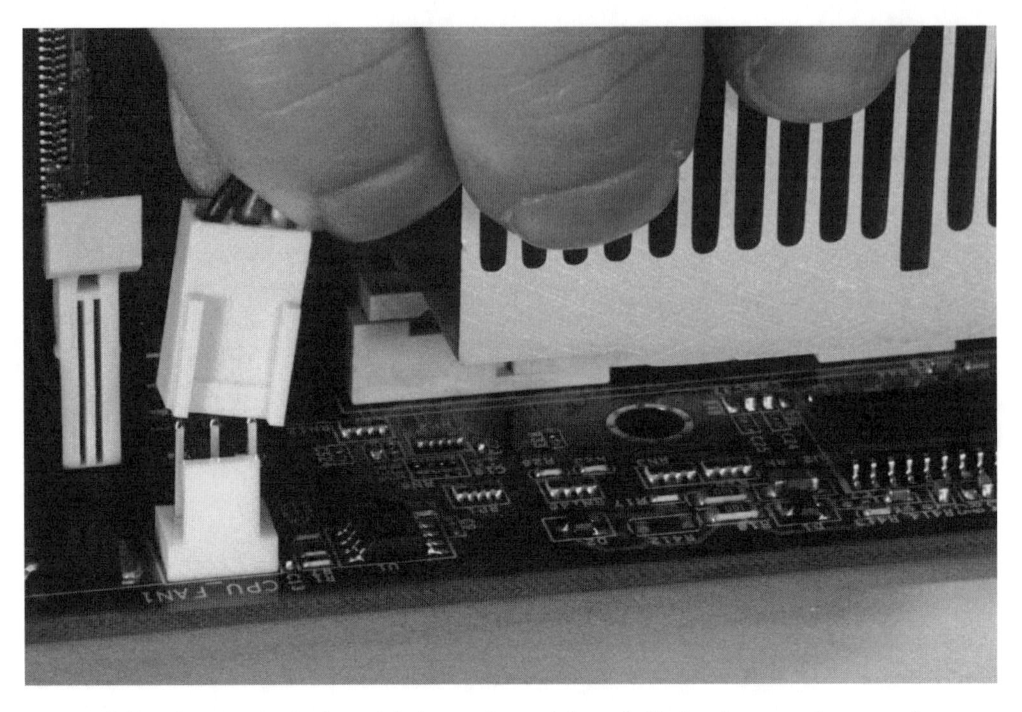

Figure 4.13. Plugging in the heatsink fan to the mainboard. Notice the post shows us the proper orientation. ***IMPORTANT! DO NOT FORGET THIS STEP!*** *Failure to properly cool the Athlon CPU will damage it. When you first start your system, leave the side panel of the PC case off and examine all fans to be sure they are spinning rapidly.*

You now have your CPU and heatsink properly installed on your mainboard. Well done!

Installing Memory (DDR)

Now that you have your CPU installed, it's time to install the RAM. Most common today is DDR memory. It's a good idea to purchase your mainboard before you purchase memory, just to be sure you acquire the correct memory. Read the manual that came with your mainboard to see what kind of memory it uses.

RAM is very sensitive to static electricity. Before picking up a RAM chip, touch both hands to a metal piece to draw any static electricity away from your hands. You might also want to wear a grounding wrist strap when you install the memory. Try to touch the RAM only on its two sides (See Figure 3.3) and the top near the sides. The sides are great for picking it up, but

Figure 4.14. RAM slots (or sockets) on mainboard.

Figure 4.15. The RAM chip has a notch to prevent inserting it in the wrong orientation.

you'll need to push it into its socket from the top. Try not to touch the chips themselves or the metal contacts. And, leave the RAM in its original packaging until you're ready to install it.

Not touching the metal leads of the memory is also important because oils that build up on your hands can damage the leads.

Examine the RAM sockets (Figure 4.14) and the RAM chip (Figure 4.15). You'll see that RAM can only be inserted in one direction, because there's a small cut out separating the metal contacts (also called leads) on the RAM chip into two sides. Each side has a different number of metal contacts, making it impossible to seat the RAM chip incorrectly. Be sure the notch in the RAM chip is aligned with the protruding part on the RAM socket.

Figure 4.16. Open the lever at the sides of the memory slot. Pushing the chip down will close the lever.

Fully open the locking levers of the RAM socket (Figure 4.16). Each bank will have a lever at each side. Push the lever gently away from the RAM socket and down until it is fully open. Now, pick up the RAM chip and place it over the RAM socket. Be sure that it's aligned in the proper direction. Press the chip straight down into the socket. If it sticks, you might find it useful to allow one side of the RAM chip to enter first, but try to keep the chip as nearly level as possible as you push it into place (Figure 4.17 and 4.18).

When the RAM chip seats itself, the levers at the side should pop into position themselves, "locking" the memory chip in place (Figure 4.16). You shouldn't need to touch these levers after opening them to insert the memory.

Figure 4.17. Inserting the memory chip into its slot. Align the chip and press straight down. Be sure to touch the metal of the PC power supply before picking up the chip to draw off any static electricity that may have built up on your hands.

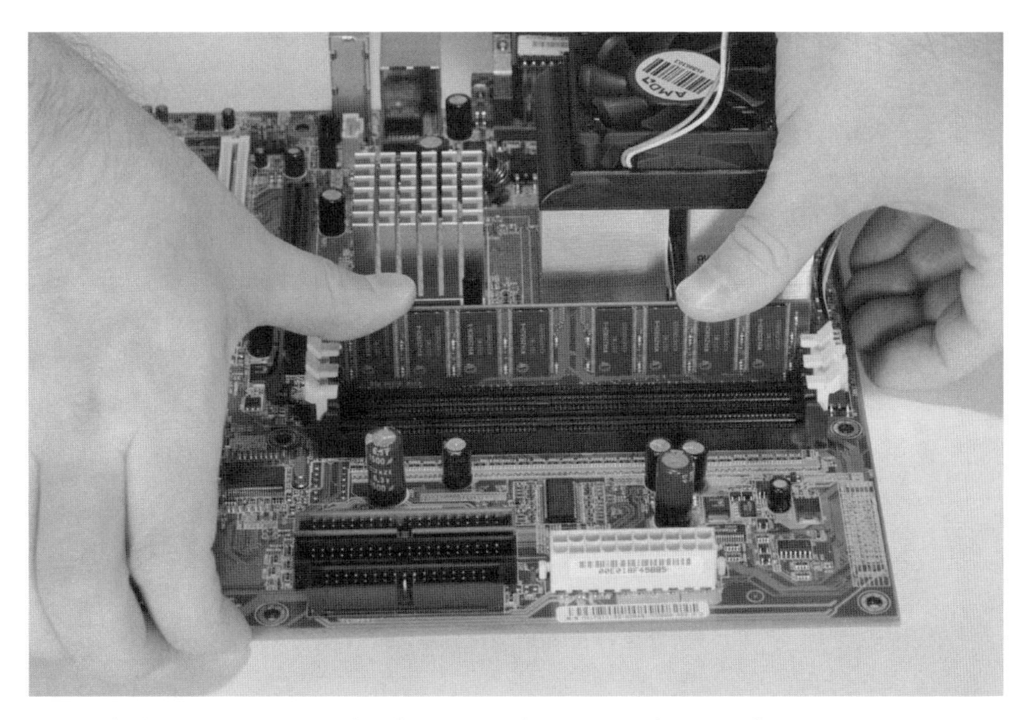

Figure 4.18. You can use your thumbs to press the memory chip into place.

Examine the memory chip to be sure it's fully seated. Sometimes one end of a chip might seat fully, but the other end doesn't. If so, just push the non-seated end in some more.

Your RAM chip is now fully installed (Figure 4.19).

Incidentally, each memory socket is called a bank. And, the banks are numbered. Examine your mainboard and its manual to see which bank is Bank 1. It's most common to place a single memory chip into Bank 1. If you install several memory chips, see which order allows the easiest installation of all the chips. This isn't usually a problem with DDR memory which is inserted straight down, but if one of the banks of memory is close to some obstruction, you might want to install that bank first. That way each chip will be easy to install.

It's usually recommended that all your memory chips be similar. For example, the memory used in this build is Kingston DDR PC2700 ValueRAM. So, if you decided to add another 256MB RAM chip to your PC and you had Kingston PC2700 ValueRAM installed, it would probably be good to use Kingston PC2700 ValueRAM for the new 256MB chip.

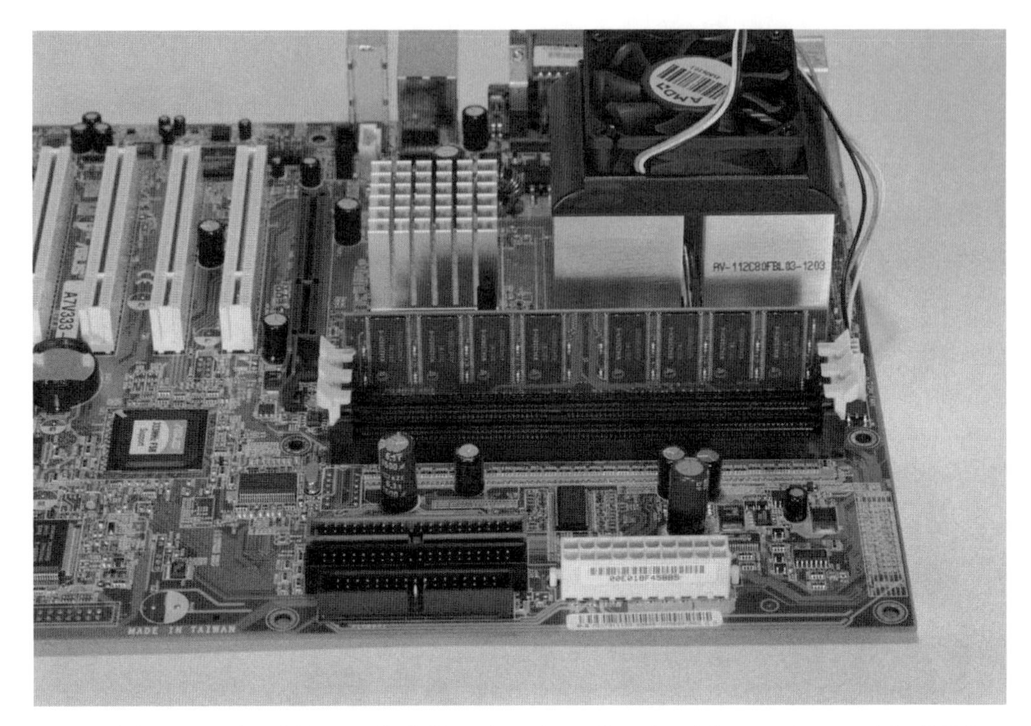

Figure 4.19. RAM chip fully installed. Note the wires off to the right aren't part of the RAM. They are for the heatsink fan which was plugged in earlier.

You can mix PC2700 chips with PC2100 chips, for example, but they'll all often run at the slowest speed. Whenever you have a question about memory compatibility, check your mainboard manual and look for the memory chip manufacturer's website with google.com.

For example, the mainboard manual for the A7V333-X says that the chips should be unbuffered non-ECC DDR SDRAM. That's the most common type. But, if you wanted to double check that the Kingston ValueRAM we purchased was appropriate, you could go to kingston.com and look up the exact Kingston model of the memory chip to see that it's non-ECC (you could get the model number from a website like BestBuy.com where you were thinking of purchasing the RAM).

Today, most memory sockets and leads will use gold contacts. You can see this by the goldish color of the connectors. It's usually recommended that you don't try to mate gold connectors with tin connectors, because the metals won't play nicely with each other. They try to steal each other's electrons which leads to a corrosive-type effect.

Congratulations! Your mainboard now has its CPU installed with its heatsink and fan. The RAM has been placed (Figure 4.20). Now we can place the mainboard in the case.

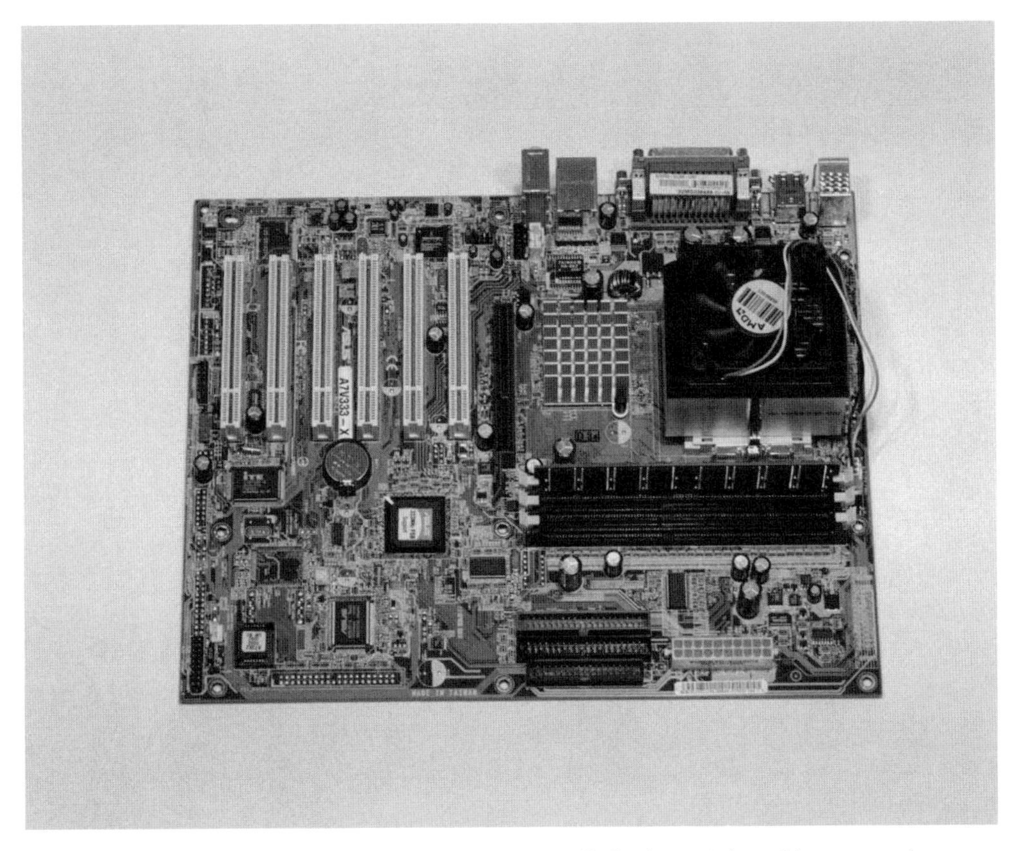

Figure 4.20. Mainboard with heatsink and RAM installed. The mainboard is now ready to place in the case.

Sometimes figuring out how to open your new PC case is the most challenging part of building your own PC.

Installing The Mainboard In The Case

After you've installed the CPU, heatsink, and RAM to the mainboard, it's time to install the mainboard in the case. Read the mainboard manual to see if any jumpers on the mainboard need to be adjusted. Usually, the board will be all ready to go.

It's also a good idea to familiarize yourself with the various connectors on the mainboard, especially the small pin connectors to the case, such as the power LED and reset switch. When the board is installed in the case, it might be harder to see the pins and the printing on the mainboard. So, it's good to know what goes where ahead of time.

Opening The Case

Figuring out how to open the PC case can be slightly challenging. If your case came with instructions, examine the instructions to see how to open it. It's always amusing to find a case with the instructions for opening it inside the case.

It's possible to overlook some simple thing, such as a hidden latch that must be opened. And, if you overlook a hidden trick, you might find yourself unscrewing all sorts of things that would be better left alone, such as the screws attaching the power supply to the case. Unless your power supply fries and needs replacement, there's no reason to remove it.

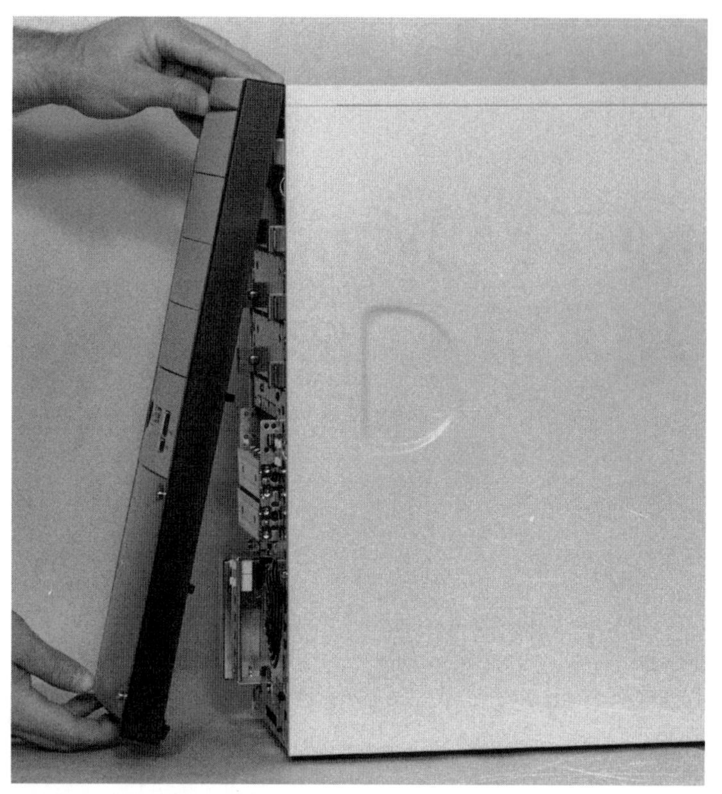

Figure 5.1. Removing the front cover of the PC case. Your case may open differently. Inspect it carefully before deciding how to proceed. Although the case is pictured lying flat on the table, it sometimes helps to lift the front of the case a few inches off the table to be able to get a good grip on the latch.

Other systems have side panels that are easily removable from the back, while the front panel (also called a "bezel") remains in place. You usually need to remove one or two screws that secure a side panel and then just slide the side panel out.

Other cases, such as some Dell cases, absolutely require finding a manual online or a Mensa-level intelligence to understand how to open the case. But, most ATX cases should open relatively easily. Just examine all sides and the top and the bottom of the case and decide how best to proceed.

Figure 5.1 shows removing the front panel of our Enlight case. There is a latch below the front of the case which allows the front of the case to be removed. Be sure to press the latch all the way so that it disengages from the case. These latches are sometimes made of cheap plastic (or, at least, it appears

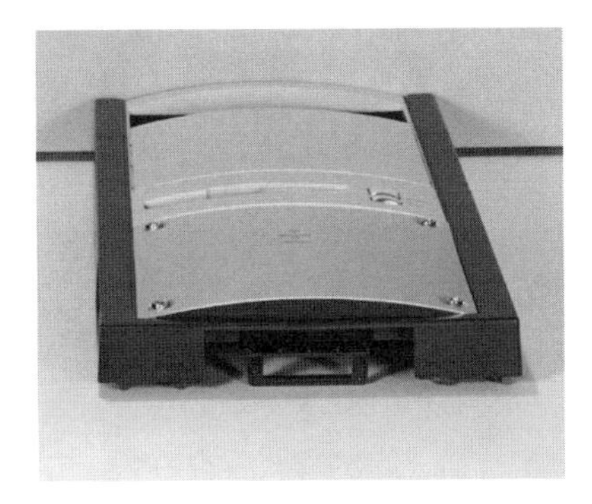

Figure 5.2. Bottom of the bezel is pictured. Notice the latches and lugs on bezels are often made of plastic. Be gentle to avoid breaking a lug or latch.

cheap to me), so don't use any greater force than necessary. With the latch pressed, pull the front cover away from the rest of the case.

After the latch has been disengaged from the case, the bezel pivots away at the top of the case. Only pivot the bezel a bit and then try to pull the bezel straight out and away from the case.

Examining Drive Cages

After removing the front panel, we see several things (Figure 5.3). First is that there is a removable cage for holding a floppy drive, hard drive, and other 3.5" drives (Figure 5.4). This particular drive cage pulls out easily after disengaging two levers at the sides. The smaller 3.5" drives will be attached to this cage with screws.

Notice that this 3.5" drive cage has three locations, called drive bays, to attach 3.5" drives. Two of the three slots are covered by RF shields which are designed to provide a metal barrier between the inside of the case and the outside world. When installing a drive, you usually remove the RF shield. These particular shields just pop out and are easily replaceable.

Notice that the top bay matches up with the slot in the front bezel for the 3.5" floppy drive (Figure 5.5). So, you can't install the floppy drive in the lower bay unless you want to use a power saw to cut out a hole in the front of the case, which you probably don't want to do! This provides a fancy looking front for the floppy drive. The actual floppy drive will sit *behind* this interface. The button on the case to remove a floppy disk will engage the button on the floppy drive, itself, and the light from the LED showing floppy activity on the floppy drive will be channeled to the front.

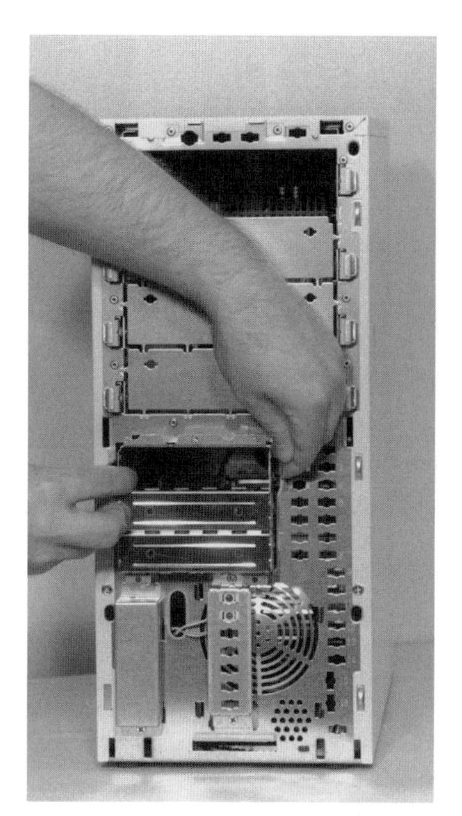

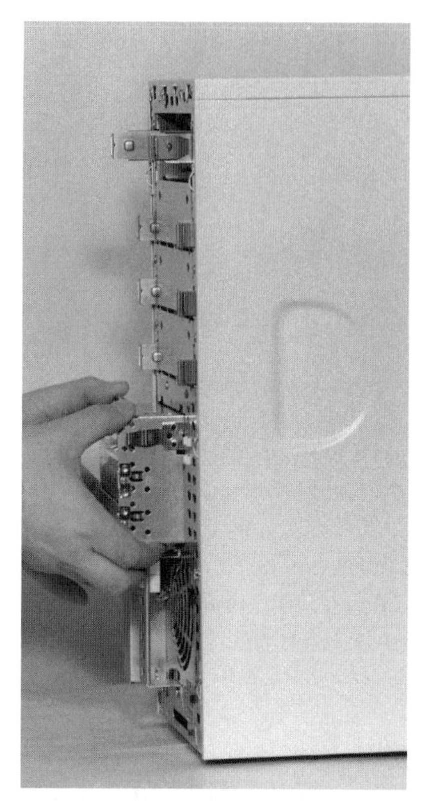

Figure 5.3. Removing the 3.5" drive cage. 3.5" drives (floppy and hard drives) will attach to this removable cage with screws.

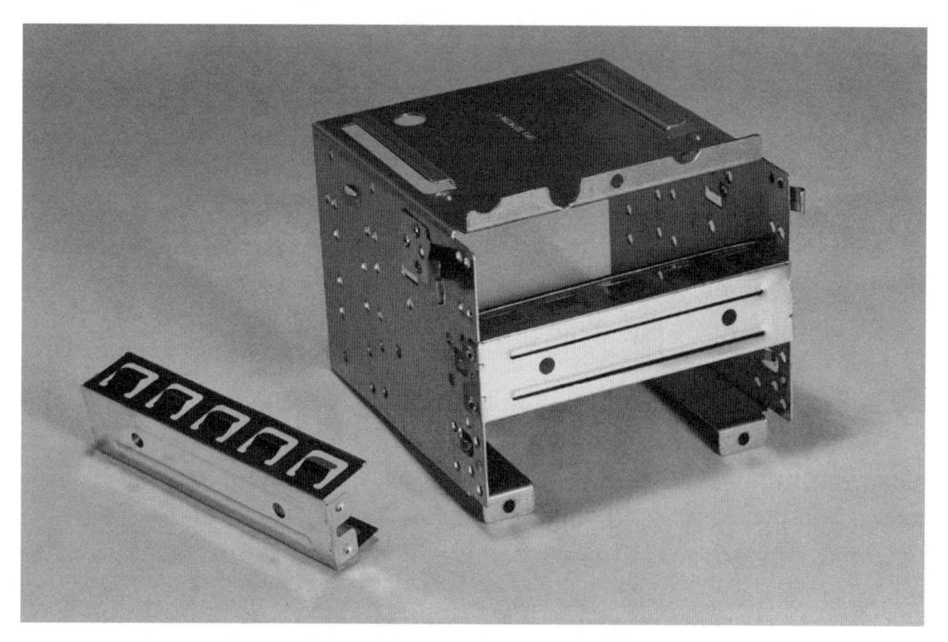

Figure 5.4. The 3.5" drive cage removed. We have also taken out the metal part known as an RF shield. In the two open spaces, we'll install the floppy and hard drives.

Figure 5.5. Front of case next to bezel. Notice that when the floppy drive is installed, it must line up with the hole in the bezel. This determines the bay in which the floppy must be installed.

Other cases just have the floppy drive sit flush with the front of the case. Either style is fine.

Some cases will also have removable cages for 5.25" drives, such as CD-RW drives. Working with a 5.25" cage is usually the same as working with a 3.5" cage. Either the 5.25" drives will be attached to the cage with screws or sometimes rails will be attached to the drive and then the rails slide into place in the cage. If rails come with your case, just attach the rails to the drive and insert the drive. Be sure the rails aren't upside down or backward.

This particular case doesn't use a 5.25" removable cage. And, it doesn't have removable rails which are attached to the sides of the drives. Rather, for each

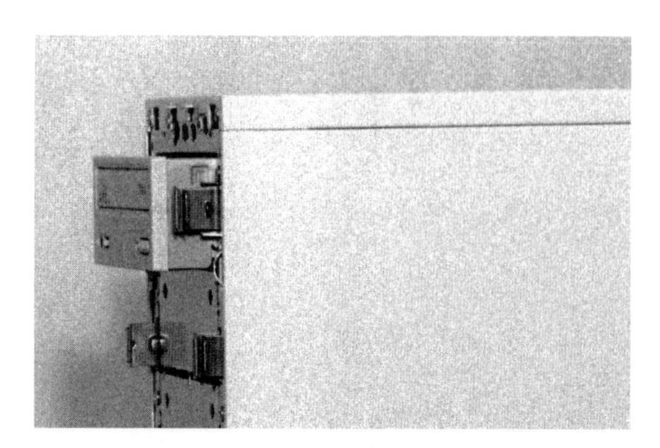

Figure 5.6. This case has little levers that pull out. Then, the 5.25" device is inserted. Then, the lever is closed to secure the drive. Your PC case will have its own method of securing 5.25" drives to it.

drive bay, it has levers that pull out. Then the drive is placed into its bay and pushed into place, and the levers are closed to engage the drive and hold it in place (Figure 5.6). This design doesn't even require a screwdriver.

Figure 5.7. These 5.25" RF shields are "removable" by breaking them off. Use a side cutter to detach the next shield, if needed. One space is already provided for one 5.25" drive. Be careful not to push too hard to remove one of these, because when it breaks off, your hand could slip and you could get cut by the sharp edges.

The 5.25" RF shields have one opening which, it is assumed, will be used for the CD-RW. The other RF shields are also removable. However, they're attached by thin pieces of metal (Figure 5.7). To remove a shield, just twist, turn, and bend the RF shield until it breaks loose. Unfortunately, sometimes, there will be sharp edges, and, once removed, such a shield can't be replaced. So, only remove this type of shield as you need the bay. And, always be careful of sharp edges on a case. We won't be using any of the other 5.25" drive bays, so we'll leave all 5.25" RF shields in place. If the metal holding a "removable" shield is particularly strong, you might need to cut it with a wire cutter with a small head (called a side cutter). Be careful not to cut yourself when breaking off one of these RF shields. Blood spurting out of your hand detracts from the fun of building your own PC.

Next, we remove the side panel. It's held in place with a single screw (Figure 5.8 and 5.9).

Figure 5.8. Removing the side panel of the case. It's held in by a single screw. You generally remove the side oppose the I/O shield which we discuss next. Pull the side slightly forward to remove it. Your case may disassemble differently.

Figure 5.9. Removing the side panel. After sliding the panel forward a bit, it will disengage.

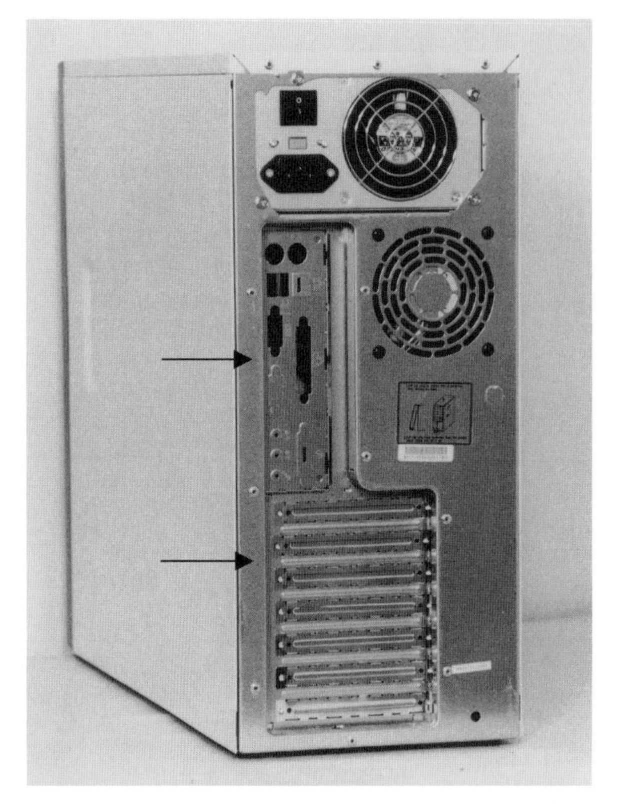

Figure 5.10. Back of case. The top arrow points to the removable I/O shield. The bottom arrow points to removable slot covers for expansion cards (PCI cards and AGP cards) discussed later.

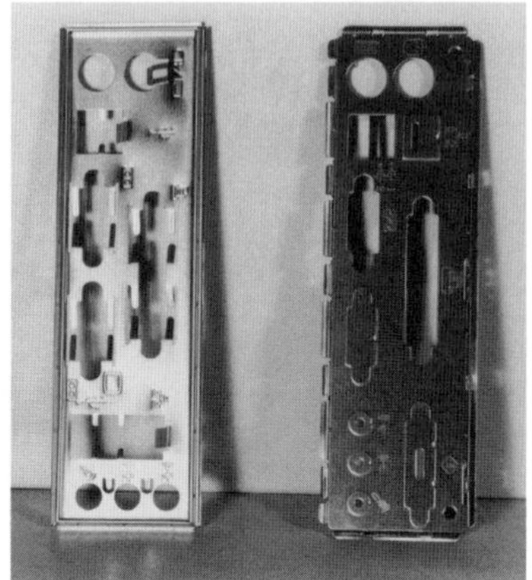

Figure 5.11. Comparing I/O shields.

Changing The I/O Shield

Now that the case is opened, we can examine the I/O shield at the back of the case (Figure 5.10). This is a metal shield through which connectors attached to the mainboard protrude. The PS/2 mouse connection, PS/2 keyboard connection, serial port, parallel port, and other connections to the mainboard will be connected through the I/O shield.

The I/O shield that comes with the case doesn't match up with the connectors on the mainboard. We can see this by comparing the I/O connectors on the mainboard to the shield. Just hold the mainboard up to the shield or place it inside the case so the connectors face the I/O shield to see if the mainboard matches the existing I/O shield. If the mainboard comes with its own I/O shield, we can hold up the I/O shield that comes with the mainboard and compare it to the one that comes with the case (Figure 5.11).

Our mainboard has built-in networking, and there is an RJ-45 network connection directly to the mainboard. The I/O shield that comes with the mainboard allows for this connection, while the standard one that comes with the case doesn't. So, we need to replace the I/O shield.

Our first step is to remove the I/O shield that comes with the case, so that we can install the new I/O shield. Many I/O shields are designed to pop into place from the rear of the case. These are removed by pushing them from outside the case back into the case. Sometimes using a small, flat screwdriver to wedge one side of the shield into the slot helps get it started (Figure 5.12).

The shield that came with this case is slightly different. It has two sides which are different and is most easily removed by first using a flat screwdriver to push one side of the shield out of the case. Then, the I/O shield can be removed by pushing it from inside the case (Figure 5.13 and 5.14).

Figure 5.12. Some I/O shields pop out easily. Others are best removed by using a small, flat screwdriver to disengage them. Be careful when pushing on these, because they often contain sharp edges.

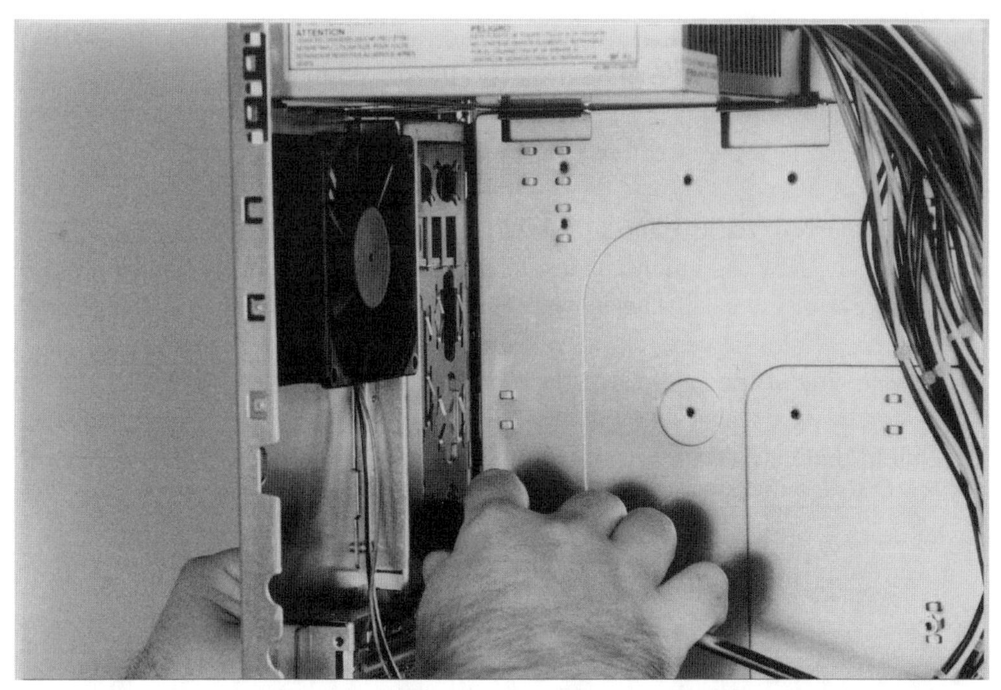

Figure 5.13. Using a screwdriver to pop out the old I/O shield. This particular shield removes most naturally from the back of the case. Some shields are best removed by pushing them into the case. Examine your shield to decide how best to proceed. Using the back of a screwdriver to do the pushing helps prevent cut fingers if the I/O shield pops out suddenly.

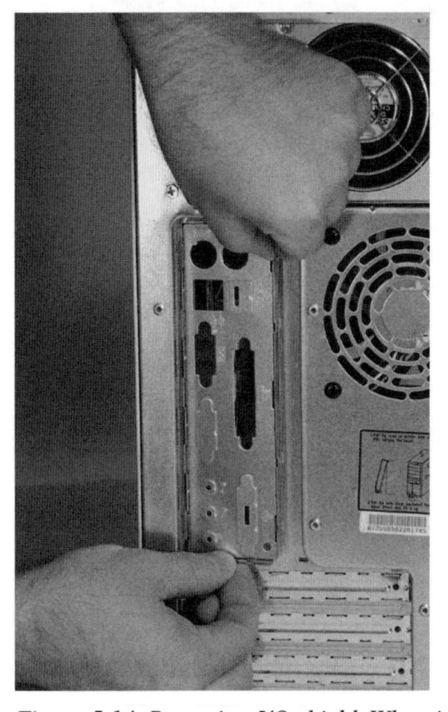

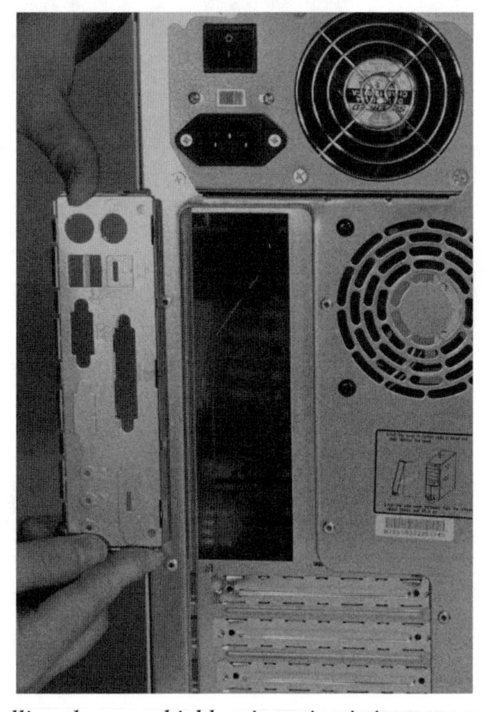

Figure 5.14. Removing I/O shield. When installing the new shield, orientation is important.

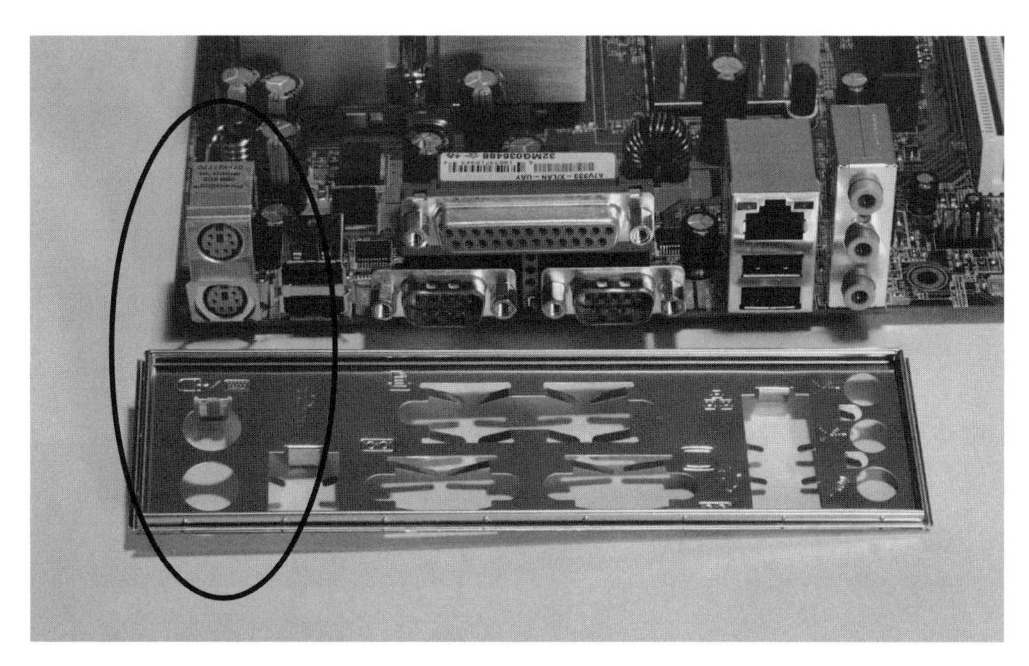

Figure 5.15. Because the corner of the mainboard must sit toward the top of the case (see Figure 5.13 to get an idea of where the mainboard sits), the new I/O shield must be installed so that the two big holes on the left (for the keyboard and mouse) are toward the top of the case. The three connectors to the right are for the mainboard's built-in sound.

I/O shields are often designed so that the metal at the edges wraps around to give the edges a natural springiness that holds the I/O shield in place. Examine your I/O shield carefully before you start to remove it to help you find the best way to remove it.

Now we'll put the new I/O shield in place. This new shield is the conventional style which pops into place from inside the case (Figure 5.16). After installing the I/O shield from the inside of the case, we could use the back of a screwdriver to push the I/O shield into place. Some I/O shields have very sharp edges, so be careful not to allow your hand to slip and hit the shield or the case when you're removing or installing an I/O shield. Remember, blood spurting out of your finger will detract from the fun of building your own PC.

Figures 5.13 to 5.15 show us that the orientation of the I/O shield is important. Typically, the PS/2 connectors for the keyboard and the mouse will sit toward the top of the case.

Figure 5.16. Popping the new I/O shield into place. Note: The orientation of the shield is determined by the mainboard. The metal fins of the shield point inward. Writing on the shield to identify the connectors is on the outside.

Test Fitting The Mainboard

Now that you have the new I/O shield installed, we can test fit the mainboard (Figure 5.17 and 5.18). Turn the case on its side so that the mainboard can easily be placed in its location. You'll know where the mainboard should sit because the I/O connectors from the mainboard will need to line up with the I/O shield. There are usually several standoffs already placed inside the case on which the mainboard will sit.

The mainboard should fit with no problem. **We need to watch out for extra standoffs that don't line up with screw holes in the mainboard.** Remove those standoffs or they will touch the bottom of the mainboard in undesirable locations. A standoff below a screw hole is acceptable (Figure 5.19 and 5.20).

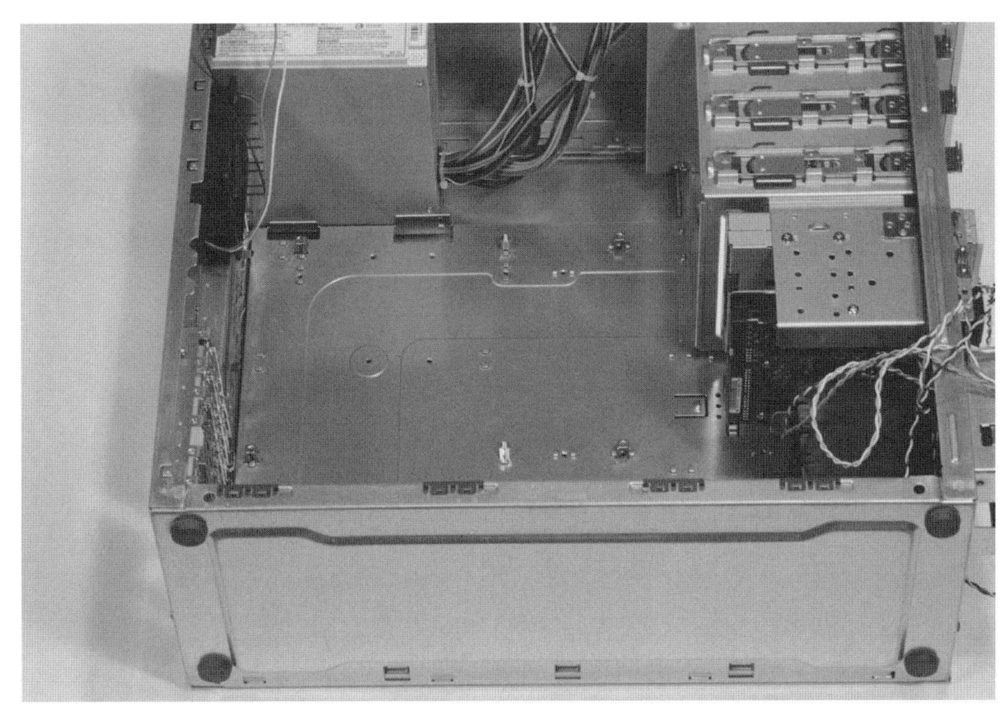

Figure 5.17. Fitting the mainboard. Place the case on its side. Push all power connectors and wires out of the way before placing the mainboard. Our initial goal is to learn where we want to place standoffs which will support the board.

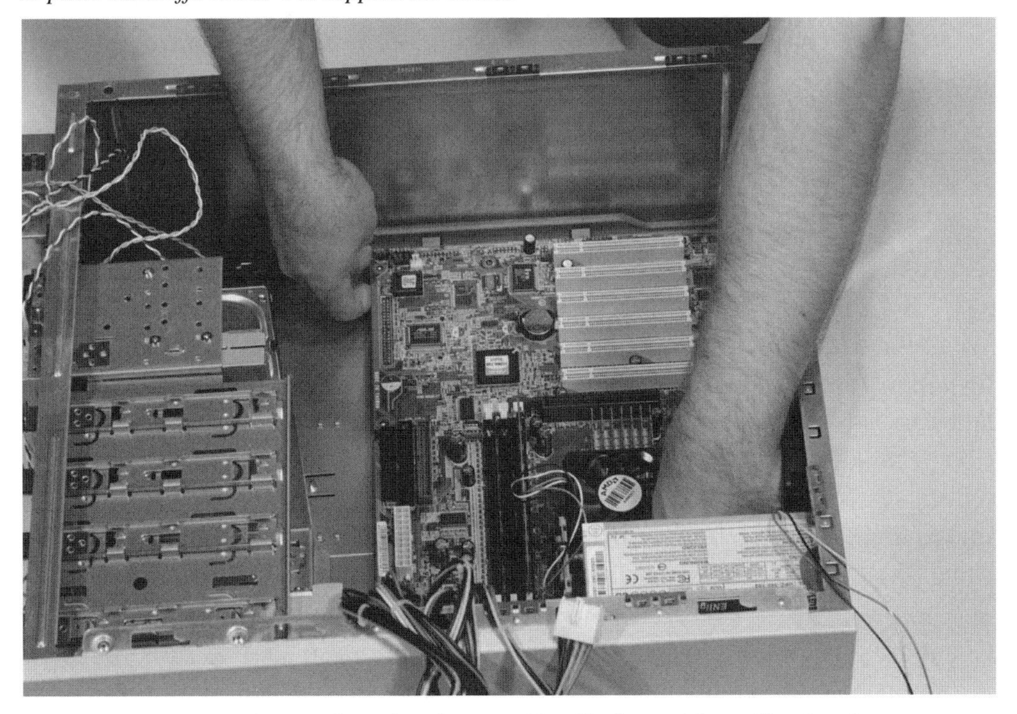

Figure 5.18. Placing the mainboard in the case. Handle the mainboard by the edges.

Figure 5.19. Every case standoff must line up with a hole in the mainboard. Remove any standoffs that don't line up. This is ***important****, because improperly placed standoffs could innappropriately ground parts of the mainboard.*

Figure 5.20. Removing an offending standoff that wouldn't sit below a hole in the mainboard. When placing the board, always look for standoffs that don't line up with holes.

We might also want to add a few extra standoffs at other locations that match up with screw holes in the mainboard. In particular, in this build, we needed to add standoffs in the area around the sockets for the ATX power supply and the ribbon cable sockets for the floppy and hard drives. These standoffs help reduce stress to the mainboard when the ribbon and power cables are plugged in. We don't want the board to bend under the force of plugging in a ribbon cable. Figure 5.19 shows a standoff near a ribbon socket.

Count the final number of standoffs that you plan to use, and be sure that there is a screw hole in the mainboard for each standoff used. Then, be sure each

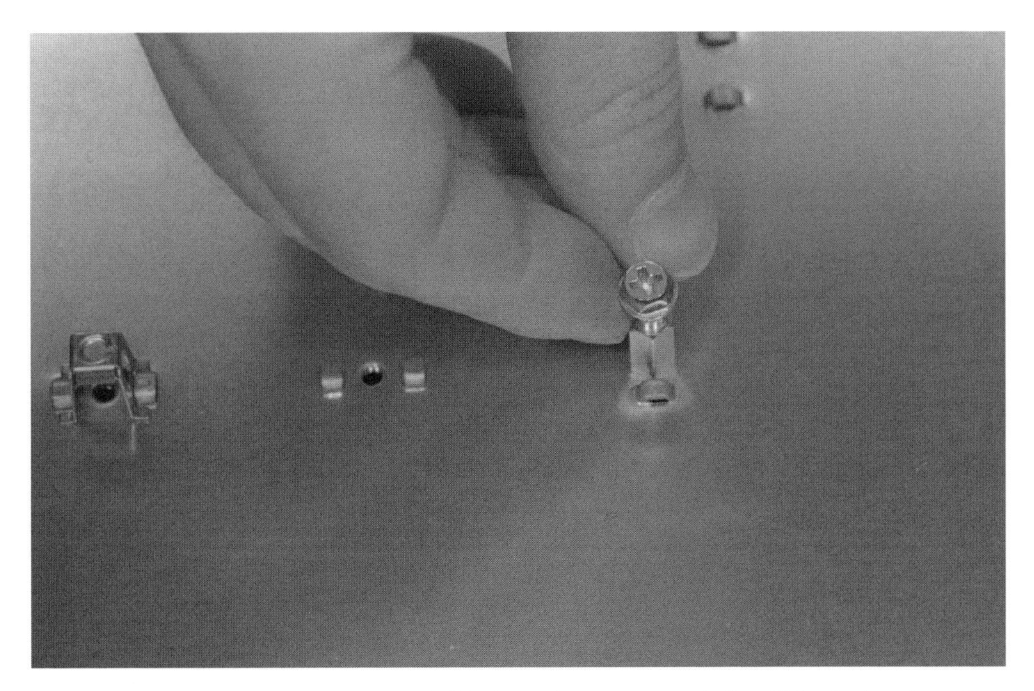

Figure 5.21. Testing a screw in a standoff hole. At least two standoffs will be designed so that the mainboard can be screwed down and secured.

standoff is visible through a screw hole. This will help you not to forget to remove a standoff without a screw hole above it on the mainboard.

Some cases come with plastic standoffs which are designed to be inserted into the mainboard first. Then, the bottom end of the plastic standoff sits on the metal case.

The Enlight case comes with two different types of standoffs (Figure 5.21). One style is designed with a screw hole in the top. This allows the mainboard to be secured to the case with a screw. These standoffs are also used for properly grounding the mainboard to the case. Screwing down the mainboard to the standoff grounds the mainboard. You'll see a ring of metal around the mainboard hole. This ring helps ground the mainboard to the case. Some experts suggest only using plastic standoffs below mainboard holes that lack a ring of metal. A variety of standoffs will usually come with your PC case.

The other style of standoff isn't designed to be screwed down. It just sits below the mainboard and provides a resting surface for the mainboard. This

Figure 5.22. Back of the case shows that as the mainboard was pushed toward the I/O shield one of the metal fins was bent and now interferes with the connector. If this happens, remove the mainboard and bend the offending fin out of the way.

case has two screw-down standoffs already in good locations, and we'll screw down the mainboard only in those two locations.

Be sure to test fit the screws that come with your case to be sure that you've selected the correct screws for securing the mainboard (Figure 5.21). If you just start a screw with a screwdriver, it's possible to strip the socket or the screw threads. So before you seat the mainboard, first test the screw with your hand to be sure it works. Then, have the two proper screws (or more) handy when you place the mainboard.

As you place the mainboard, you might notice that it wants to sit about a quarter inch back from the I/O shield. This is natural. Move the board around just a bit, and push it toward the I/O shield. It should pop into location. Then, the screw holes of the standoffs should be centered under the screw holes of the mainboard.

The I/O shield has little fins sticking out which are designed to press against the I/O connectors of the mainboard. These fins help ground the mainboard (in theory, at least. If your I/O shield is plastic, I don't see how this can work!) Plus, the pressure from these fins helps secure the mainboard in place.

After you push the mainboard toward the I/O shield and the board is properly lined-up, examine the connectors through the I/O shield. Sometimes, one of the metal fins will get in the way and be smashed so that it sits in front of the I/O connector, effectively preventing the connector's use (Figure 5.22).

Simply remove the board and bend any offending I/O fins back and out of the way and try again to seat the mainboard. Be sure that any fins you bend back don't touch any part of the mainboard, or, if they do, try to make the fins only touch the metal case of the I/O connectors on the board.

Also when securing the mainboard, be sure all case wires are out of the way. Don't allow any case wires to remain below the mainboard. And, if you drop any screws or anything else, be sure they're removed before installing the mainboard. Any little metal parts inappropriately floating around under the mainboard could cause problems, because they could inappropriately ground the bottom of the board. Also be sure that your screwdriver is clean and has no metal shavings or grease on it from previous projects. Little metal shavings are also bad for mainboards.

Now screw the mainboard to the case (Figure 5.23). You'll only need two screws. But, feel free to use more.

You now have your mainboard installed in the case (Figure 5.24). Unless you decide to upgrade the mainboard, you'll probably never need to remove it. If you do, be sure to prepare a clean surface to set the mainboard on and be sure to ground your hands by touching a metal surface before touching the mainboard.

Figure 5.23. Screwing down the mainboard secures it to the case.

Figure 5.24. Mainboard installed in the case.

Finally, your case should have a case fan. The fan connector is usually the type that slips over three pins on the mainboard. See your mainboard manual to locate the case fan connection. **Connect your case fan (Figure 5.25). Double check to be sure your CPU fan is also connected.** Some case fans connect to wires directly from the power supply.

Connecting Case Leads To The Mainboard

Finally, there are several leads from the case that must be attached to the mainboard (Figure 5.26 and 5.27, also see Figure 2.7). These leads include:

1) Power Switch (PW)
2) Reset Switch
3) Power LED
4) Speaker Connector
5) HD LED

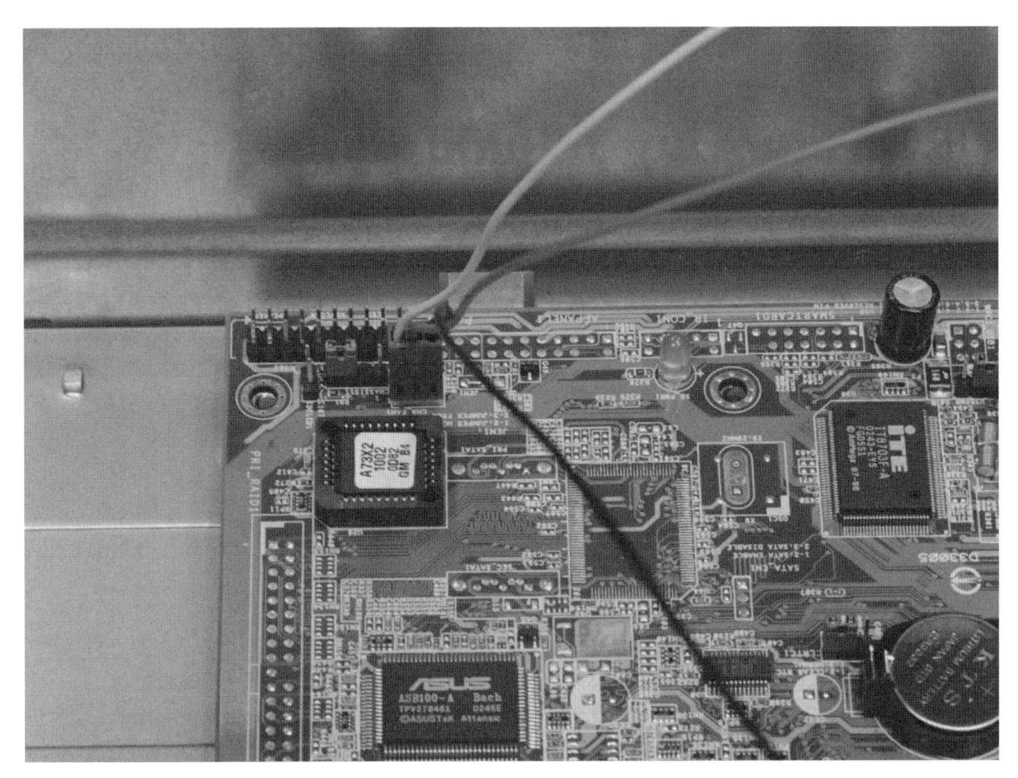

Figure 5.25. The PC case fan is connected. See your mainboard manual to determine where the case fan is connected. The case fan is typically connected with a three-pin connector similar to the CPU fan you connected earlier.

You'll need to consult your mainboard manual to determine which pins these leads are connected to. Most of the leads, such as the power switch and the reset switch, can be connected in either orientation. There is no "Pin 1" or side to these connectors.

Otherwise, if connected in the wrong orientation, something just won't work. For example, it's possible to have the HD LED backward. If this is backward, when you start the PC, it's likely your HD LED light won't go on at all, or it will go on and stay on. Usually, we expect to see the HD LED on the front of the case blink with hard drive activity. However, these connectors, if oriented incorrectly, will not damage the system.

These connectors were discussed in the component overview section. It's important to inspect the little pins carefully before installing your mainboard, because it's easy to be off a pin and you'll have a better view of the pins before the mainboard is installed.

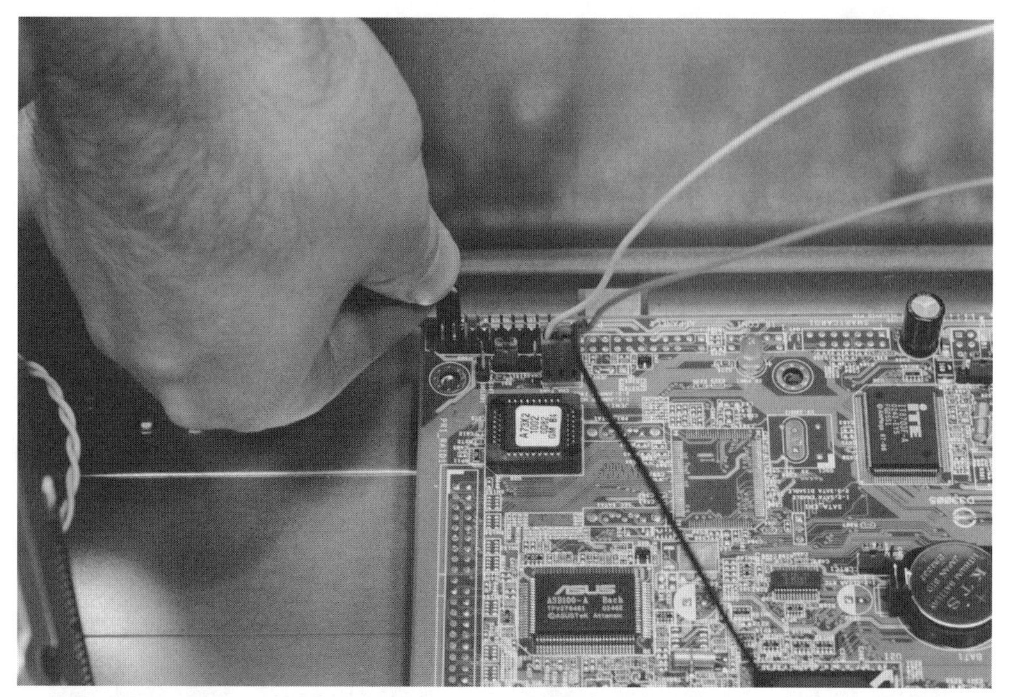

Figure 5.26. Connecting the reset switch from the case to the mainboard. Pushing the reset switch on the case restarts your system.

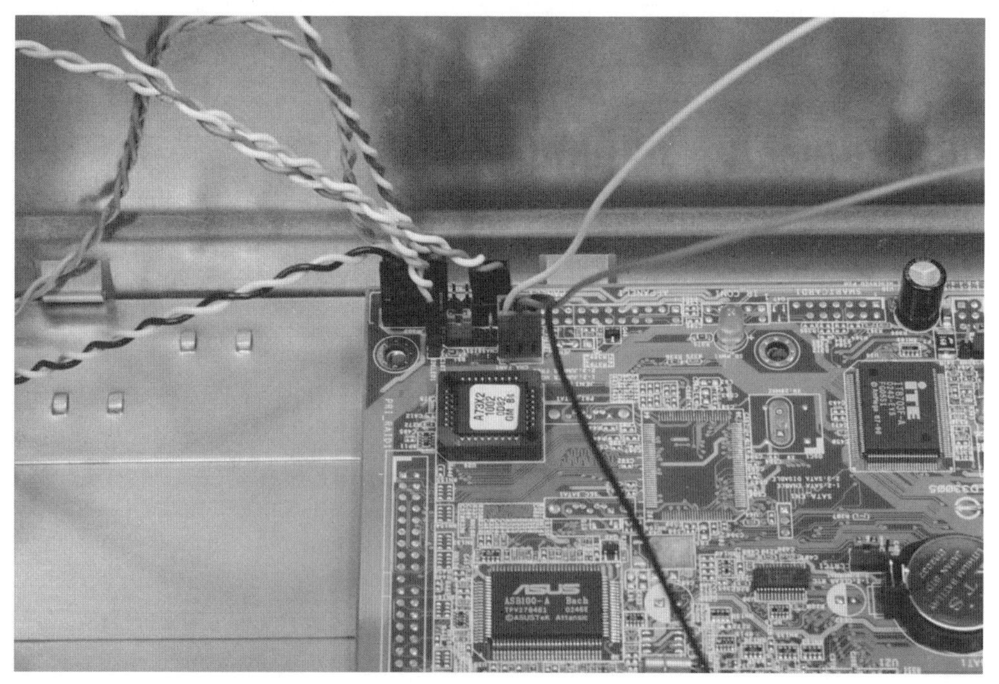

Figure 5.27. Connect all the thin-wire connectors from the PC case to the mainboard. See your mainboard manual to determine the proper connections. Often, the pins are also marked on the mainboard. These connectors were discussed during the component overview.

Figure 5.28. Testing a screw in the floppy drive. Before installing any drive, have the proper screws handy. The floppy drives use fine thread screws. The hard drives and other drives use coarse screws that typically come with the drive. Notice the screwdriver is slightly magnetic allowing it to hold the screw. Don't worry. That small magnetic field won't hurt your drives.

Installing 3.5" And 5.25" Drives

Floppy Drive

Next up, we'll install the 3.5" drives in their cage. Each side of any drive has screw holes which will secure the drive to the cage. Let's start with the floppy drive. The floppy drive uses the fine thread screws that came with your case. Most floppy drives don't come with screws. Pick up one of the fine thread screws and test it to be sure you have the correct screw (Figure 5.28). Just see if you can get it started with your fingers or with light pressure from a screwdriver. Find three similar screws. If a particular screw won't go, it's probably the wrong thread or, possibly, the thread of the screw or the nut has been stripped. Try another screw. Try to avoid forcing any screws.

Now, insert the floppy drive in its cage in the proper orientation (so you can put a disk in it from the front) and secure the drive by tightening the four screws (Figure 5.29 and 5.30).

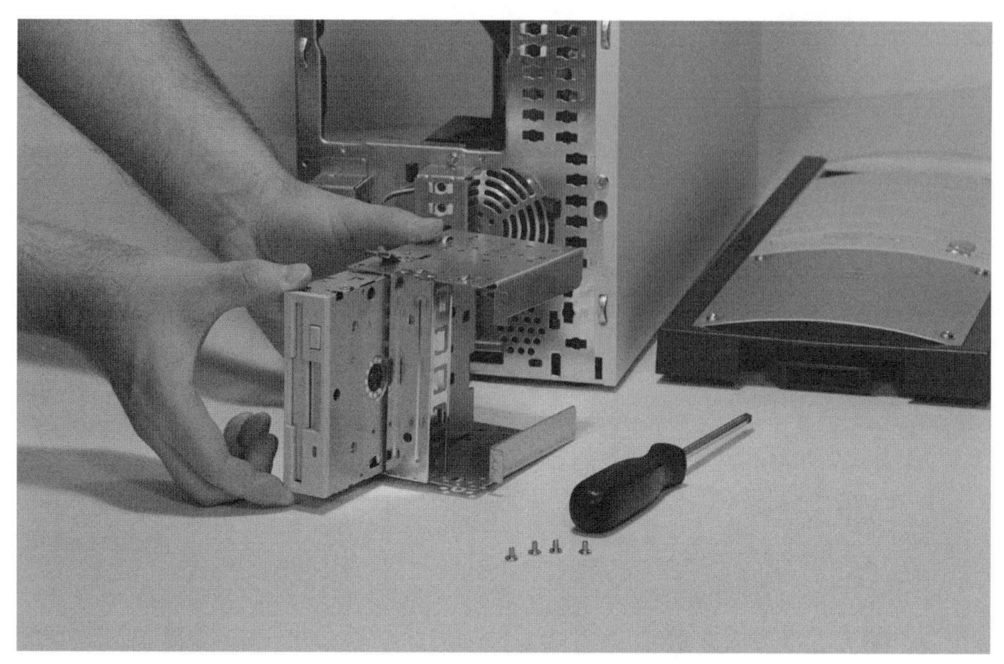

Figure 5.29. Insert the floppy drive into the 3.5" cage. The bay the drive must occupy is determined by the position of the floppy hole in the front of the bezel (See Figure 5.5).

Figure 5.30. Screwing the floppy drive into the 3.5" drive cage.

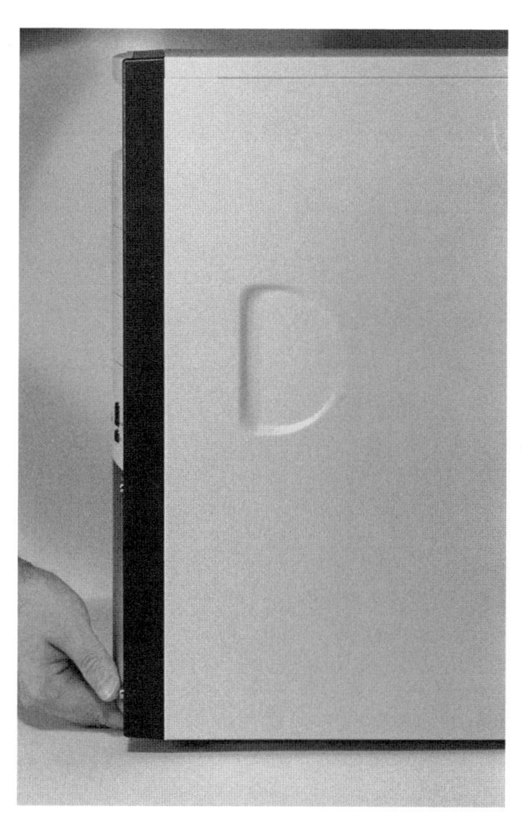

Figure 5.31. After installing the floppy in the cage and replacing the cage in the PC case, we gently try to close the bezel. This step isn't formally required. But, we want to be sure the floppy sits at the correct depth. If it sits too far forward, the bezel won't shut. Or, it could break. When closing the bezel, it's handy to lift the case up in the front and use your fingers to depress the bezel latch before closing the case. This saves wear and tear on the latch. Some people just slam it shut, which is bad.

Whenever closing anything, always keep an eye out for wires or anything else that could get pinched and be sure obstructions are moved out of the way.

The Enlight case has the floppy drive sit behind the bezel. This means the floppy drive can't protrude too much or you won't be able to close the front of the case. To get the depth correct, this cage has exact holes in the cage to position the drive and tighten it into place. But, just to make it challenging, there are two different sets of holes to allow the drive to seat at two different depths. If, as you close the bezel, you find the floppy drive doesn't sit at the proper depth, just remove the floppy and try the other set of cage holes. I'd recommend starting with the set of holes that puts the floppy the farthest back. When closing the front of the case (bezel), never force it. It could be that the floppy drive protrudes too far.

Other cages, where the front of the floppy drive is flush with the front of the case, often have slots which allow you to adjust the drive back and forth until it's exactly flush with the front of the case. Then you can screw the floppy drive into place. Sometimes the slots are a bit oversized and the small screw heads will have a poor grip on the slot.

Let's put the cage back into the PC and gently try to close the front (Figure 5.31). If the front doesn't close properly, we can see the drive

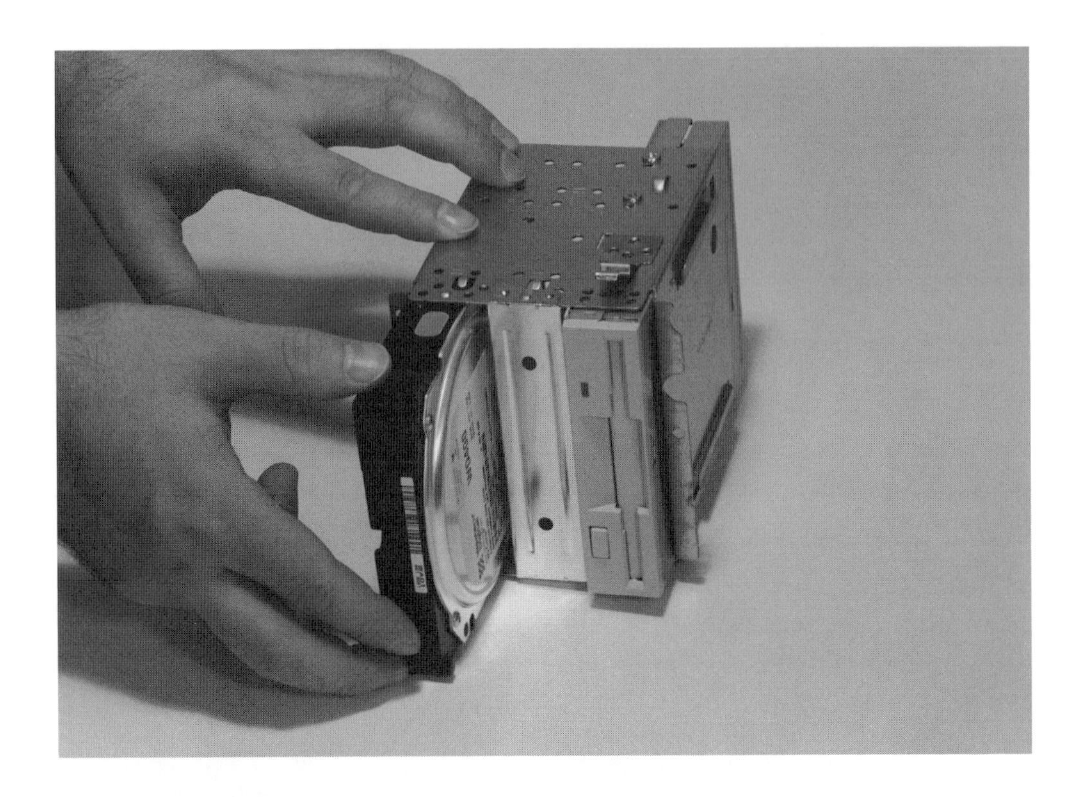

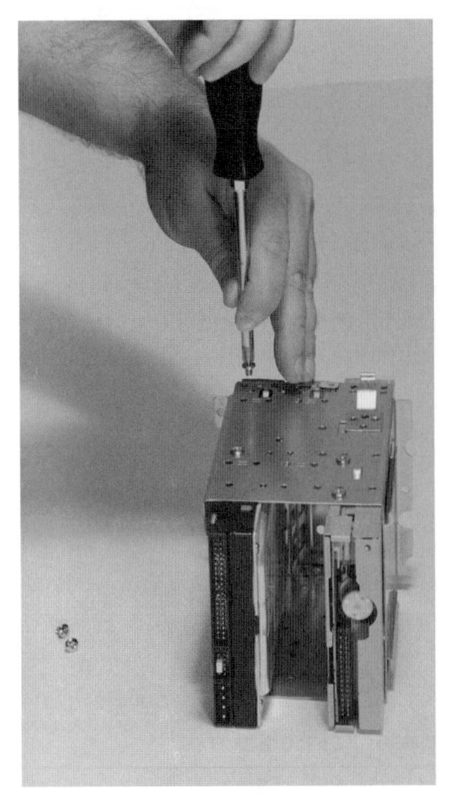

Figure 5.32 (above). Inserting the hard drive into the 3.5" drive cage.

Figure 5.33 (left). Screwing the hard drive into the 3.5" drive cage. Try to avoid touching the bottom of the hard drive which contains a circuit board. It's also good to ground yourself before handling the hard drive.

protrudes too much, and we'll need to use the other set of cage screw holes to move the drive back. Be sure when you close the front of the case that something isn't preventing it from closing, such as a floppy drive that's sticking out too far. With too much force, it's possible to break the bezel. You might want to close the front with no drives installed, just to get a feel for how much force it takes to finally pop the bezel into place.

Hard Drive

Now we'll install the hard drive in its bay. Remove the 3.5" cage from the case, if it isn't removed already. While we could put the hard drive immediately below the floppy, we'll skip one bay and place it in the last bay farthest away from the floppy. The extra air space between drives should help with cooling.

Remove the RF shield (or, if the drive sits far enough back, you could just leave the shield in place. It shouldn't matter. The drive itself will act as a shield). Insert the drive (Figure 5.32). Screw the drive to secure it to the 3.5" cage (Figure 5.33). The back of the drive has connections for the ribbon cable and power connector. Those should point to the inside of the case.

As with the floppy, before screwing in the hard drive, pick up a screw and test it by hand or with very light pressure from the screwdriver. Find three similar screws. It's best to use screws that came with the hard drive.

This is a good time to examine any instructions that came with your hard drive to see if any jumpers need to be adjusted. Jumpers are little connectors which connect adjacent pins. They "jump" between the pins. The jumpers are probably set fine, but it's a good idea to check them, just in case.

The usual jumper settings for a hard drive are:

1) Cable Select
2) Primary
3) Secondary

Cable select means that the mainboard will choose whether to make the drive primary or secondary. Most mainboards today support cable select. And, most drives will have their jumpers already set to cable select. You can just have all your drives set to cable select, and the mainboard will take care of the rest.

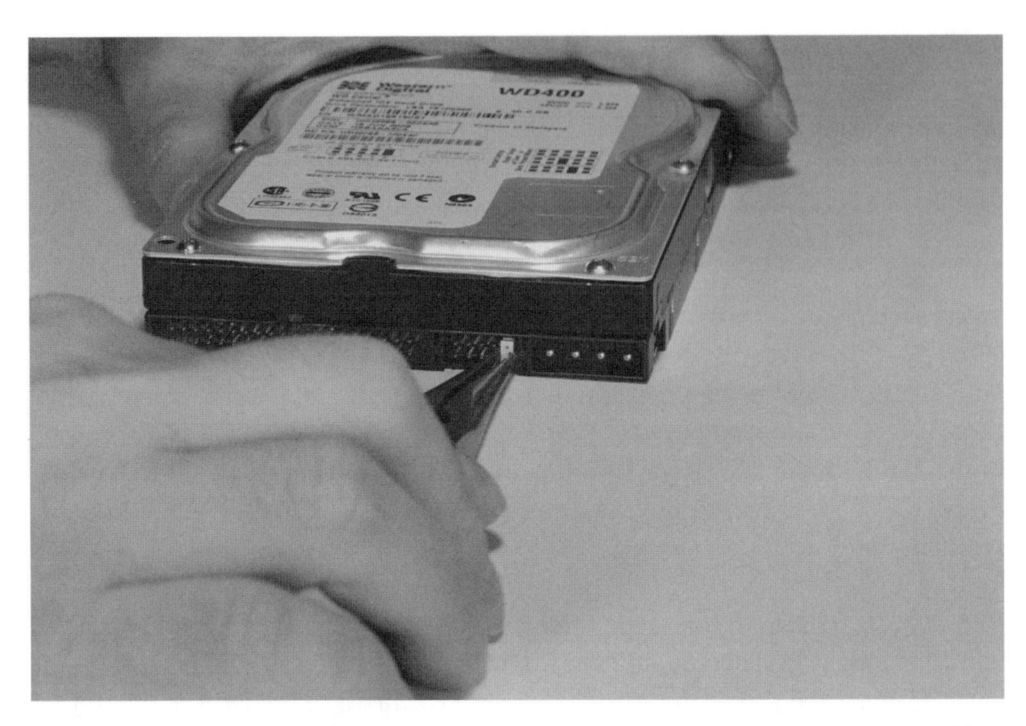

Figure 5.34. Changing the jumper on the hard drive from cable select to primary. We could have left it as "cable select" and it would have worked fine.

Figure 5.35. The jumper is changed. It sits across the bottom row of pins when set to primary. We learned this from the instructions that came with the hard drive. We could have left the jumper remain set to "cable select."

“Primary” means first and most important. Think of the primary as the one that usually takes control of the cable and gets its way. The secondary is like a little brother who must usually wait.

You usually want your main hard drive set as primary, or set it as cable select and have the mainboard set it as primary. Because we know we want this hard drive set to primary, we read the Western Digital instructions which tell us how to set the jumper. Rather than going up and down, as it looks like it should, the jumper in this case goes across pins on the lower, longer line of pins. We set the jumper to primary.

Incorrectly set jumpers are a common problem when building a PC. So, double check the orientation. Does the jumper go on the top row, bottom row, or across the top and bottom rows? Does the jumper go closer to the side of the drive with the power supply connector, or is the jumper closer to the side away from the power connector? Count pins on each side of the jumper. All this will help assure you have the jumpers set as you want. Be sure to push the jumper in all the way.

To remove jumpers, longer nails are handy, or you could use a small needle nose pliers (Figure 5.34 and 5.35). Be gentle. There’s no need to crush the little feller, no matter how frustrating he is to deal with.

If we were to place another hard drive in the system, we could make it secondary and put it on the same cable as the primary drive. Use the fastest drive with the largest buffer as your primary drive to maximize the speed of your operating system.

With drives cheap today (you can get a 40 GB drive for $40), you might want to install a second hard drive as a back up. Then, just drag and drop copies of your most important files to the second drive. Of course, you can also back up to a CD-RW or DVD burner. The chances of both drives failing and your losing data is very slim.

Some mainboards support RAID, which means redundant array of independent disks. RAID writes data to more than one hard drive at the same time, so that if one drive fails, you won’t lose data. However, if you make back ups regularly, you probably won’t need RAID for a home system. The chances of one hard drive failing is pretty slim.

Figure 5.36. Inserting the full 3.5" drive cage into the PC case.

If you want RAID, you can choose a mainboard that supports RAID or else purchase an expansion card that gives RAID capability.

While some hard-drive cables (IDE cables) have only a connector at each end, most have a connector at each end and a connector at the center. The primary drive is usually connected at the far end of the ribbon, and the secondary drive is connected to the middle connector.

Most mainboards support two IDE connectors. Because each IDE connector can run two drives (one as primary, one as secondary), you'll be all set to add up to four hard drives, CD-RWs, DVDs, etc. If you want more drive capability, you'll probably need to add an expansion card giving you another IDE connector. Four drives are usually more than adequate for most systems.

One handy PCI expansion board is an IDE, serial, parallel, and other multiple function I/O controller board. This board will give you more of every type of port, if you find you need them. These PCI expansion boards were more common in the past (before internal CD-RWs and USB ports) when people often ran an external zip drive from the parallel port and a printer from another parallel port. If the devices got into arguments, putting one on its own controller board solved the problem. Today, expansion boards adding extra USB ports are common.

With the jumpers properly set and the hard drive screwed into the cage, we can insert the cage back into the case and turn our attention to the 5.25" drives (Figure 5.36).

Installing The CD-RW, DVD, And Other 5.25" Drives

The only 5.25" drive we'll install in this system will be a 52x24x52 CD-RW (Figure 2.18). This means that it can write data at 52x speed, it can rewrite data at 24x speed, and it can read data at 52x speed. 1x speed is some standard set long ago in a time far away. Few remember exactly what that speed is. But, we remember that higher multiples mean a faster drive.

If you purchase CD-R disks that are rated at a slower speed than your maximum CD drive write speed, you can often use your operating system to adjust the speed at which the CD-RW drive will write. For example, in Windows XP, use the control panel to find the CD-RW and look at its properties. It will usually say it's running its CD-RW write speed at its fastest possible setting, which is usually what you want. Simply find a slower setting, if the CD-R media requires it. This is handy if you have a 52x drive but can get a bunch of CD-R media free that writes only at 48x. Similar speed reductions can occur within your burning software, such as Nero.

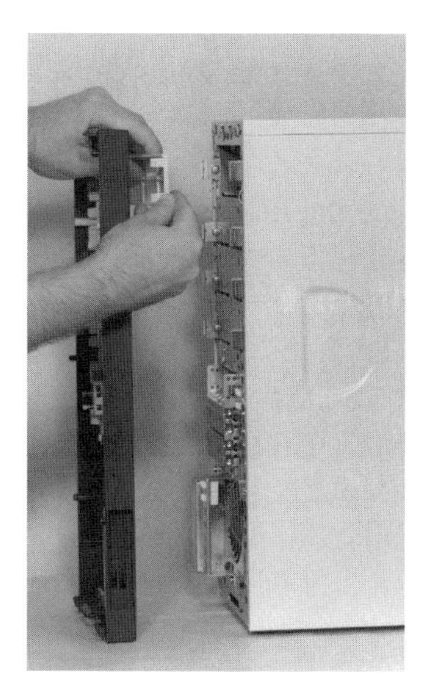

Figure 5.37 and 5.38. Removing the bay cover from the bezel. The 5.25" CD-RW drive will occupy this bay.

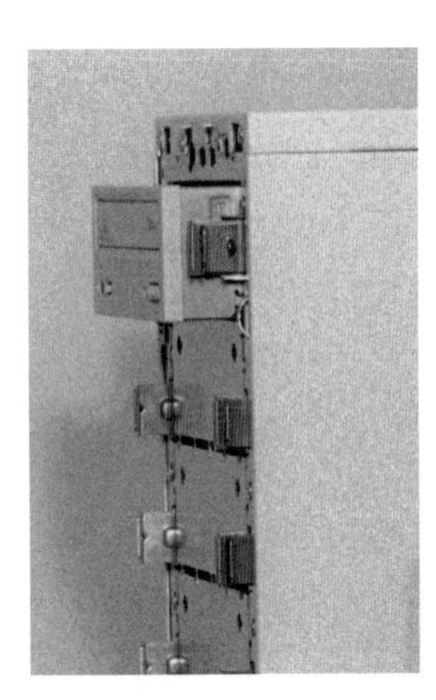

Figure 5.39 and 5.40. Inserting the CD-RW drive into its bay. This PC case uses a screwless system where the drive simply inserts and is secured by closing some levers. Your case may differ. Many PC cases use four screws on the side of the CD-RW to secure the drive to rails. Then the rails insert into slots in the case. Notice that the drive protrudes from the front of the case. It will be flush with the front of the case when we replace the bezel.

Incidentally, if you examine advertisements from Best Buy and other computer stores, you'll often find CD-R media really cheap, like free, after a mail-in rebate. These offers can be a bonanza for a PC person. You can even find 256 MB RAM chips free, after mail-in rebate. These offers are designed to draw customers into the store in the hope they'll buy other things. I just head straight to the rebate items. Many times you can also purchase the item online, download the rebate, and skip the trip to the store.

Before we can install the CD-RW drive, we must remove the plastic slot cover on the bezel over the 5.25" bay it will use (Figure 5.37 and 5.38).

This Enlight case has a screwless system for securing the 5.25" drives. We simply pull out the levers on each side of the drive. Be sure the levers are all the way out. Then we insert the drive and push it into place (Figure 5.39 and 5.40). We then close the levers which lock the drive into place. It's possible to get this wrong. For example, not locking the drive in fully. So, we'll grab the drive and tug it back and forth to be sure it's fully secured. It is. Little nipples come out to engage the screw holes in the drive and further tightness is provided by the sides of the levers which push against the drive.

Notice that the front of the drive will protrude slightly. This is normal. When the front bezel is replaced, the front of the drive will appear flush with the front of the case. It's often necessary to gently push the plastic of the bezel slightly up or down if it's hitting the face of the drive or to push the plastic of the drive just up or down slightly. Don't slam the bezel shut without checking for minor obstructions to it closing.

Similarly, install any other 5.25" drives you desire. This PC case has one open slot for a 5.25" device. If you wish to install multiple devices, you'll need to remove one of the metal RF shields that covers the other 5.25" drive bays.

RF shields are often held in place by thin pieces of metal. To remove the shield, the metal holding the shield must be broken. If the metal connecting the shield to the case is too tough to remove by simply twisting and turning it by hand (it is in this case), then using a small side cutter works well. A side cutter is essentially like a pliers but with a cutting edge. Be very careful when removing one of these shields, because after cutting the metal, sharp edges are often exposed. If you push too hard with your hand on such a shield, when it breaks, your hand could hit one of the remaining metal barbs. This can lead to nasty cuts. Thus, if you wish to push on a shield to remove it, using the back of a screwdriver handle is sometimes a good idea, because it helps keep your hand a safe distance away from sharp edges.

Never use a Dremel tool or an electric cutting device to remove a metal shield, because these tools kick up metal shavings which can be harmful to the mainboard. If a remaining barb is in the way, try to use a needle nose pliers to bend it out of the way. Don't sand it down.

In this chapter, we've learned how to install the mainboard in the case (Figure 5.41). We've also learned how to install the drives. In the next chapter, we'll learn how to connect the drives to the power supply and to the mainboard. We'll also learn how to install expansion cards.

Figure 5.41. The mainboard installed in the case.

Installing The Mainboard In The Case: Part 2: Ribbon Time

Because we have two IDE connectors on the mainboard, we'll use one for the hard drive and the other for the CD-RW. Each device will be set as primary on its own cable. Each ribbon cable can have one primary and one secondary device.

The jumper options on CD-RW drives are the same as for the hard drive, because both are IDE devices. The choices are 1) primary; 2) secondary; and 3) cable select. Double check your jumpers before installing the 5.25" devices. You can put two CD-RWs on one cable or more commonly a CD-RW and a DVD on one cable.

It's common to have both a CD-RW and a DVD. That allows you to play DVDs and record to CDs as well as read CDs. Unless you plan to make movies on your PC, you probably won't need a DVD burner. However, prices for DVD burners have come down significantly. We'll discuss DVD burners in another chapter.

If you operate two devices on one cable, just be sure each device is set to cable select or be sure one is set to primary and the other to secondary. If you ever have a conflict, sometimes it helps to change the order of the devices. Make the one that's currently primary secondary and vice versa.

Examining the back of the CD-RW (Figure 6.1), we also see there is a connector for a sound cable (Figure 6.2). The other end of this cable will connect to the mainboard if you have built-in sound (Figure 6.3), or to a sound card.

Figure 6.1. Back of CD-RW drive. The circle shows a four-pin connector for a sound cable, which will connect to your sound card or mainboard. To the right of the sound connector are pins for jumper settings for master, slave, and cable select options. See the instructions that came with your drive for setting jumpers. Farther to the right are pins for the ribbon connector. At right is a 4-pin power connector.

The instructions for the CD-RW say that the cable can only be plugged in one way. And, a sound cable is included. But, examining the cable, we see they lied (Figure 6.2). It can be plugged in two ways. Some sound cables can be plugged in only one way, because they have notches in them which identify the top. Others are just flat little suckers that will go in in either direction.

If your CD's sound doesn't work, try reversing the cable, if you have a flat, notchless connector. It should work in either orientation, however, because the four pins are usually denoted RGGL, right speaker, ground, ground, and left speaker. Right is often red in color. If a device doesn't work, always check to see that it's properly connected.

Sometimes instructions for PC components, such as CD-RWs, make little sense, because the instructions don't seem to match up with the actual device you're holding. Sometimes the instructions were written and a vendor was changed and the components changed, but the instructions weren't updated. This can happen with software also.

We now have all our 3.5" drives and 5.25" drives attached to the case. The next step will be to connect all devices to the mainboard using the appropriate cables. Ribbon cables will transfer signals between the drive and the mainboard. Other connectors will supply power.

Figure 6.2. Connectors on sound cables, which will connect the CD-RW to either a sound card or to the mainboard (if the mainboard has built-in sound). The instructions say the cable can be plugged in only one way, such as the cable on the right. But, in reality, the cable in the box is the one on the left. They lied!

Figure 6.3. Sound connected to mainboard. After connecting all ribbon cables and power connectors, don't forget to connect CD sound to your mainboard or to the sound card.

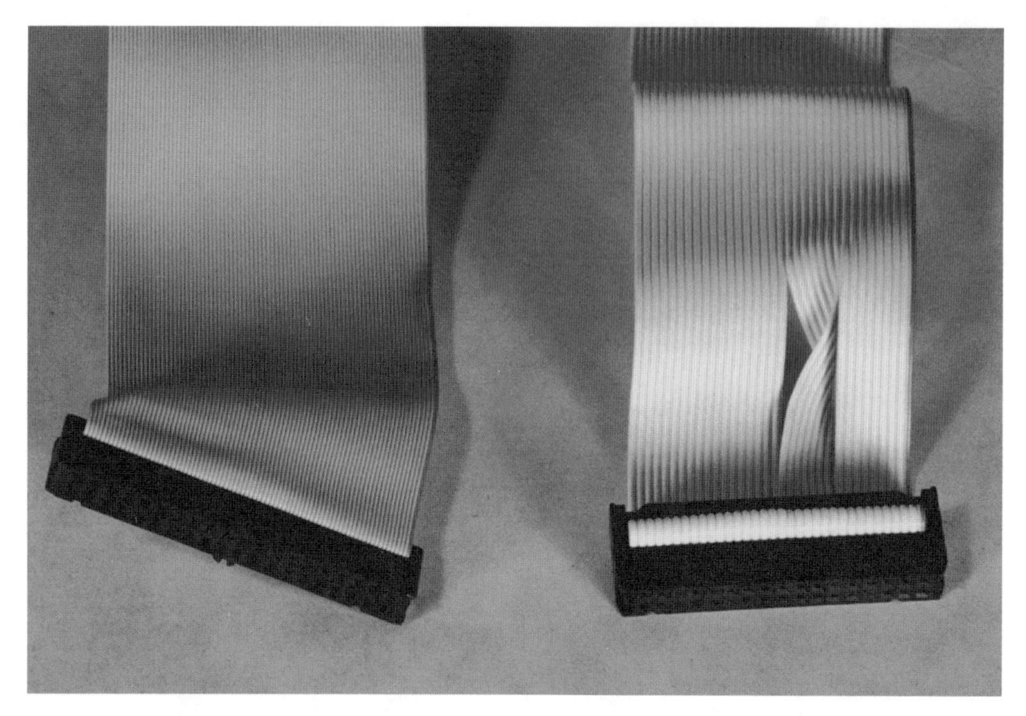

Figure 6.4. Ribbon cables. Cable on right is a 34-pin floppy ribbon cable. The end with the twist plugs into the floppy drive. The other end plugs into the mainboard.

The best order to connect the devices is the order that's easiest for you. Sometimes one device will be hiding in a corner of the case, and it's best to connect that device first. Other than that, the order in which you make these connections is unimportant. Just double check to be sure you haven't forgotten anything.

Connect The Ribbon Cables

Floppy Ribbon Cables

Let's start by connecting the IDE ribbon cables and the floppy cable. These cables look like decorative party paper ribbon, except they come in boring colors and aren't made from paper.

The floppy drive is connected with the 34-pin ribbon cable (Figure 6.4) which comes with your mainboard. It won't plug into the forty-pin socket used for the hard drive and CD-RW drive. They'll be pins left over.

Figure 6.5. Connecting a ribbon cable into the floppy drive. The end with the twist goes to the drive. The other end will go to the mainboard. This figure also shows the power cable connected to the floppy drive. The order in which you connect the ribbon cables and power cables doesn't matter. If it's easier for you, you can put the case on its side to make the connections. Here the case sits upright.

If you examine the floppy cable, you'll notice one side of the cable looks like it's torn (Figure 6.4). It's not. It's just designed with a twist. This end of the cable will connect to the 3.5" drive. Connect the end with the twist to your floppy drive (Figure 6.5). The other end will connect to the mainboard (Figure 6.6 and 6.7). Figure 6.8 shows the floppy ribbon cable fully connected.

If you examine one end of the floppy cable connector, you'll see that there is a single hole missing in the connector. If I recall right from math, a negative times a negative is a positive. So, lack of a hole means material still remains. The other end of the cable is also missing a hole. This missing hole can be matched with a missing pin (on a drive or mainboard) to help orient the connector.

There is also sometimes a protruding notch on one side of each connector at the top and outside part of the connector. This notch will match up with a notch in the mainboard floppy socket. This helps to assure the ribbon cable is installed in the proper orientation. Sometimes, your ribbon cable will also have a red stripe down one side. Red means Pin 1. Or, sometimes, there will be something else, such as a red triangle, showing Pin 1. Pin 1 will be noted in your mainboard manual.

Find the 34-pin floppy connector on your mainboard. When in doubt, consult the mainboard manual. Examine the pins carefully. You'll see there is a

Figure 6.6. IDE and floppy connector sockets on mainboard. The bottom connector is for a 34-pin floppy ribbon cable. Notice the cut-out notch on one side which helps orient the cable. Be careful not to bend any pins as you press the connector into place. The light-colored 40-pin connector is the mainboard's primary IDE connector and should be connected to the hard drive. The two 40-pin IDE connectors support up to four devices.

Figure 6.7. Connecting the floppy ribbon cable to the mainboard. Push the connector straight down. Here the case sits on its side.

Figure 6.8. Floppy ribbon cable fully installed. Here the case is sitting on its side.

missing pin. That's normal. It will match up with the lack of a hole in the ribbon connector.

Be careful not to force a connector in the wrong orientation, or you might damage or bend a pin.

You'll also see a cut-out notch on one long side of the socket. This is designed to help assure proper orientation of the floppy cable. However, some cables don't have notches. So, sometimes the cut out isn't much help.

If there is a notch on the cable, use it to determine the proper orientation of the cable. If your cable has no notch, either match up the missing hole with the missing pin, or else use your mainboard manual to determine Pin 1 of the floppy connector and match that to the red stripe of the floppy cable. One way or another, you'll get that sucker installed in the proper orientation.

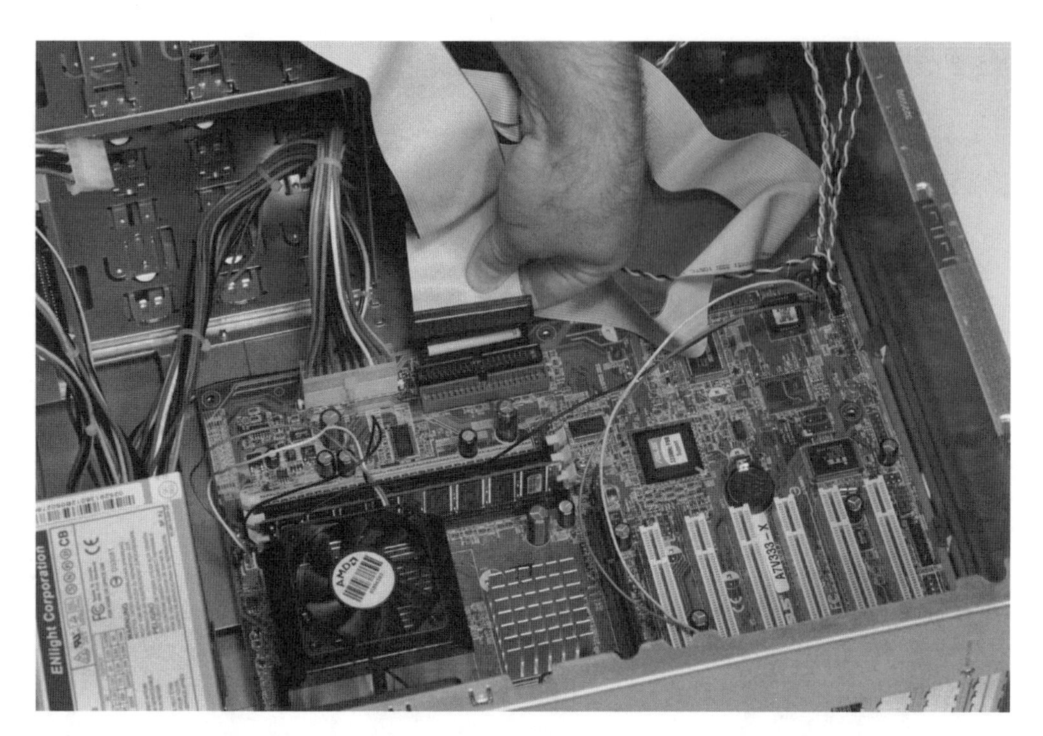

Figure 6.9. Connecting the CD-RW ribbon cable to the secondary IDE connector on the mainboard.

Similarly, the floppy drive itself is missing one pin on the connector, so you can use that as a guide for the proper orientation of the cable to the drive. Other floppy drives have Pin 1 marked in some other way. Pin 1 always goes to the red line side of the cable. And, if you really must confirm orientation yet another way, you can do a search on google for your particular floppy drive to find a manual for your floppy or more information about it. Most floppy drives don't come with any documentation.

With bootable CD drives today and the limited capacity of floppies, they're not used very often. But, they can be useful for creating an emergency boot disk. And, if you have a case, such as the Enlight case for this build, with a hole for a floppy, it's probably good to have something installed behind the floppy hole, because someone will eventually try to insert a floppy disk. Plus, for $15, a floppy is inexpensive.

It's probably most common to plug cables into the drives first and then to the mainboard, but you can do it either way you prefer. Using your thumbs and fingers, push the floppy cable fully into place on the drive. Sometimes it's easiest to get one side of the cable connector started first. But, as you push

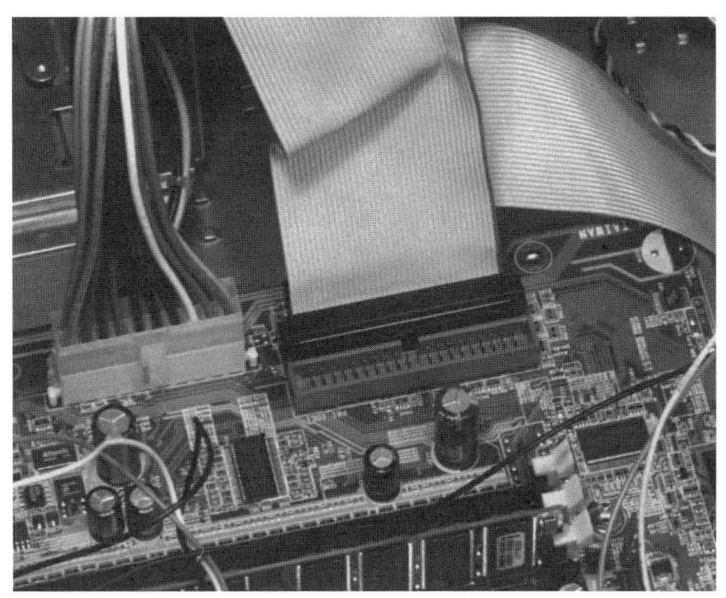

Figure 6.10. CD-RW ribbon connected to mainboard.

down, try to apply equal force to each side of the connector so that the whole connector seats fully. Try not to touch the mainboard with your fingers as you plug in the cables.

Installing The CD-RW Ribbon Cable

Connect the 40-pin ribbon cable to the CD-RW drive and then connect it to the mainboard's secondary controller (the second IDE connection on the mainboard) (Figure 6.9, 6.10, and 6.11). Ignore any connectors in the middle of the cable and use the ends of the ribbon cable (unless you plan to connect a secondary device to the middle cable connector).

While each ribbon connector can have a primary and a secondary device on it, most mainboards also support two IDE connectors on the mainboard, which are also referred to as primary and secondary. We'll connect the secondary IDE to the CD cable first, because it's between the floppy connector and the mainboard's primary IDE connector (see Figure 6.6). Then, we'll connect the primary mainboard IDE connector to the hard drive. To determine which IDE connector is primary, consult your mainboard manual. Any IDE ribbon cables you connect in the future will be similar to these.

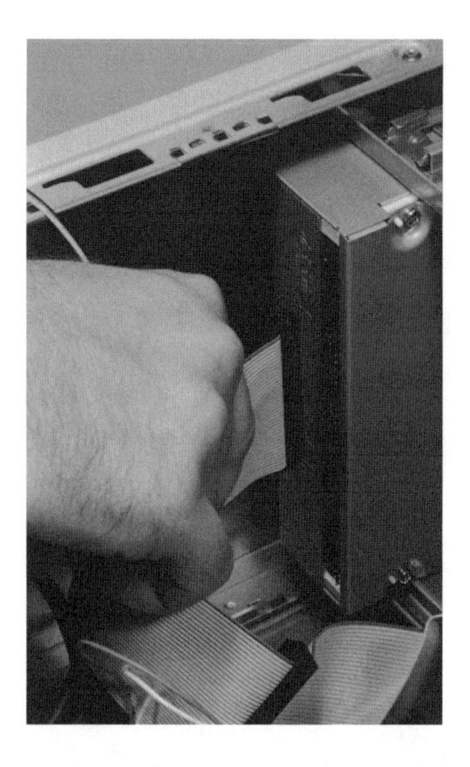

Figure 6.11. Connecting the ribbon cable to the CD-RW drive. Hold the connector by the black end to push it in. We intentionally had the model hold the connector by the cable so the hand didn't completely obscure the picture. Also, when removing cables, don't pull them by the ribbon, which could damage wires. Rather, pull them out by holding the black connector.

(Figure 6.1 shows the back of the CD-RW drive, where the ribbon cable goes.)

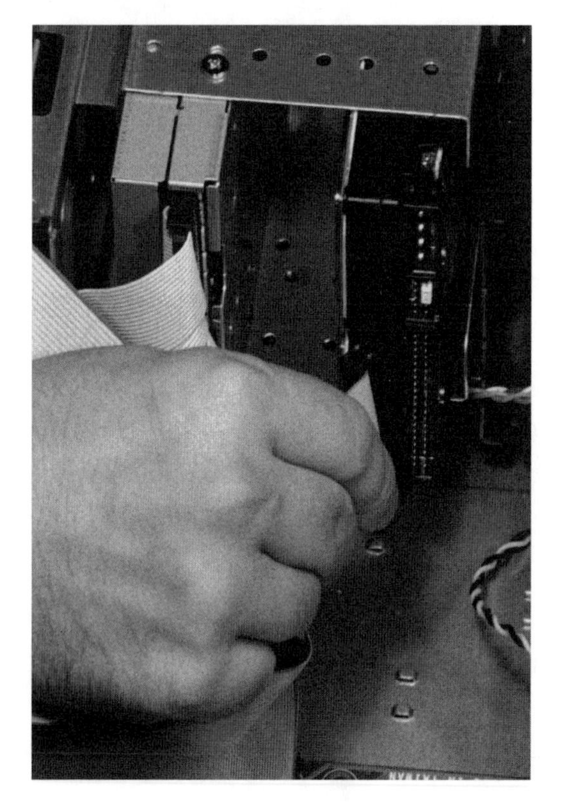

Figure 6.12. Connecting ribbon cable to the hard drive. The black end of the 40-pin ribbon cable should be connected to the hard drive. Use the ribbon cable which came with the hard drive. The other end of the ribbon cable should connect to the mainboard's primary IDE controller. In addition, you should set the hard drive to the primary device on the primary controller.

(Figure 2.17 shows the back of a hard drive.)

Installing The Hard Drive IDE Cable

Next up, we'll examine the hard drive IDE cable. Depending upon the layout of the connectors on your mainboard, it might be easier to install the hard drive cable first. Order doesn't matter, as long as everything gets plugged in properly. For example, if the cable from the floppy will go across the sockets for the IDE cables, you can install the floppy cable last. Sometimes ribbon cables will push and shove amongst themselves for space. That's normal. By now, you're an expert on connecting ribbon cables.

A cable for a hard drive probably came with both your hard drive and with the mainboard. Don't throw out the extra cable. Rather, keep all your extra parts and manuals together. This will make future repairs easier. You can usually use either ribbon cable.

These 40-pin IDE connectors have 80 connectors today (Don't ask me how. It's magic! Actually, each pin has a dedicated ground). Some older IDE hard drive cables might not work with newer IDE drives. If your hard drive instructions say you must use the cable that came with it, go ahead and use that one.

Today, one end of the hard drive connector is usually blue and the other black or gray. Connect the blue end to your mainboard. Connect the gray end to the drive.

The same tricks you used with the floppy cable are used to properly orient the hard drive cable.

The hard drive ribbon cable will have a red stripe down the side with Pin 1. And, Pin 1 is usually identified in the manuals for both the hard drive and the mainboard.

Also, the cable is likely to have a notch that will match up with a cut-out notch in the drive and a similar cut-out notch in the mainboard socket for the IDE connector. Often, there is a missing pin at the top center of the connector.

Plug in the hard drive ribbon cable to the drive (Figure 6.12) and connect it to the mainboard (Figure 6.13 and 6.14). Be sure to seat it fully by pushing it in with your fingers or thumbs. Use the connectors at the ends and ignore the connector in the middle of the cable, unless you wish to install another device

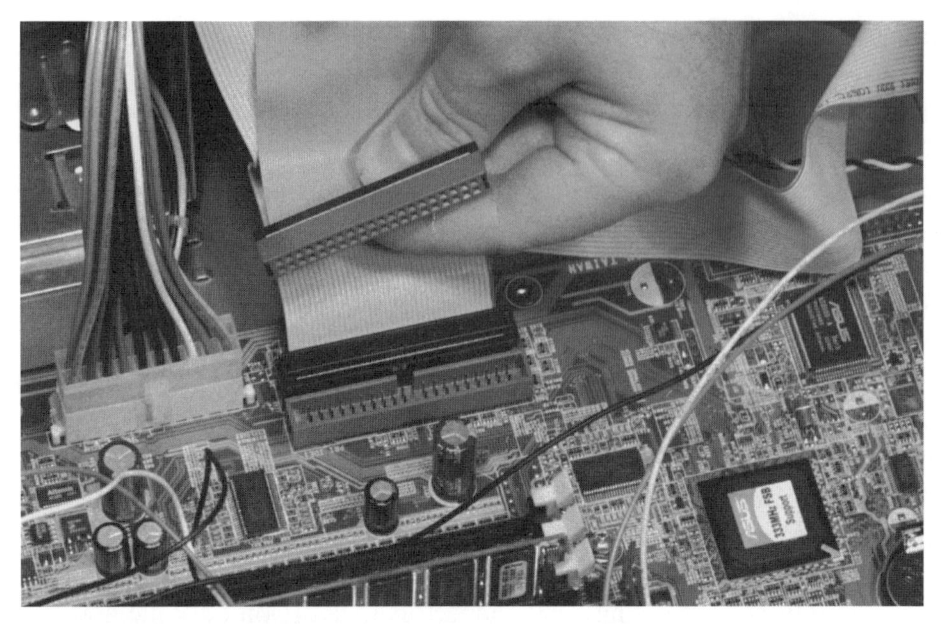

Figure 6.13. Connecting the hard drive ribbon to the mainboard.

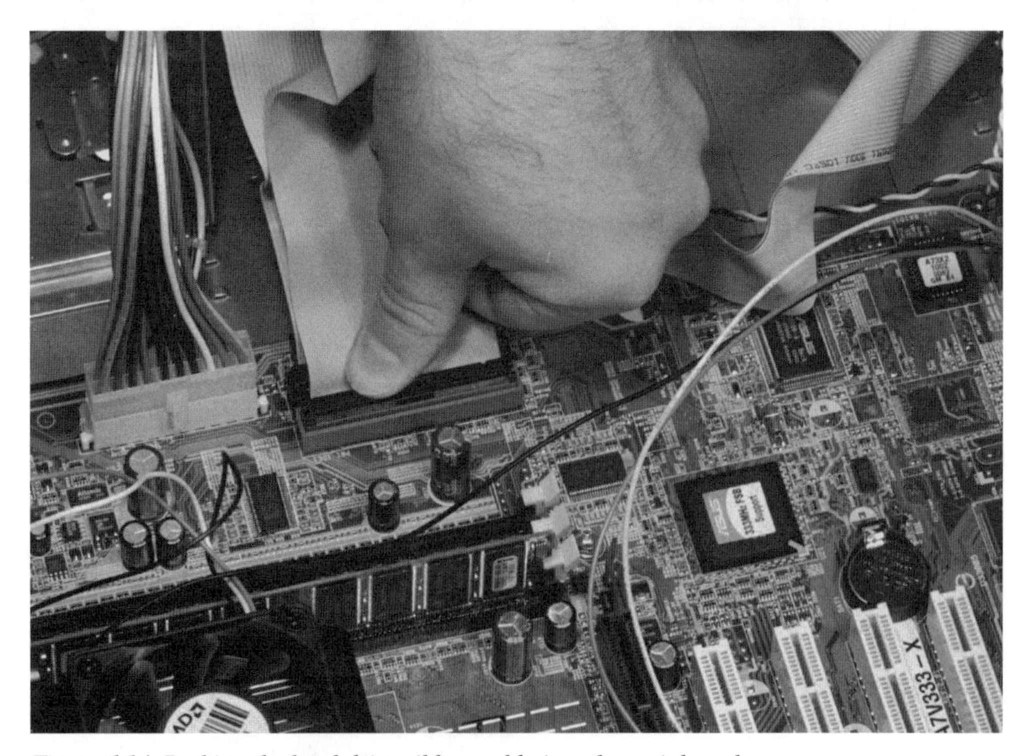

Figure 6.14. Pushing the hard drive ribbon cable into the mainboard.

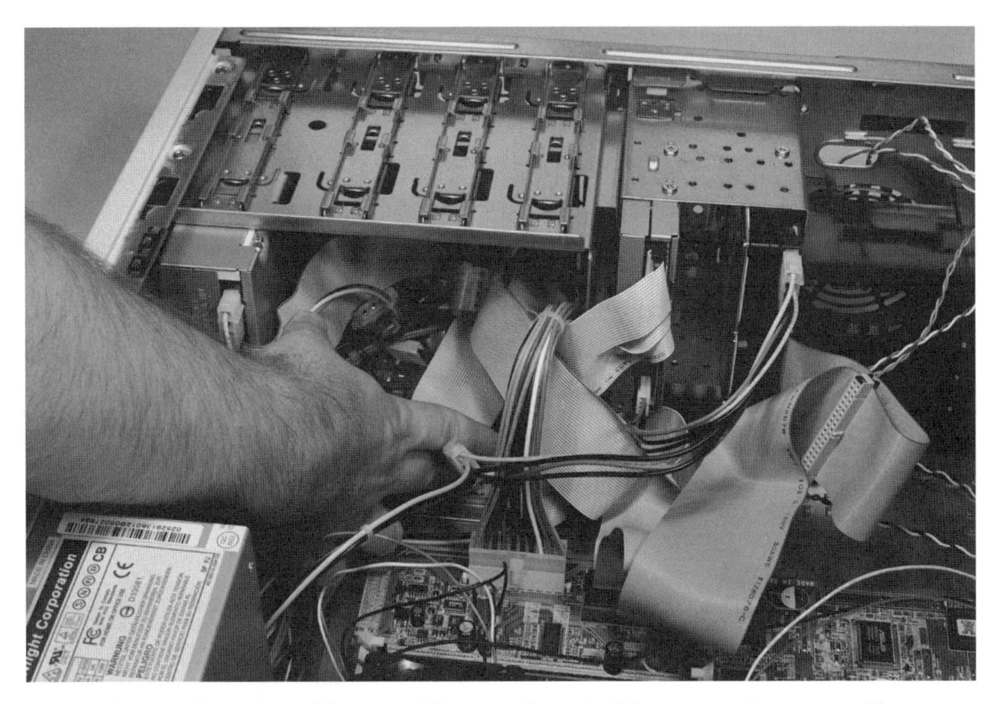

Figure 6.15. Pushing the cables out of the way. Some builders argue that poor cable management can lead to improper airflow within the case.

such as a secondary device on the cable. If you wish to install a second drive on the cable, it's usually easiest to connect the middle connector first, before connecting the end connector to the primary drive.

Ribbon Cable Summary

You've connected the floppy, hard drive, and CD-RW ribbon cables. Each cable can be pushed out of the way so that it doesn't hit fans, the mainboard, etc. Figure 6.15 shows pushing cables into the empty 5.25" bay area. It's good to have your cables out of the way of anything that gets especially hot, such as heatsinks. Some people will bundle their cables together to make the inside neater, but most builders just let all the cables hang out and have a good time.

Figure 6.16. Connecting ATX power to the mainboard. Here we are connecting the power before the ribbon cables have been installed.

Power Connectors

Power To The Mainboard

Now we must add power to each device.

First, we'll add power to the mainboard. The standard ATX power supply connector is a 20-pin connector (Figure 2.5) which can be plugged in correctly by noticing the clip on one side of the connector lines up with a notch on the socket. Push the connector down and it will click into place (Figure 6.16 and 6.17).

Pentium 4 systems also make use of a special four-pin connector (Figure 2.6). If you're building a Pentium system, connect the four-pin connector. It also has a clip to help show orientation. If you're building an Athlon system, you won't need this four-pin power connector.

When in doubt, examine your mainboard manual to see where power connectors go.

Figure 6.17. ATX power connected to mainboard. This is the only power source the Athlon mainboard needs. Pentium 4 mainboards will also use a special 4-pin power connector. To prevent damaging your system, these connectors are designed so they can only be plugged in one way. A little clip will help you orient the power connectors.

Power To Floppy

All other devices, the floppy, hard drive, CD-RWs, etc., will also need power. The floppy makes use of an odd looking power connector (Figure 6.18). Plug in the floppy power connector (Figure 6.19 to 6.21). See the figures for the proper orientation of this silly connector.

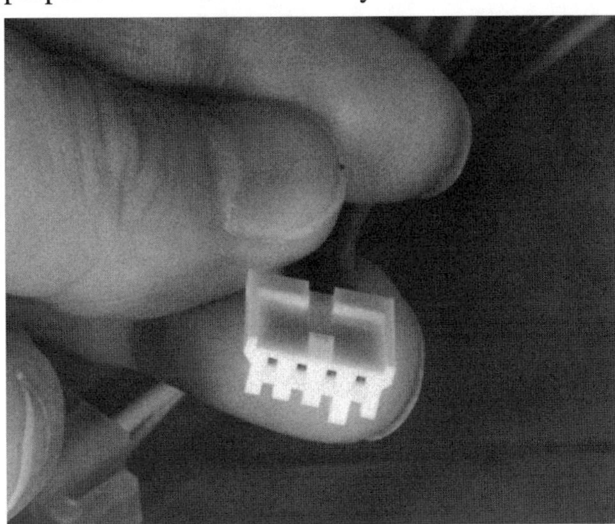

Figure 6.18. Floppy power connector. Here it's held upside down. The five notches will point upward when it's installed. One notch sits higher than the others. The bottom of the connector looks a little like the bottom of a space ship with two fins pointing outward.

Figure 6.19. The floppy connector held with the top pointing up and the bottom pointing down. It will plug into the four pins at the left of the floppy drive. Notice one of the five notches at the top is slightly higher. This is one of the few power connections that can confuse new builders.

Figure 6.20. From Figure 6.19 we have simply rotated the connector around to show how it's installed.

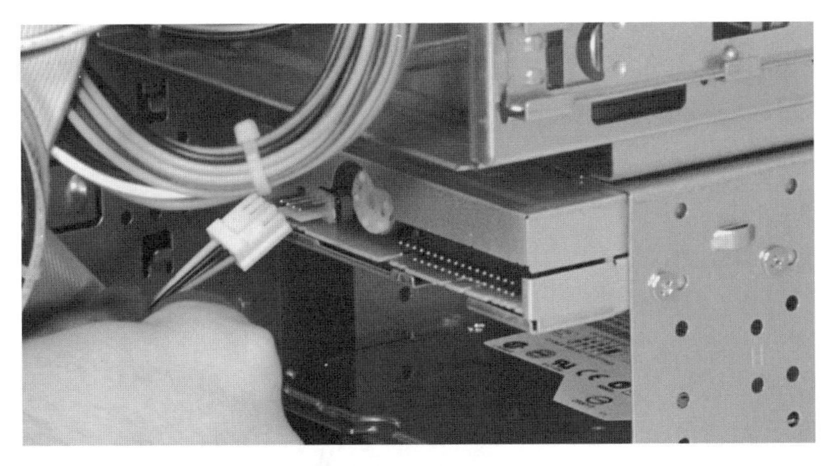

Figure 6.21. Plugging in the 4-pin floppy power connector. We have removed the floppy ribbon cable to get a better look. For photo clarity, we are also holding the cable by the wires. You'll hold it by the white end to plug it in. Also, when you remove power cables, try to pull them out by the white part of the connector. Don't pull connectors by the wires or you may damage a wire. Here the case sits upright.

Power To Hard Drive and Other Drives

The standard four-pin power connector is called a molex (Figure 6.22). One side of the connector is rounded, while the other side is square. This prevents the connector from being plugged in the wrong way.

Plug in a molex power connector to the hard drive (Figure 6.23 and 6.24) and attach another molex power connector to the CD-RW (Figure 6.25 and 6.26).

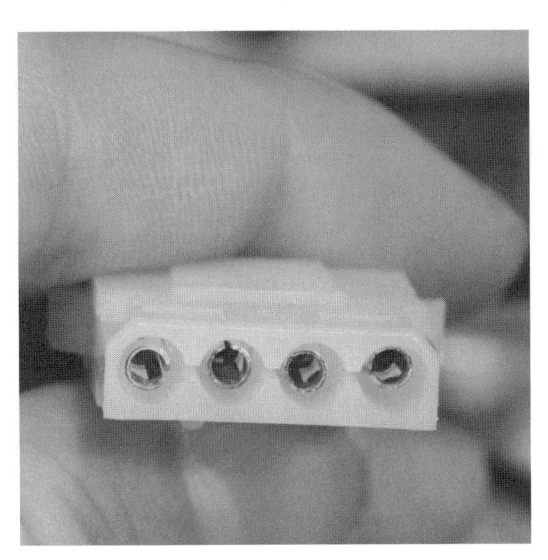

Figure 6.22. Four-pin molex power connector provides power to most drives, including 3.5" hard drives, CD-RW drives, DVD drives, etc. One end has rounded corners so that it can only plug in in one direction. Sometimes, it takes a bit of force or wiggling them about to plug them in or remove them.

Figure 6.23. Plugging in a molex power connector to hard drive. Case sits on its side.

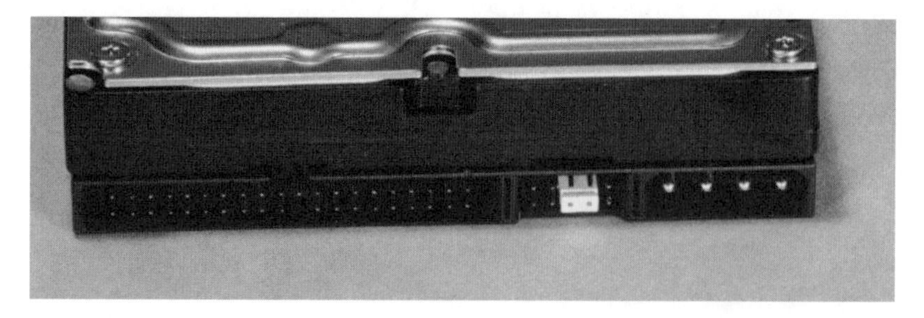

Figure 6.24. Back of hard drive. The four pins on the right are for a molex power connector.

Sometimes it takes a bit of force to push a molex power connector all the way in. It sometimes helps to wiggle it from side to side as you push it in. They can also be difficult to remove. When removing any cable or power connector, always try to grab it by the connector and not by the actual ribbon or by the

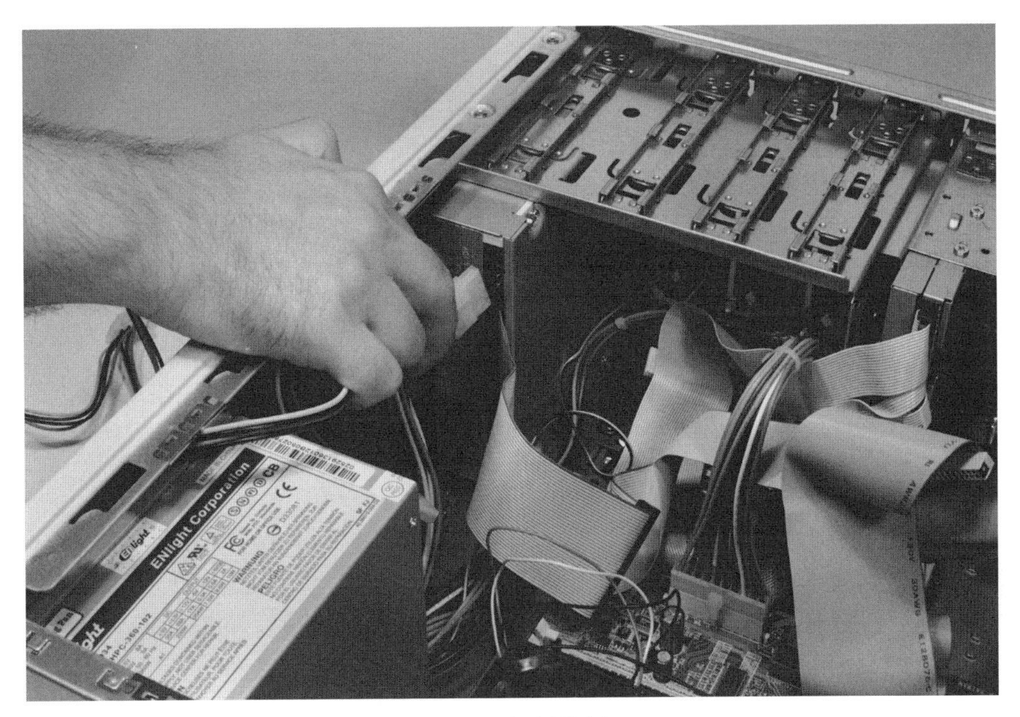

Figure 6.25. Plugging in the molex power to CD-RW drive.

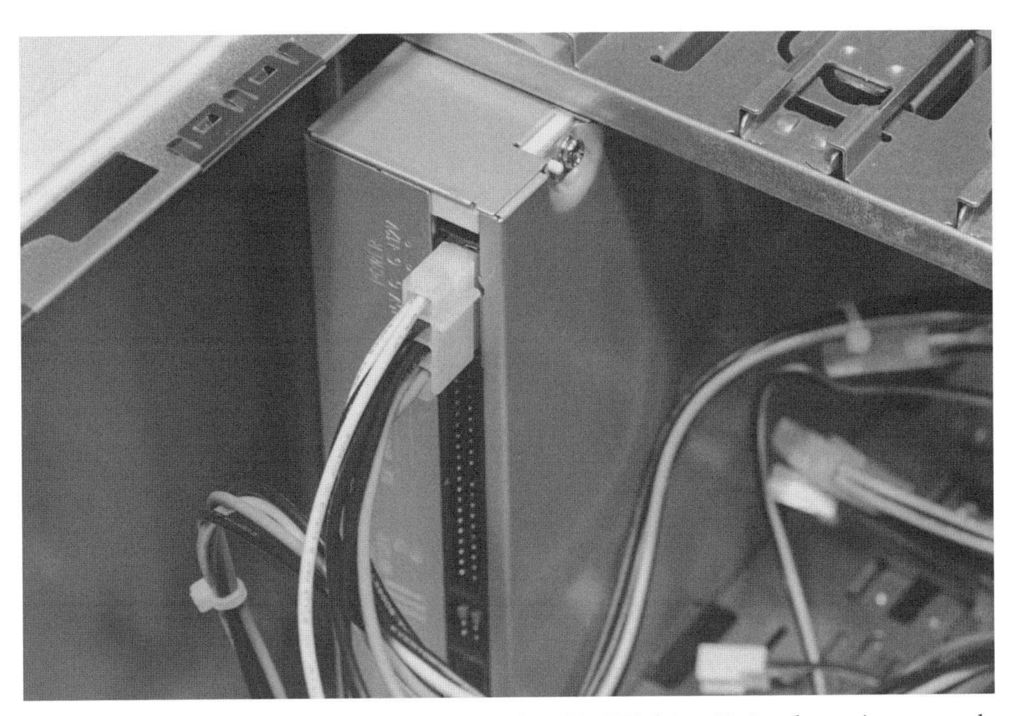

Figure 6.26. Close up of molex power connected to CD-RW drive. Notice that we've removed the ribbon cable to the CD-RW for photo clarity.

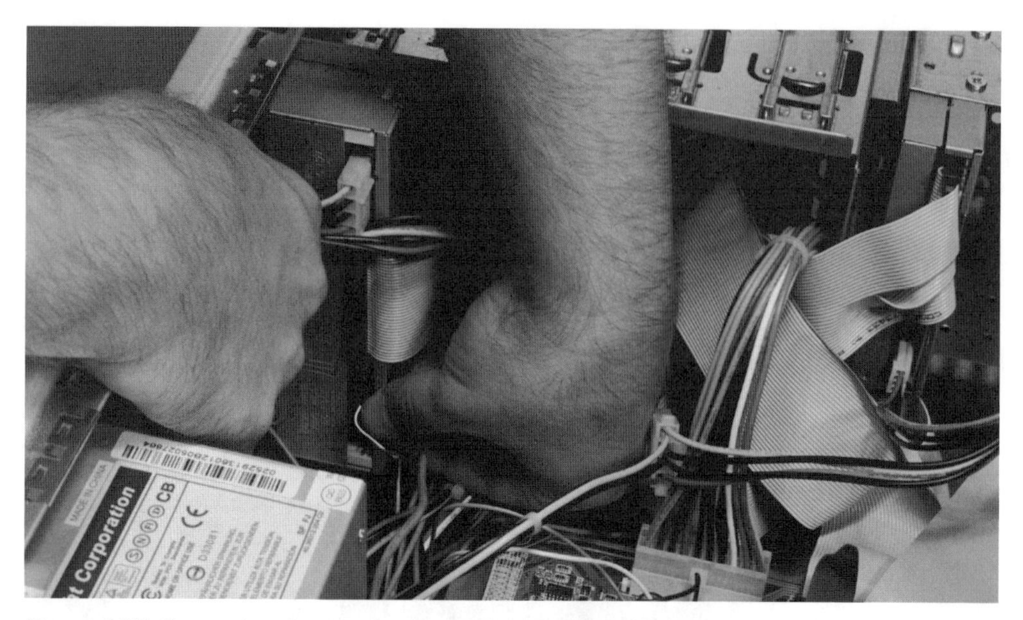

Figure 6.27. Connecting the sound cable to the CD-RW drive. The other end connects to a sound card or to the mainboard. See the discussion at the beginning of this chapter for more information. Here, the thumb is pushing the sound connector into place.

Figure 6.28. Close up of sound cable connected to the CD-RW drive. Notice that we've removed the ribbon cable for photo clarity. Also see Figures 6.1 and 6.2.

wire. Pulling too hard on a ribbon cable or on the wire could damage the wires inside. Pulling on the connector shouldn't hurt anything.

Now all of your drives have power.

If you haven't already done so, it's a good time to connect the sound cable to your CD (Figure 6.27 and 6.28) and to your mainboard if it has built-in sound. If you're using a PCI sound card, you'll need to install it before you can connect the sound cable between it and the CD-RW.

Summary So Far: All Drives Ready To Go

The two things all disk drives need are power and a signal ribbon cable. We've connected ribbon cables for sending signals and information between the drives and the mainboard, and we've connected power to each device.

The next step will be to install all AGP and PCI expansion cards. Figure 6.29 shows the AGP and PCI expansion slots on the mainboard.

Installing The AGP Video Card

Take your AGP video card out of its static proof bag (Figure 2.16 shows an AGP video card). As with all expansion cards, touch your hands to a metal surface to draw off any static electricity that might be on your hands before handling the card. It's best to handle cards by the edges and corners. One side of the card is attached to a metal piece that will sit toward the back of your PC's case. Try to pick up the card using the metal piece only.

You'll notice that the card has a funny notch toward its back (the end far away from the metal end). That is unique to the AGP card. It will match up with a small protrusion on one side of the AGP socket that is controlled by a slight plastic lever. You'll also notice that the AGP slot sits farther back than the PCI slots.

Place your AGP card above its AGP slot to determine which expansion slot cover it uses on the back of the case. Carefully set the AGP card down and remove the appropriate expansion slot cover from the case (Figure 6.30 and 6.31).

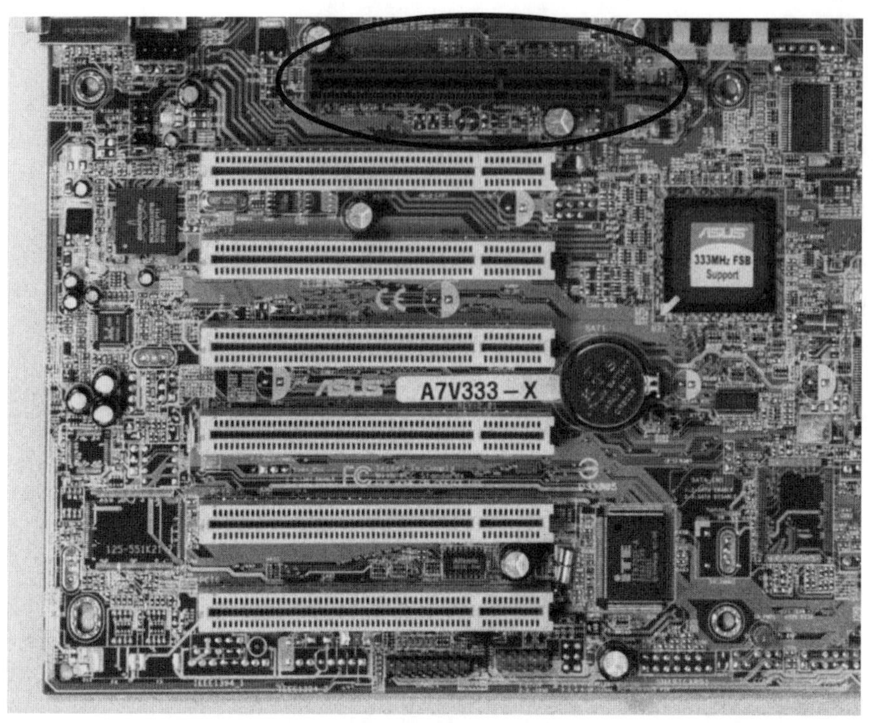

Figure 6.29. Close up of the AGP and PCI expansion slots on the mainboard. The darker slot which sits farther back from the edge of the mainboard is the AGP slot (circled). The six white slots are PCI slots.

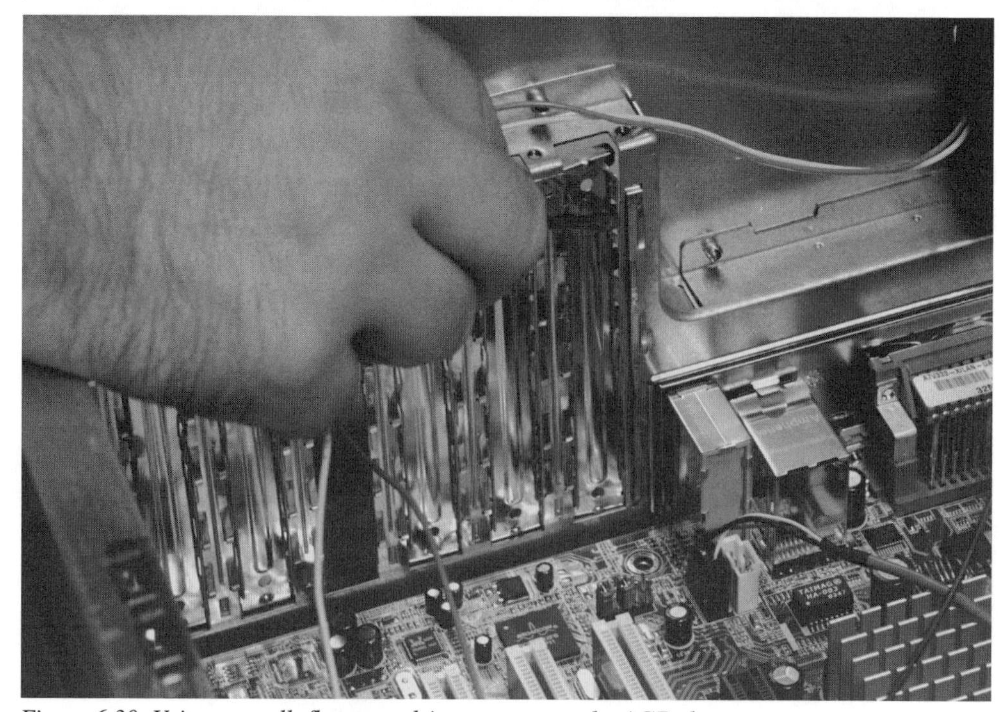

Figure 6.30. Using a small, flat screwdriver to remove the AGP slot cover.

Figure 6.31. The AGP slot cover and one PCI slot cover have been removed from the back of the case. External devices can connect through the back of the case to connectors on expansion cards. This allows your PC to interface to any external device.

Sometimes it's necessary to hold the card up to the slot to determine the correct slot cover to remove. It's easy to be off by one slot cover just by eyeballing it. Often, there will be a single AGP slot at the far end of the PCI expansion slots on the mainboard. If so, just remove the cover at the far end. You can sometimes just count from one end to determine which slot cover to remove. For example, this case has seven slot covers which exactly match up with the six PCI expansion sockets and the one AGP socket.

The Enlight case shown here has expansion slot covers that are replaceable. Once removed, they can be put back if you change your mind. Some slot covers are held in place by a single screw, while others just hold themselves in. Unscrew the slot cover to remove it, if it's held in place by a screw.

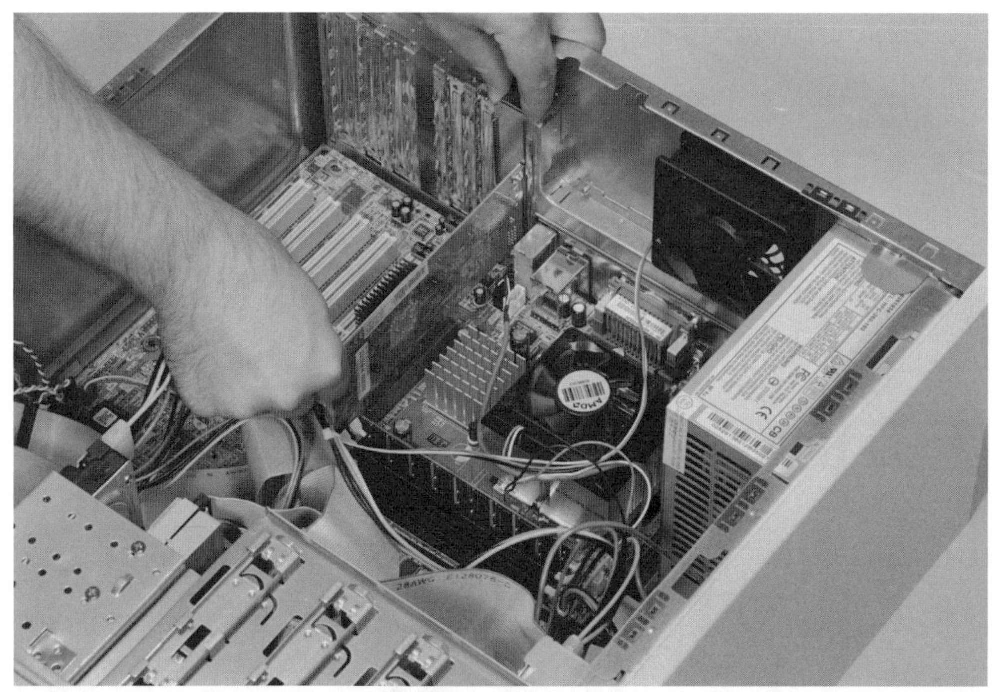

Figure 6.32. Placing the AGP video card in its slot.

Figure 6.33. Pushing the AGP card down with the thumbs.

Some cases have metal covers that are held in by very tiny pieces of metal. Once removed, these covers can't be replaced. (You can always purchase solid metal covers that screw into a slot closing it off, if you want). For this type of slot cover, you need to bend the slot cover until the metal breaks to remove the slot cover. Be careful of sharp edges.

After removing the slot cover, find a small, coarse screw from the set of screws that came with your PC case. It's a good idea to test the screw above its slot. Some cases have poorly tapped threads, and the screws sometimes cut their own path into the case as you tighten them. Other cases are better. The screws go in easily and come out easily.

Now that you have a screw and your Phillips screwdriver handy, pick up the AGP video card and position it above its slot. Push down on the card to get it to seat in its slot. The slight lever with the protrusion at the back can be pressed in with your fingers to allow the card to clear the protrusion (Figure 6.32 and 6.33).

Sometimes pushing one end of the card in first helps seat it more easily, but toward the end when you're pushing the card into its final place, you want uniform pressure at both ends of the card so that the leads seat fully along the entire card. Give the card an extra little push to be sure it's fully seated.

Now, hopefully, the screw hole notch in the metal rim of the card lines up with a screw hole in the case. If not, you might need to push the card around just a bit to get the screw to clear the card notch and be able to screw it in. Try to avoid putting too much pressure on the card.

Screw in the AGP video card (Figure 6.34) to hold it in place.

The AGP video card is now installed. From the back of your PC, you'll see that the video connector of the video card is now accessible (Figure 6.35). Later, you'll plug in your monitor here, when your system is fully built. The video connector shown is the 15-pin analog connector which will work with any monitor. Some of the newer video cards come with DVI connectors which are designed to send a digital signal to LCD monitors. That way the signal always remains digital. These video cards also typically come with a DVI to 15-pin adapter if you wish to use an analog monitor.

Figure 6.34. Screwing in the AGP video card. The AGP card is now fully installed.

Figure 6.35. Back of PC case with AGP video card installed. This is a 15-pin analog video connector. Your system may use a digital connector.

Expansion cards, unlike drives, do not need cables for power or for signal transfer. All power and signal connections are provided by the metal leads between the expansion card and the card slot in the mainboard.

Installing PCI Expansion Cards

Next, we'll install any PCI expansion cards you have (Figure 6.36 to 6.39).

If your system doesn't have built-in sound, you'll probably have a PCI sound card. If your system doesn't have built-in networking, you might want to install a PCI network card to connect your computers together.

There are many PCI cards that add functionality to your PC, from video input and output cards for home video producers (see videoguys.com for example) to special cards that interface to external mechanical devices.

For example, many experiments at universities are computer controlled, where the computer might control various optics or other mechanical devices, such as spectrometers or gas chromatography equipment. Such control is usually through a PCI card. Other cards might allow your PC to control a home security system.

Once you've installed one PCI card, you've essentially installed them all. They're all installed in the same manner. Because the mainboard in the demonstrated build has onboard sound and onboard networking, we'll install a PCI internal modem card, which gives the computer dial-up access to the Internet.

Remove the PCI card from its static proof bag. As with all other devices sensitive to static electricity, touch something metal before touching the card, such as the back of the case or a metal railing. (No, a can of beer doesn't count!) If you want, you can also wear a grounding wrist strap, but it isn't necessary. Try to handle the card by the edges and in particular by the metal strip at the end.

Position the card above a PCI slot you plan to use. You'll probably find that some slots won't be accessible after some cards are installed. For example, your AGP video card might have its own heatsink which protrudes too far out to allow the PCI slot next to it to be accessible.

It's good to plan ahead and decide how many cards you need. While you'll usually have room to add another card later, I usually try to skip a slot between cards, if possible, so they get better air circulation. If this isn't

Figure 6.36. Pushing the PCI modem card into place.

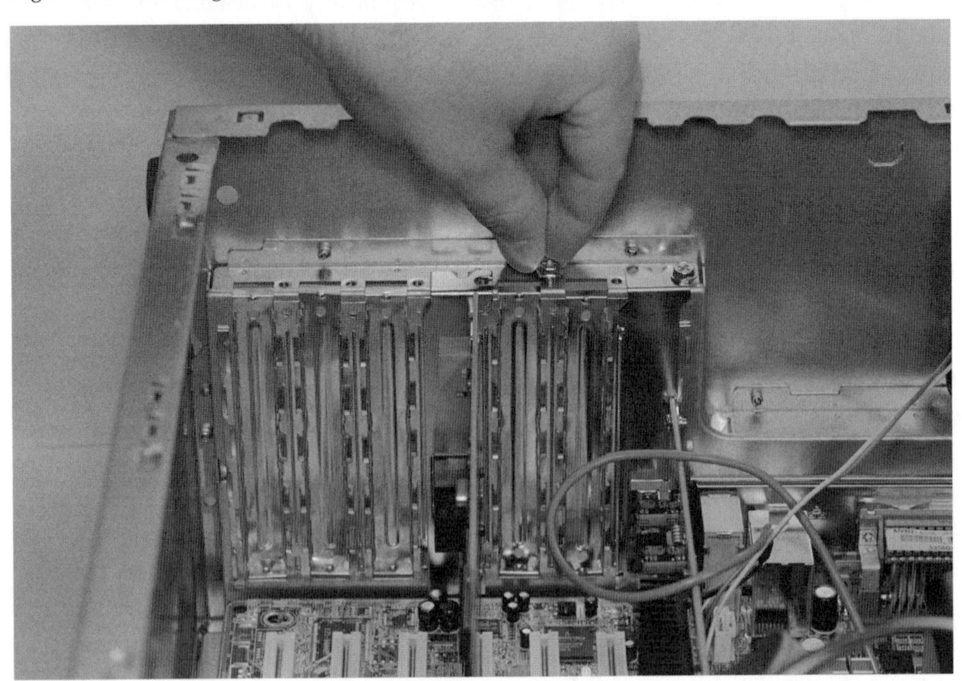

Figure 6.37. Testing a screw from the set of screws that came with the PC case. We are testing the screw in the hole next to the installed PCI card. All slot covers should use the same type of screw, usually a short, coarsely-threaded screw. Sometimes a screw won't go easily because of poorly tapped threads on the case.

Figure 6.38. Screwing in the PCI modem card.

possible, you might want to see that the cards that will generate a lot of heat have an extra, unused slot around them (as with the AGP card). Thinner cards can be used in adjacent PCI slots. Other than these considerations, feel free to use whatever slot you prefer.

Remove the PCI slot cover just as you did with the AGP slot cover. Take a coarse screw from the set of screws that came with the case. Test the screw to be sure it goes in properly (Figure 6.37). For cheaper cases which have poor threads and expansion slot covers that permanently come off, I've found testing the screw can often save you from trying to use a slot where the screw hole doesn't seem to be properly tapped. (A tap is a little device that turns a hole into a screw thread.)

Now, with the slot uncovered and the test screw removed, position the PCI card above its slot and push it straight down (Figure 6.36). Sometimes putting one end of the card in first, by just a little, helps. Push the card straight down to seat it fully. Give an extra uniform push to be sure the card sits properly.

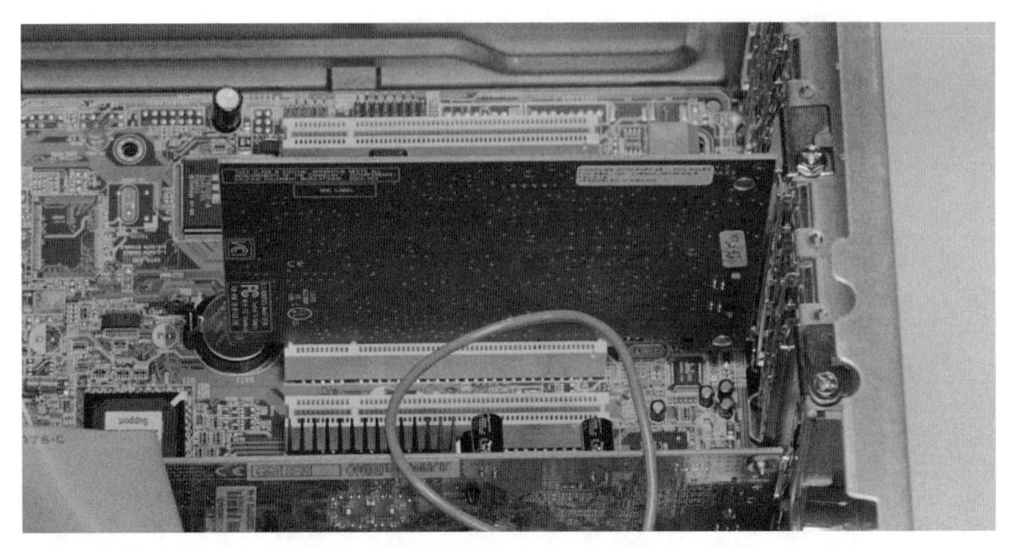

Figure 6.39. PCI modem card installed. By examining the edges of the card where it sits into the socket, we see the card is fully seated. Sometimes if an expansion card device doesn't work, it's because the card isn't fully seated.

Now, secure the card to the case by screwing it into its expansion slot (Figure 6.38).

The PCI modem card is now installed (Figure 6.39). Proceed in the same manner to install any sound cards or other PCI cards you have.

Your system is now essentially built. The mainboard and drives have been installed and connected. The expansion cards have been added.

Many builders suggest assembling and testing your basic system before installing unnecessary expansion cards. For example, you might just install the sound card and test the system at this point. Then, open it up later and add your video production and other PCI cards. The idea here is that you want to test the basic system first to be sure it works. You don't want to introduce any conflicts created by an extra add-on card.

Then, if you add cards and find something doesn't work, you're more certain that the problem was introduced by the newly-added card, because your system worked fine before adding the card. This is a general rule of trouble shooting. If you want to know the source of a problem and you change several things at once, you can't easily know which change made a difference. If you change only one thing and the problem disappears, it's likely the problem was due to the thing you changed.

Sometimes you don't really know or care what creates a problem. You just want the problem to go away. For example, while working one day, your system unexpectedly crashes. You reboot the system and continue working as if nothing happened. You don't know or care to know what caused the unexpected crash.

Figure 6.40 shows the inside of the case of the fully-built system. We'll sit the case upright, test it, and then replace the cover and bezel. There's still a bit to do, such as installing an operating system.

Figure 6.40. The system is essentially built. The mainboard has been installed. The drives have been installed, with ribbon cables and power cables connected. We've installed the AGP and PCI cards. Now, we test the system. Be sure the CPU fan is spinning before closing the side. You can run the system in any orientation. When closing the case, be sure no cables are pinched by the cover.

Testing The System

For the Enlight case, the side of the case should be replaced before the front bezel is replaced. However, we wish to see that the CPU fan is turning rapidly, so we'll leave the side of the case off for now. We will replace the front of the bezel, although we could just as easily push the start/stop button with the bezel off. The front cover is purely decorative. If in doubt which button is for on-off and which is the reset, you could just hold up the bezel and see which button is which.

There is ongoing debate about whether or not you should run a system with its internals exposed. Some say that modern cases are designed for effective cooling, sucking the air in from one side of the case and blowing it out the other side. They say that with the side removed, the proper sucking and blowing airflow isn't maintained and the system can overheat.

The other group says that, with the side of the case off, there is great air circulation between the inside of the case and the outside, and that's about the best ambient temperature you'll ever get inside the case anyway, and so its fine. (If you have a program to measure CPU and mainboard temperature, you can test this to see which is cooler. See Figure 4.7) We'll compromise and lay the removed side panel of the case up against the exposed side of the case. It's generally agreed if the PC has a hard drive smaller than 20 GB, the case should be fully covered to protect the PC from embarrassment.

Now, we plug in the monitor to the back of the video adapter card. We plug in the power cord to the back of the case (Figure 6.41). And, we plug in the monitor to give it power.

It's recommended that you not plug your computer and monitor directly to a wall outlet. Rather, you should purchase a UPS (uninterruptible power supply). The UPS serves as a surge protector to prevent your system from being damaged if a power spike is delivered to it. And, sometimes power will fail unexpectedly. The UPS gives you time to save your work and properly shut down your system.

If a system is turned off and back on rapidly, it's probably not good for the system. A very short power drop could mimic this effect and could be hard on both the computer and the monitor. A UPS prevents this.

Figure 6.41. Plugging in the power cord to the back of the case. Above it is the ATX power supply on-off switch. Between the cord plug-in and the power switch is a selector for setting the incoming voltage. For the U.S., it should already be set to 115 volts when purchased.

The big moment has arrived. We're set to test our new system. We push the power button and ... nothing happens. Hmpf. We take off the front bezel to be sure it hits the power switch. We test the switch directly without the bezel. The system doesn't respond. At a point like this, it's smart to check the basics. For example, does the wall socket have power? You could purchase a fancy gizmo to test an outlet, but a hair dryer, radio, or a lamp works just as well.

Examining the back of the PC case, we see that there is a switch with two positions, 0 and 1. Zero often means off, and one often means on in the computer world. We turn the switch from 0 to 1 and push the power button again. The system boots up. Older AT power supplies seldom had power switches at the back and if you're used to an AT system, it's easy to miss the switch at the back of the case.

The system powers up. We see the CPU fan is spinning, and BIOS recognizes that it's the first time the system has been started. It asks us to confirm the CPU speed setting. Our system is built on an Athlon 2000+ chip, and the menu offers 1.67 GHz and 2.08 GHz as options. Neither of those corresponds to 2.0 GHz which is what we might expect a 2000+ chip to run at. We usually don't want to run a chip faster than it's rated, so the higher value is out.

AMD has an "effective" measure of CPU performance. That's what the plus sign means after the 2000. 2000+ means it's comparable to a 2.0 GHz Pentium. The 2000+ Athlon actually runs at 1.67 GHz. However, the Athlon is more efficient because it can do more during each clock cycle than can a Pentium. So, the correct setting is 1.67 GHz.

BIOS Settings

The BIOS settings on your PC are probably fine. If you want to examine them, you can, but your mainboard probably recognizes all it needs to know about your hard drive, etc. To enter BIOS setup, a key, such as delete, is usually pressed when the system first starts up. Consult your mainboard manual if you want to learn more about BIOS setup.

Unless you've placed a Windows XP CD into the CD-ROM, you probably receive a message that says the system can't find a bootable disk. We'll change that in a moment.

Replacing The Side Of The Case And Bezel

Now that your system is tested and we've visually seen that the CPU fan is spinning properly, we can shut down the system and replace the side of the case (Figure 6.42 and 6.43) and the bezel (Figure 6.44). We could also leave the side off temporarily and continue to install an operating system. To replace the side of the case, examine the back of the side carefully (Figure 6.45). Often, the back of the side will have notches or rails that must engage for the case to close properly.

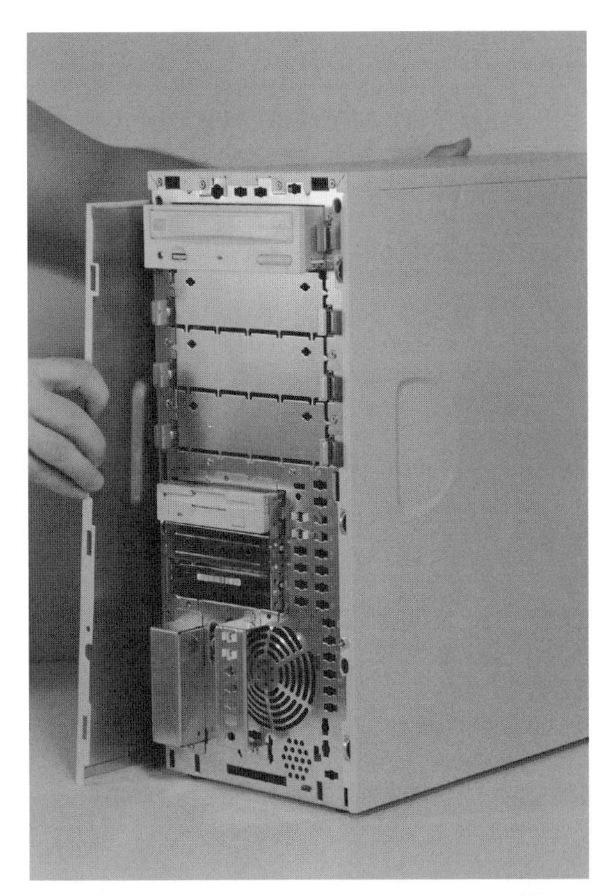

Figure 6.42. Replacing the side of the case. This case side must be pushed toward the back of the case to engage lugs on the case.

Before closing the case, be sure no wires or cables are near the edges where they might get pinched.

Figure 6.43. Screwing in the side of the case. Some cheaper cases have poorly tapped threads for the screws, so use only minimal force to tighten the cover screws.

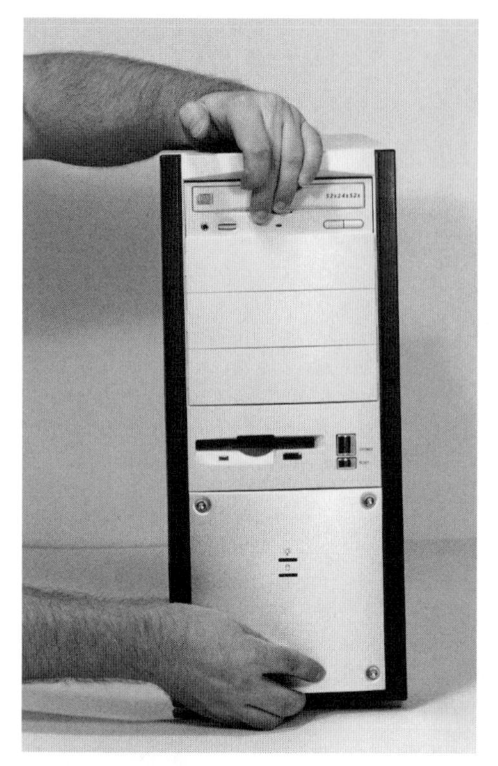

Figure 6.44. Closing the bezel. Here the lip of the bezel hits the CD-RW drive and we need to gently lift up the CD drive to close the bezel. Don't just slam the bezel to close it. Close it gently to be sure nothing interferes with it closing.

It also saves wear and tear if you depress the front cover latch as you close it. Tilt the front of the case upward to get a good grip on the latch.

Figure 6.45. Back of the side panel. If you have difficulty replacing the side of your case, examine it carefully to see how the lugs engage the rest of the case.

Installing Windows XP

Now that the hardware of the computer is together and running, we need to install an operating system. An operating system will allow your PC to run other software, such as games, word processors, spreadsheets, and graphics software. Think of the operating system as the interface between your software and the computer hardware. Actually, there is one more level of interface called the BIOS or the basic input output system. The operating system communicates with the BIOS. The BIOS communicates with the hardware. However, for practical purposes, you can consider your operating system as connecting your hardware and software together.

The most popular operating system is Microsoft Windows, and its most current version is Windows XP. We'll install Windows XP Home Edition, which is slightly less expensive than Windows XP Professional. Windows XP Professional does allow dual-processor support, if you anticipate using two processors on your mainboard.

Be sure to purchase Windows XP, in either flavor, as OEM software from the place where you purchase your mainboard and other components (unless you plan to install only Linux). OEM software is less expensive than retail boxed software, and it's not an upgrade, so you won't need a previous version of Windows installed on your system to install OEM software.

Other software, such as MS Office, can also be purchased as OEM software.

The Western Digital hard drive has not been partitioned or formatted and has no software on it.

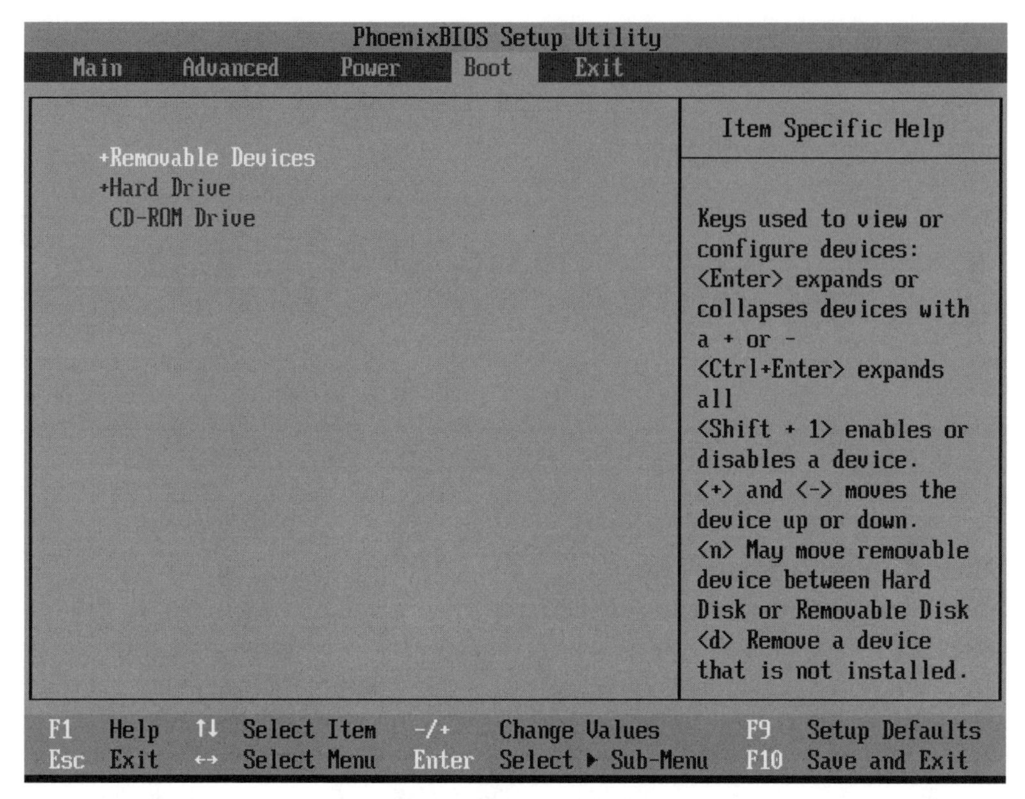

Figure 7.1. BIOS settings show boot order. Here the system tries to boot from the hard drive before the CD drive. Use arrow keys and plus/minus keys to switch the boot order if desired.

When you start your system for the first time, you'll probably receive a message that the computer couldn't find a bootable disk or an operating system (unless you already put the Windows CD in the CD tray).

Your computer's BIOS specifies the search order that your computer uses to find a bootable operating system (Figure 7.1).

This system seeks an operating system first from the floppy drive, second from the hard drive, and third from a CD. You can enter BIOS to change it so that the CD drive is checked before the hard drive, if you find that desirable.

Because there wasn't a floppy disk in the floppy drive, no operating system was found there. Then, the computer examined the hard drive, which is brand new, and it didn't find an operating system. Then, the computer examined the CD drive and found no operating system, because there was no CD in the tray. The result is that no operating system can be found.

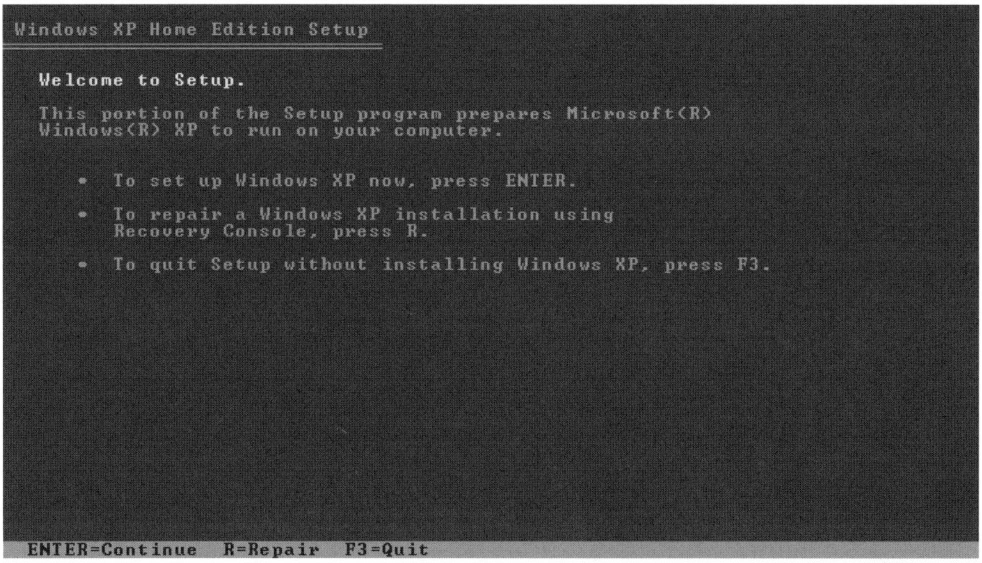

```
Windows XP Home Edition Setup

  Welcome to Setup.

  This portion of the Setup program prepares Microsoft(R)
  Windows(R) XP to run on your computer.

      •  To set up Windows XP now, press ENTER.

      •  To repair a Windows XP installation using
         Recovery Console, press R.

      •  To quit Setup without installing Windows XP, press F3.

  ENTER=Continue   R=Repair   F3=Quit
```

Figure 7.2. Microsoft welcomes you to setup. Press ENTER to setup Windows on a new hard drive.

We'll open the CD drive, insert the Windows XP CD, close the drive, give the drive a moment to get up to speed, and push the reset button to restart the system. (As a general rule, try Alt+Ctrl+Delete to restart the system. If that doesn't work, use the reset switch. Alt+Ctrl+Delete is a Windows or DOS operating system command, and a new system without an operating system won't recognize it). Try not to use the on-off button to restart your system, because this is harder on the components.

Today, most mainboards support booting from the CD. And, most OEM software also supports booting from the CD. Installing an operating system is as easy as inserting the Windows CD and restarting the system. If your system doesn't support booting from CD, you'll need to make a bootable floppy disk on another machine and use that to boot the new system.

With Windows XP, installing the operating system from the OEM CD is a snap. Upon restarting with the Windows XP CD in the drive, you're immediately taken through a series of introductory screens. First, a "Welcome" screen lets you know your PC sees the Windows CD (Figure 7.2). You're all set to install Windows. Press "Enter" or "Next" to continue whenever that's the only option! However, if other options exist, take a moment to consider them before accepting the defaults.

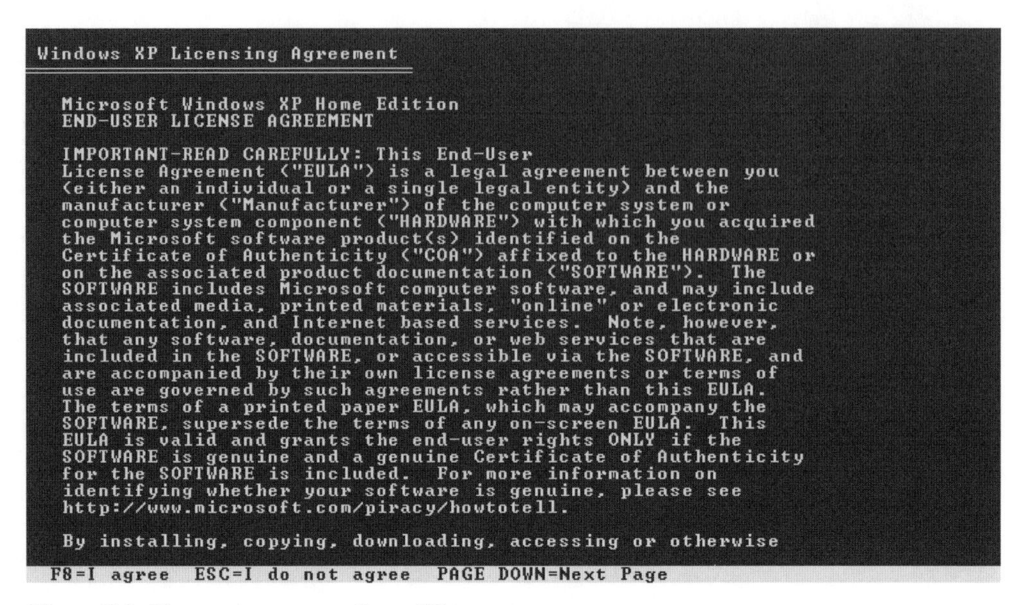

Figure 7.3. License Agreement. Press F8 to accept.

We must also accept Microsoft's license agreement by pressing F8 (Figure 7.3).

Next, we're taken to a menu that allows us to partition your new hard drive (Figure 7.4). Think of partitioning a hard drive as breaking it up into sections. After partitioning, each partition or section will then be formatted so that it can be read by various operating systems. One of the original purposes of partitioning a hard drive was to allow the hard drive to support multiple operating systems. Each operating system could be given its own partition, which could then be formatted for that operating system.

The onscreen message says "Press C" to partition and we do. The screen tells us that 76309 MB is available for partitioning our 80 GB drive.

NOTE: For the photos in this book, we partitioned a 4 GB virtual drive which shows 4095 MB as available (Figure 7.4). That's about 4 GB. We'll make the Windows Partition 2000 MB (about 2 GB) (Figure 7.5). We'll leave 2000 MB unpartitoned to demonstrate a dual boot operating system, where Linux is installed into the unpartitioned and unformatted part of the disk. Your PC will show far larger numbers for available space. Today, a 2 GB partition is small!

The screen (Figure 7.5) asks us how much of the drive we want to use to create the partition. Notice that at this point your keypad numbers will not

Windows XP Home Edition Setup

The following list shows the existing partitions and
unpartitioned space on this computer.

Use the UP and DOWN ARROW keys to select an item in the list.

- To set up Windows XP on the selected item, press ENTER.
- To create a partition in the unpartitioned space, press C.
- To delete the selected partition, press D.

4095 MB Disk 0 at Id 0 on bus 0 on atapi [MBR]
Unpartitioned space 4095 MB

ENTER=Install C=Create Partition F3=Quit

Figure 7.4. Notice we only have 4095 MB (about 4 GB) of unpartitioned space. This is because we partitioned a virtual hard drive (VMWare) so we could get screen captures for this book. For an 80 GB drive, expect to see a number like 76309 MB, rather than 4095 MB.

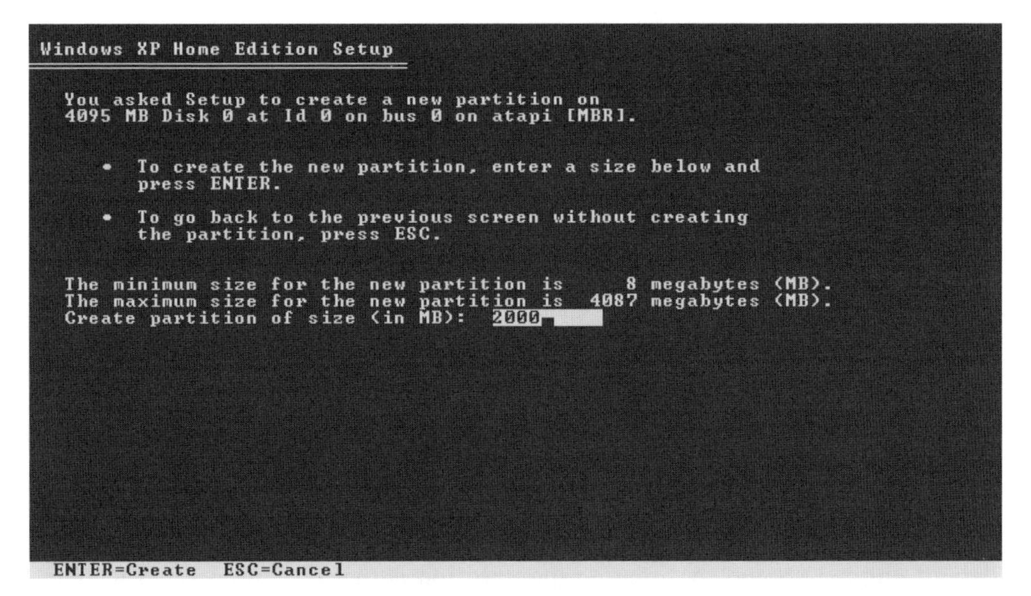

Figure 7.5. Choose the size of the partition you desire and hit ENTER. If you only plan to install Windows XP, you can use the full amount as one partition. Save some unpartitioned space if you plan to install a Linux dual boot. Here, we created a partition of 2000 MB on our virtual drive. For XP, you'll probably want at least 40000 MB (about 40 GB).

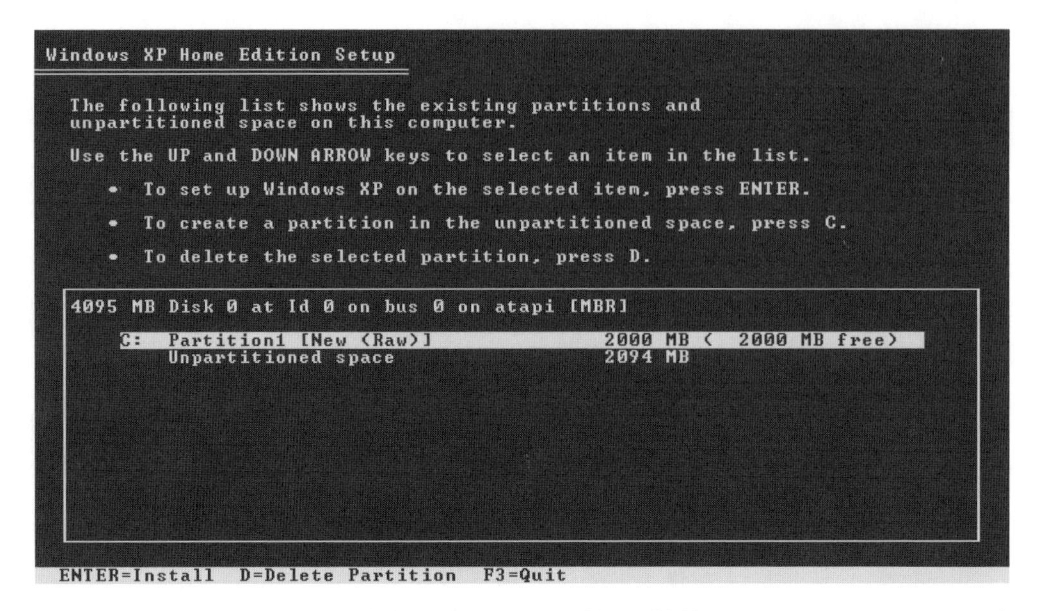

Figure 7.6 . We've created the 2000 MB partition and have 2000 MB remaining unpartitioned for Linux (to be installed later). If you change your mind and want to use a smaller or larger partition, hit D. Otherwise, hit ENTER to begin formatting and to set up Windows XP. Notice: Our 2000 MB partition is small, because we're actually partitioning a virtual drive. Your partition should probably be at least 40000 MB.

work, and you'll need to use the numbers above the letter keys. That's normal. Also, you can use the backspace key to delete the default number, which is just the maximum size of a partition on your hard drive.

We'll make the partition 40 GB (about 40000 MB) or about half the available space. That's plenty of space for what we intend to do, and we'll be using the other half of the drive to install Linux later to give us a dual boot operating system.

If you plan to use only one operating system, or if you have a smaller hard drive and need all the space, you can go ahead and use all available space for the Windows partition and then make that correspond to the C:\ drive. The default number shown for creating the partition is the maximum size of your drive. Just hit ENTER to create this maximum-sized partition if you plan to install Windows XP as the only operating system.

If you plan to install a dual boot operating system, it's good to decide how much hard drive space you want allocated for each system. For example, if

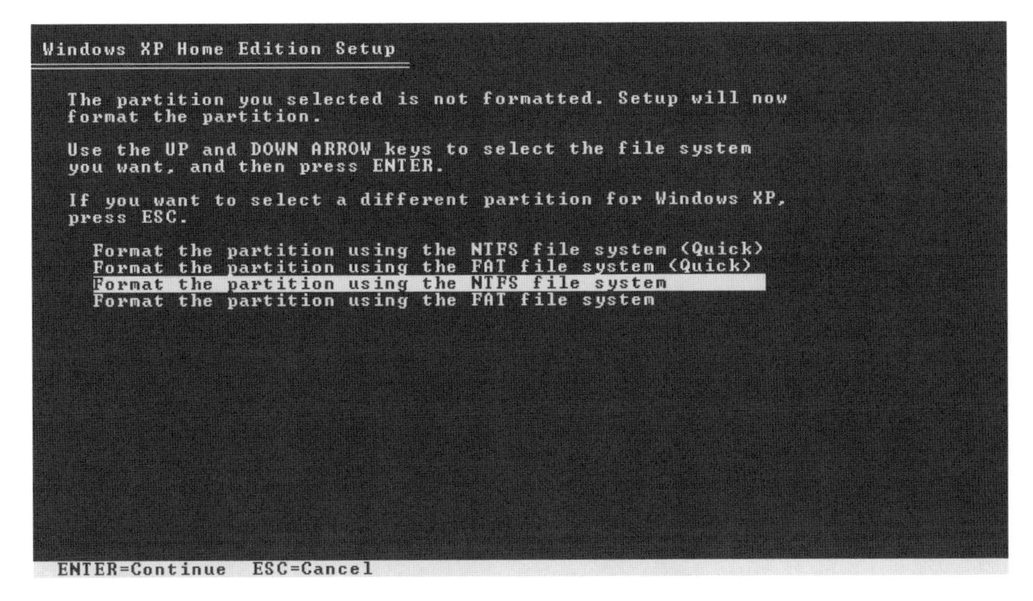

Figure 7.7 . We choose to format the partition with NTFS.

you have an 80 GB drive, and you primarily run Windows, but you'd like to experiment with Linux, you might allow 60 GB (about 60000 MB) for a Windows partition. Then, use the remaining 20 GB for installing a Linux partition. If you plan to actively use both Windows and Linux, you might decide to enter half of the maximum disk space as the Windows partition. Then, the other half can be used for Linux.

If you plan to dual boot with Windows 98 and Windows XP (or triple boot Windows 98, Windows XP, and Linux), you'll want to leave enough drive space for another partition (which will be FAT formatted), because Windows 98 only recognizes FAT formatted partitions. Install Windows 98 first.

After we choose how large to make the Windows partition, we hit "enter" (Figure 7.6) to see the new partitioning information. To do the actual partitioning, we hit "enter" again which installs the partition to the hard drive.

After partitioning the hard drive, a format screen appears automatically (Figure 7.7). To format 40 GB as one partition, we'll use NTFS file system, which stands for New Technology File System. OTFS or Old Technology File System is called FAT. FAT stands for File Allocation Table.

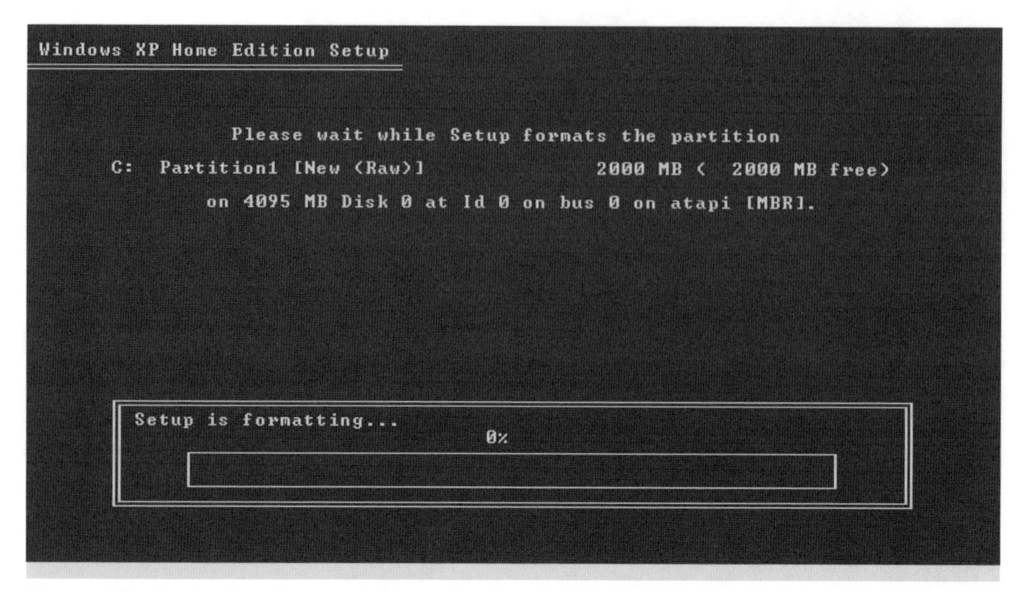

Figure 7.8. Formatting. The status bar will tell you of the progress. For a large hard drive, feel free to take a break and check back on the progress later.

We select NTFS, press "ENTER," and let the computer partition the hard drive (Figure 7.7). A status bar shows us the formatting progress (Figure 7.8).

Either NTFS or FAT is basically a way of keeping track of where information is stored on the disk. Information is divided into what are called clusters. NTFS or FAT lets us find clusters of information on the hard drive.

Imagine having a big house and a small notebook. Each room in the house corresponds to a cluster. Every time you purchase something to put in the house, you place it in one of the rooms and record which room the item is in in your notebook. Then, if you ever want to get the item, you look at your notebook to find the room. NTFS has a bigger notebook than FAT. NTFS also has better security, so people don't break into your house.

NTFS allows us to make larger partitions, and it's generally considered superior to FAT. If the partition must be read by Windows 98, FAT is necessary. FAT16 volumes are limited to 2 GB. That is why systems running Windows 95 that had large hard drives needed to have many drive letters: C, D, E... each only containing 2 GB. You can have one big C drive with NTFS. There are also two versions of FAT known as FAT16 and FAT32. If you use

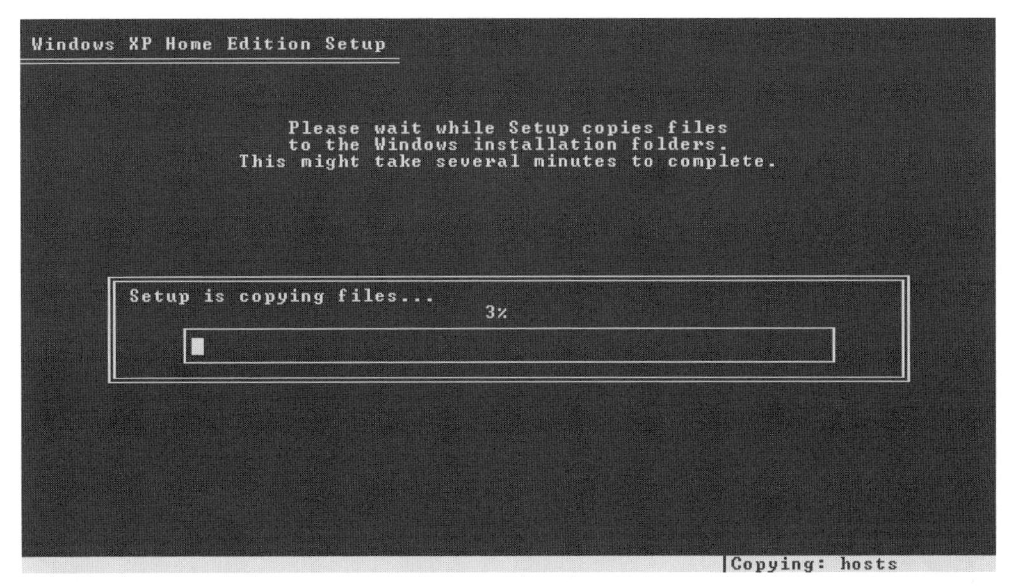

Figure 7.9. Setup is now copying files to your hard drive. After this, Windows XP will restart to complete the installation.

Windows 98, you'll probably use FAT32. However, if you don't need to use Windows 98 and only plan to use Windows XP, use NTFS as your file system.

All you really need to know about NTFS is that when you're prompted to format the system, you select the NTFS option. The format program will also ask if you want to do a quick format or a full format. Select full format. That is usually the best option and also the default option Windows offers.

Formatting the hard drive takes some time, so you might want to go get a Pepsi or some coffee. After the formatting is finished, XP begins copying operating system files to the hard drive (Figure 7.9). Then, your system will reboot to continue the installation process.

After the system reboots, you are prompted to provide some information for Windows. You'll be asked for your regional and language settings (Figure 7.10). And, you'll be asked to enter your name to personalize your computer (Figure 7.11).

You'll need to enter your Windows XP key code (Figure 7.12). Be sure to write this number down in case you need it later. I find writing this number in the Windows manual is handy. If your CD comes in a cheap floppy paper

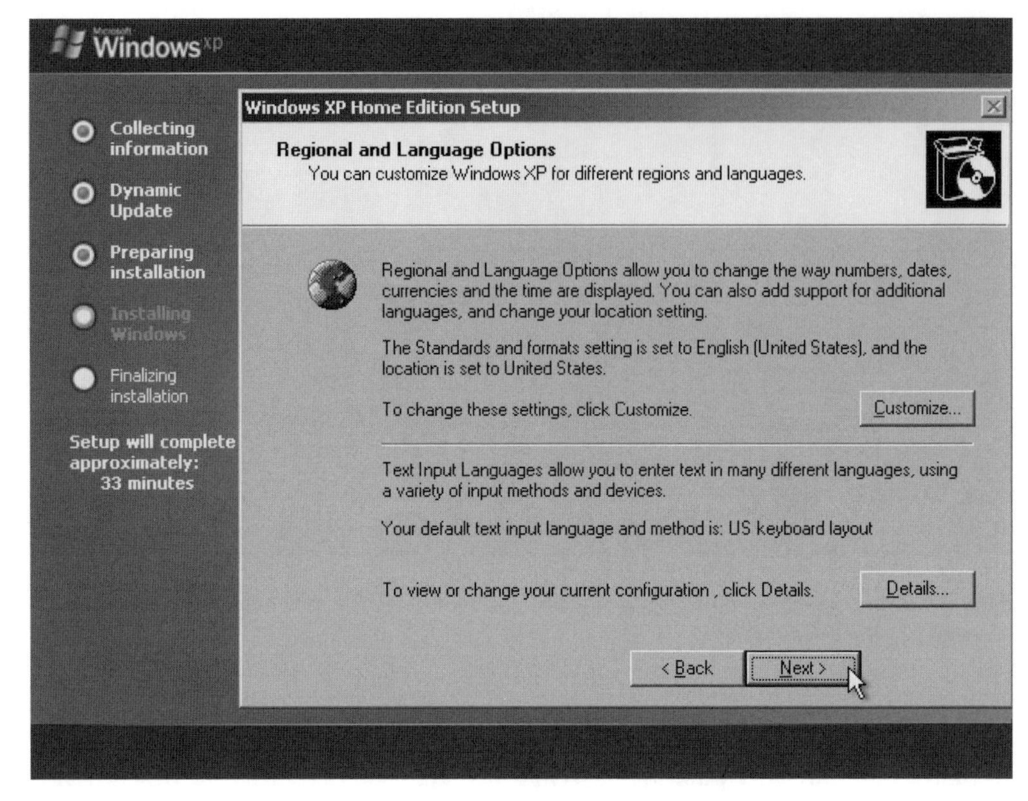

Figure 7.10. Regional and Language Options. Just hit "Next" to choose English as your language.

holder and you transfer the CD to a jewel case, be sure to copy the number onto a paper inside the jewel case. It's also a good idea to keep the original CD holder. (Keep all the stuff that's left over after the build in its own box, in case you need it later.)

If your key code number is rejected, it probably means you misentered it. Try again. And, again. And, possibly, again. Be alert for tricky letters like "I" which could be mistaken for a "1." Or a "B" for an "8."

You'll be asked to name your computer (Figure 7.13). Computer names are useful if your computer is on a network. We named our PC "ASUS." Another screen appears asking for date and time settings (Figure 7.14).

Windows will then copy some more files to your hard drive. You can see the progress of the install by the status bar at the left of the screen. Depending upon your point of view, either useful information or Microsoft propaganda

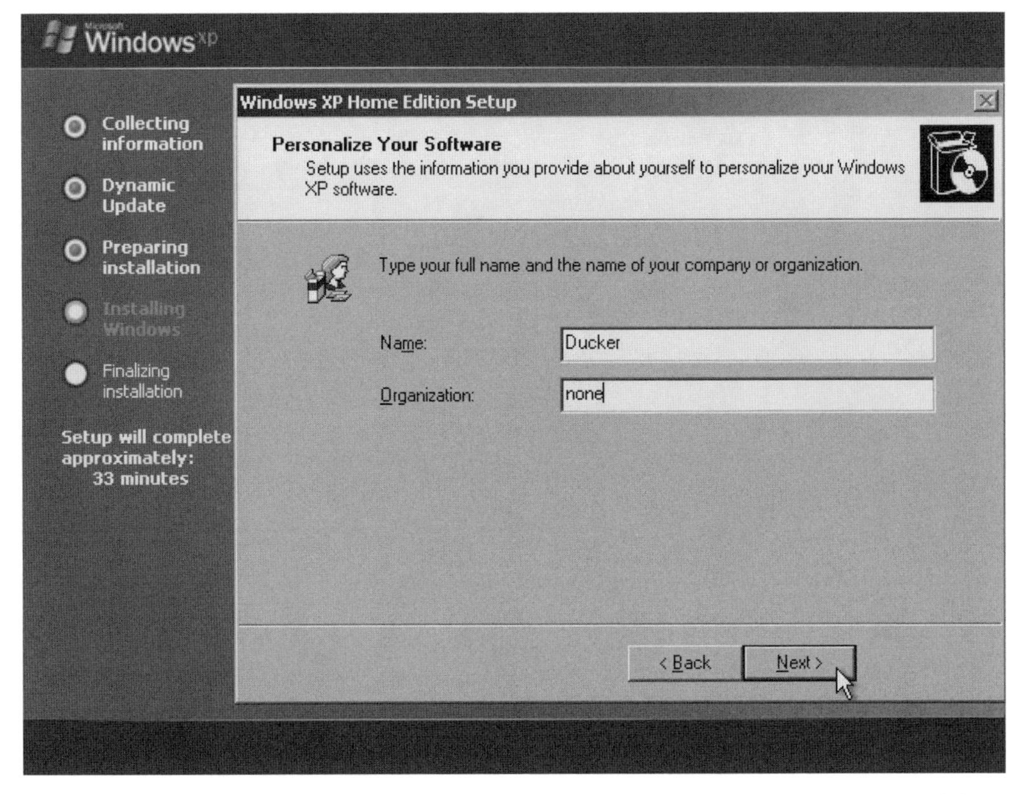

Figure 7.11. Enter your name and your organization. You can enter your full name. You'll be able to create user accounts later, where you can enter your username.

appears at the right of the screen. Don't worry about reading this. It's not important.

Next, you'll be asked if you wish to "activate Windows." You can choose to activate Windows now or you can do it later. I'd probably do it later, after you're fully satisfied with the install. Just select to activate later and continue. We'll discuss activation in more detail later.

The computer might ask you if it can adjust the settings of your monitor. If it does, you'll have only an "OK" box to select (Figure 7.15). Then, another screen will test whether or not the screen is readable with the new settings (Figure 7.16). If the screen isn't readable, don't worry. The settings should revert to the previous settings. We discuss the importance of having the correct monitor identified and how to install video drivers later.

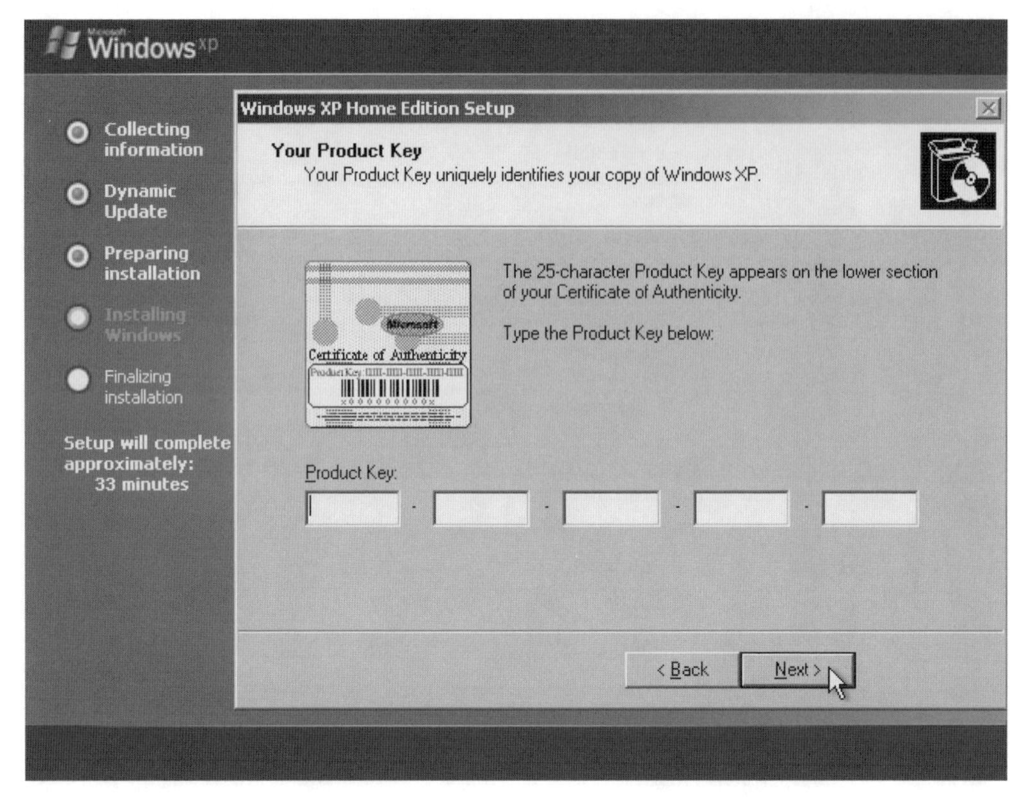

Figure 7.12. Enter your product key.

Next, we add users to the computer (Figure 7.17). Users allow several people to use the same PC, and each user can have his or her own files and settings. I added a user for "Charlie." I also added a user for "Ducker." A username should not be the same as the computer name.

When the computer is finished copying files, you can remove the Windows XP CD and restart the system, and it will now boot from the hard drive (Figure 7.18 and 7.19).

You've now successfully installed Windows XP onto your computer. You can operate your computer and install software. Congratulations!

It's crucial to note that when you purchase a PC with software already installed, the manufacturer has probably taken several steps to be sure the PC works well. For example, all necessary drivers will be installed. You'll need to do some of these things yourself when you build your own PC. But, in so

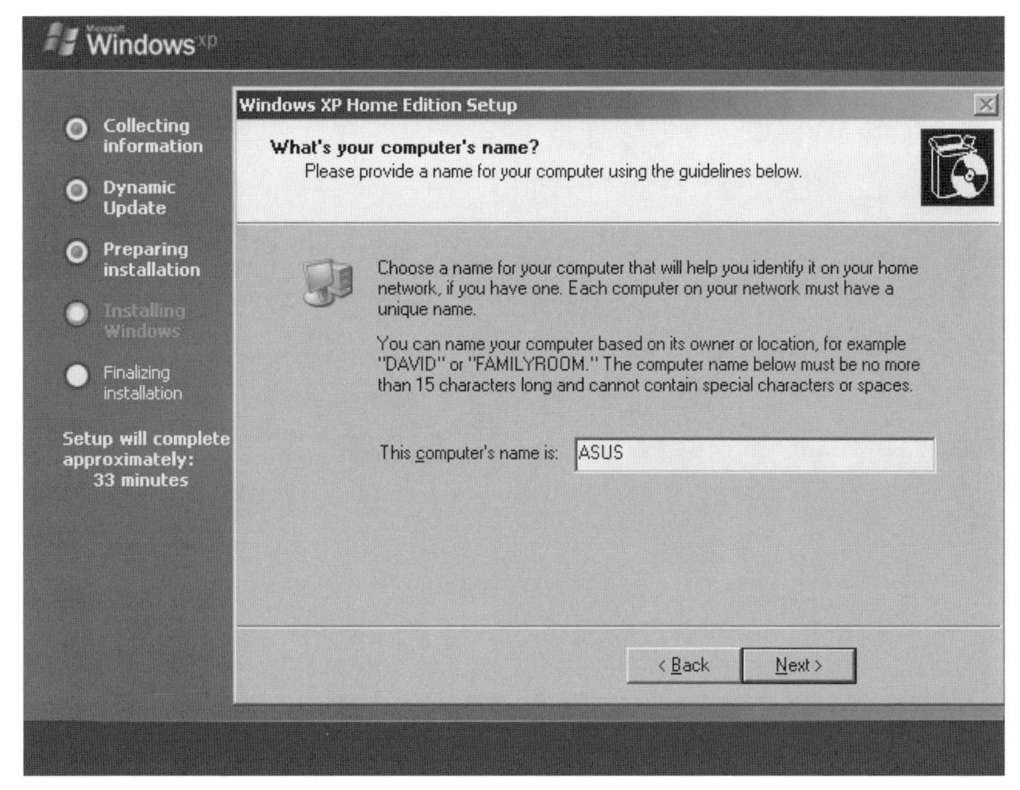

Figure 7.13. Like a proud new parent, you can name your PC. The name will identify the PC on a network.

doing, you'll know more about your PC and be a better PC troubleshooter in the future.

A few things should be done. The order isn't particularly important.

First, after installing a modem and getting your modem connection working, go to the Start Menu and find "Windows Update." You may be familiar with Windows Update already. Basically, you go online; Microsoft scans your system; and then Microsoft installs any improvements it's made to your operating system since your last operating system update.

For us, Windows update finds 29 MB of critical system and security updates. Go get another Pepsi or coffee as it downloads and installs your updates.

It's a good idea to run Windows update regularly and install any critical updates, because malicious hackers find new ways to infiltrate and attack

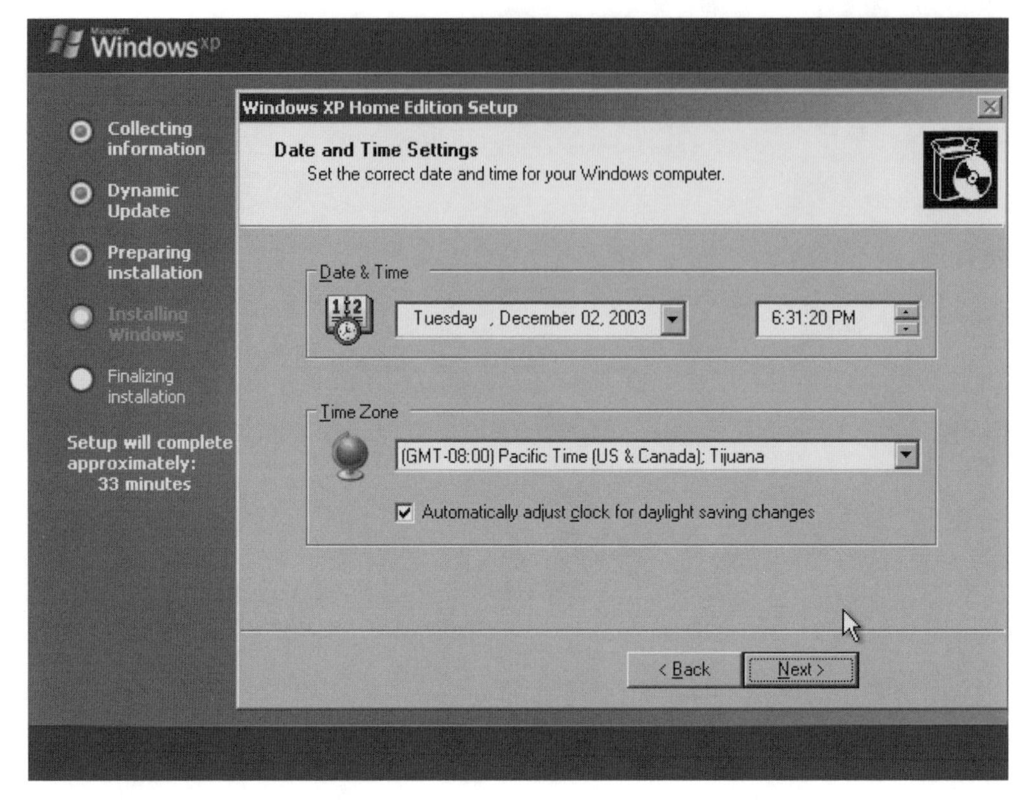

Figure 7.14. Date and Time Settings.

Windows. Microsoft usually then finds a defense which is made available via a software "patch." Not regularly updating your Windows operating system could leave your computer vulnerable to attack.

Similarly, you should regularly update your antivirus software so that it can recognize new viruses and protect your computer from them. You should purchase an antivirus program for your PC. I like Norton AntiVirus. You should also purchase a firewall, such as Zone Alarm. XP has a built-in firewall, but I like Zone Alarm better. Finally, you should go to download.com and get a free program such as Spybot Search and Destroy, which removes spyware from your system.

Next, go to "Activate Windows" (Start...Programs...Accessories...Program Tools...Activate Windows). A certain number of days after the first install, you must "Activate" Windows XP or else it stops working completely. You'll want a modem to Activate Windows online.

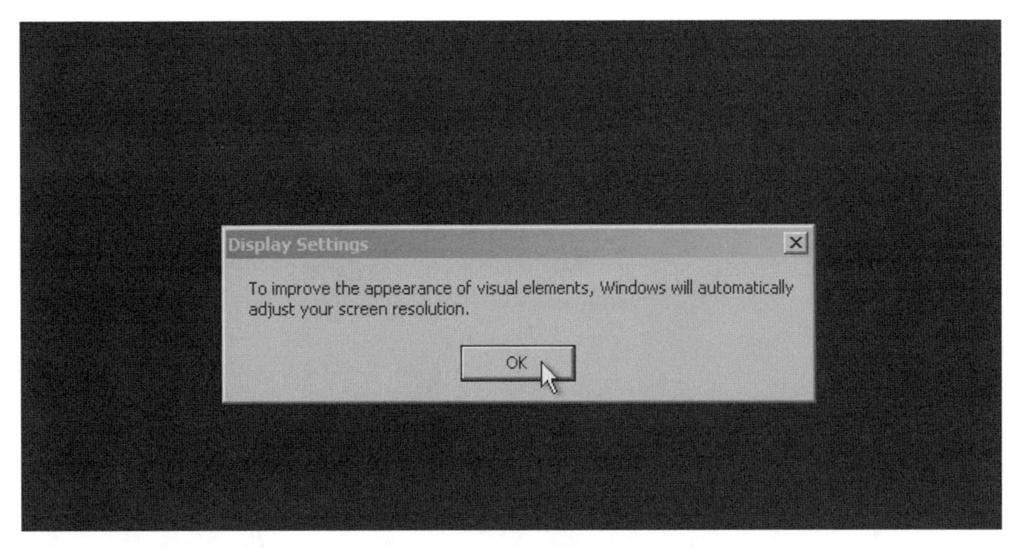

Figure 7.15. When "OK" is your only choice...hit OK.

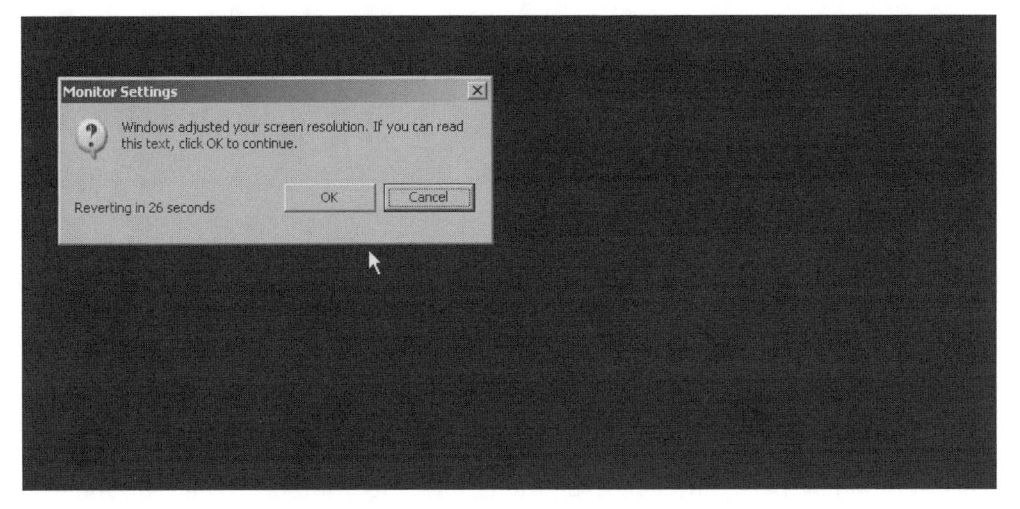

Figure 7.16. After adjusting your display settings, you're asked to hit OK to confirm that you can read the display. If the display is unreadable, the settings should revert.

Basically, "Activate Windows" is a way to protect Microsoft from software piracy. When you "Activate" Windows, your PC logs onto Microsoft's website and Microsoft takes a snapshot of your computer's hardware. Then, if someone later tries to activate that particular copy of Windows XP on another computer, it won't allow activation, because it won't be able to match up the

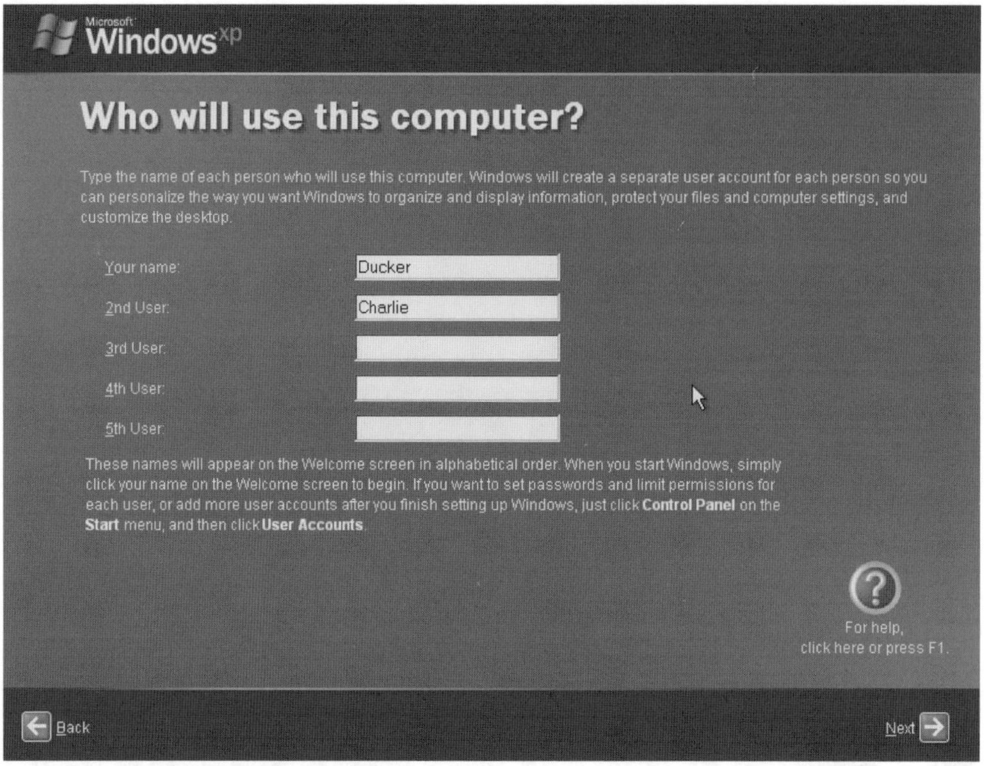

Figure 7.17. Adding users to the computer.

hardware on that computer with the hardware information that Microsoft has stored in a database.

An interesting question: What if you upgrade your system by adding a new mainboard, a new hard drive, and a new DVD drive? The "snapshot" Windows has of your old system might think you're trying to install the operating system onto another computer, even though the old components are no longer in use.

One possibility is adding only one part at a time to the old system, for example, the new hard drive. Then, hopefully, Microsoft will recognize that you're just upgrading an existing system. Then, activate Windows. If an activation fails, you can always call Microsoft and explain the situation to them. No promises this will help you!

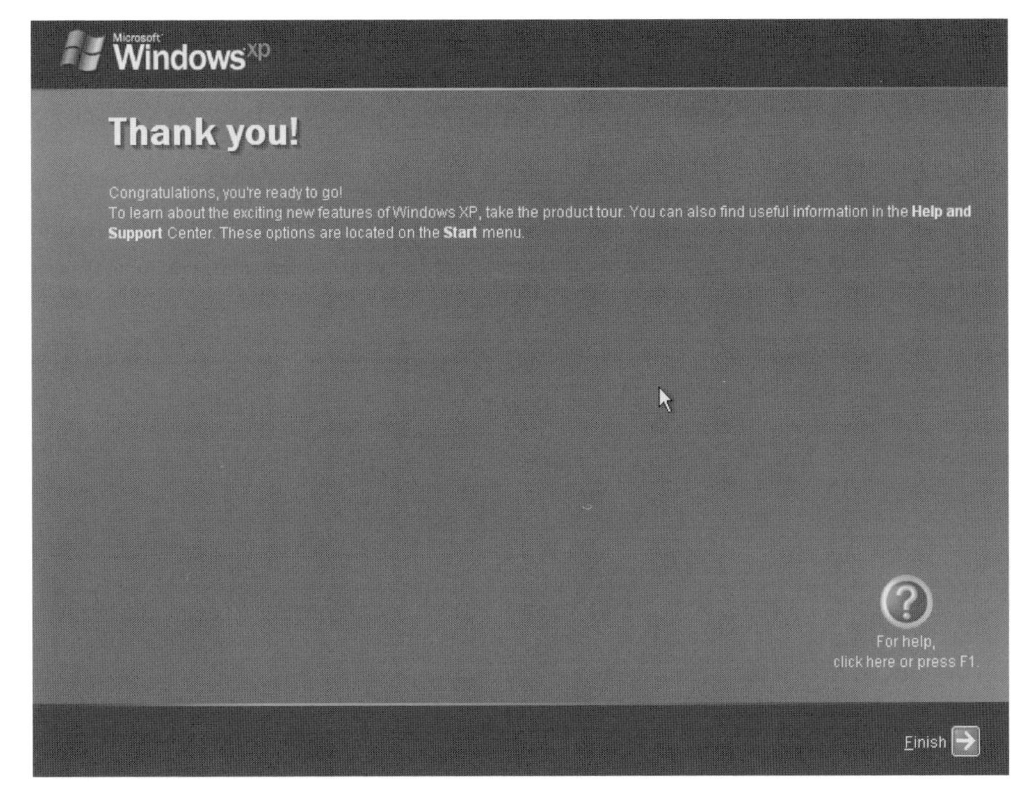

Figure 7.18. Hit the little arrow to finish.

Be aware that if you retire an older computer and try to do a full installation of Windows XP from the CD onto your new computer, the activation will fail. To me, that seems unfair.

You will need to go through the activation process only if you need to reinstall Windows XP from the CD to a hard drive. Another good option is to back up your full Windows system, using MS backup, to be discussed later.

Installing Drivers For Your Devices

Now that you have an operating system installed, you'll need to install drivers for your devices such as Video Cards, Network Interface Cards, Sound Cards, etc. In many cases, if Windows recognizes the device, drivers will be installed automatically. In some cases, generic drivers are installed and they will work fine.

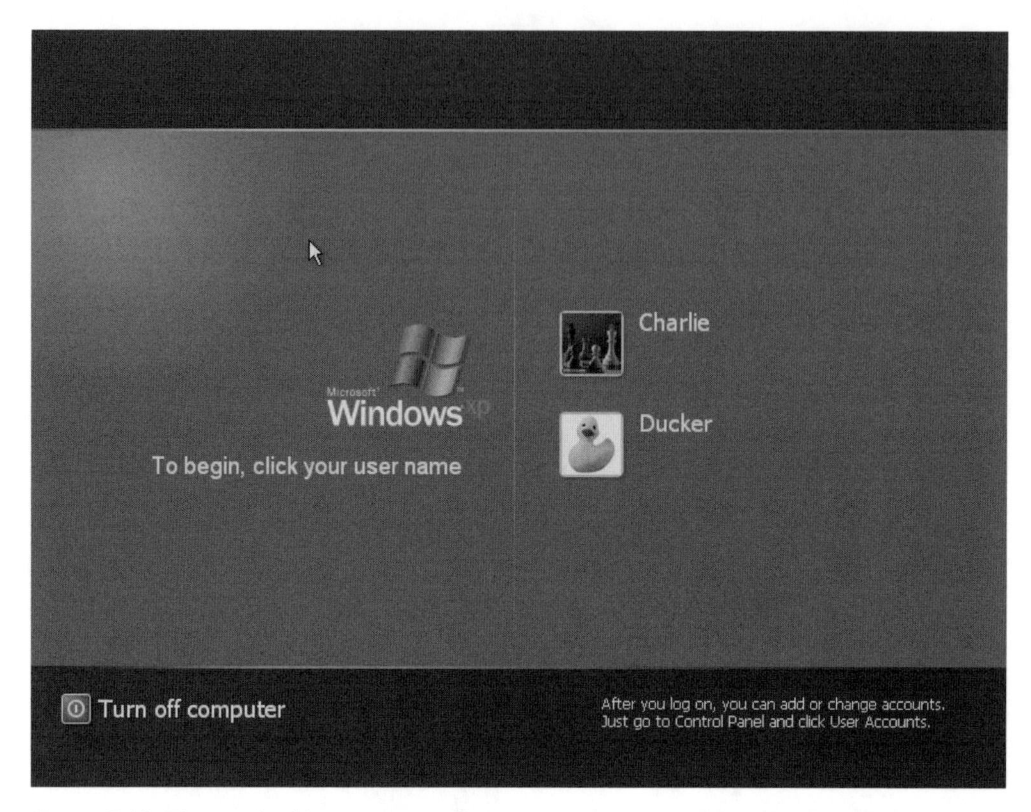

Figure 7.19. The standard login screen. Click on your user icon to log into Windows. Each user can have his or her own personalized settings. (You can change your login picture later if you wish. Just go to "Control Panel" and select "User Accounts.")

Drivers are small software programs that help the operating system use or "drive" the device. Whenever a device doesn't work properly, ask if the proper driver has been installed.

Notice that when you purchase a PC from a major manufacturer, such as Gateway or Dell, they'll be sure your system has working drivers installed for all hardware. But, when you build your own system, you might need to find and install drivers to get your hardware working properly. This will actually help you learn more about your PC, and, if things go wrong later, you'll have a head start in solving PC problems.

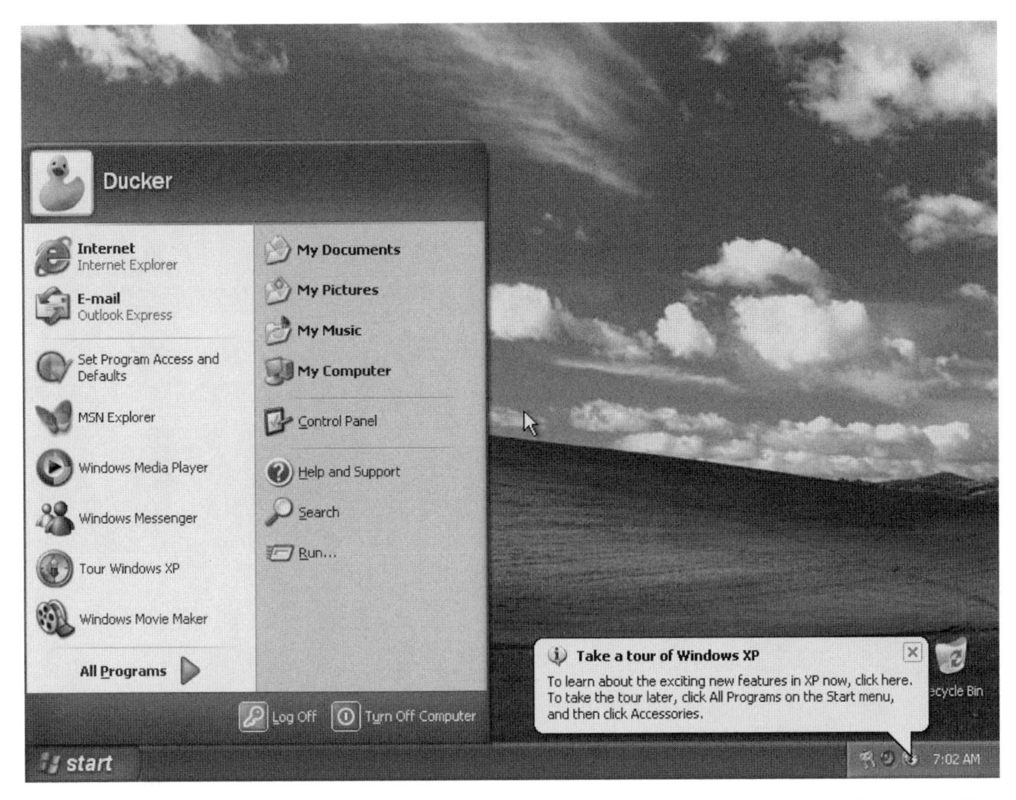

Figure 7.20. Ducker has logged on. Hitting the start menu brings up the menu of options. Go to "Control Panel" to get to Device Manager. Note: First, we'll get the proper monitor recognized. But, if you want to change the desktop later, right click on the desktop and select "Properties."

Monitor Information

We'll use the Monitor, which is actually driven by the video card, as an example. The monitor purchased for this PC build is a ViewSonic A70f+ 17" monitor.

If you look under Control Panel...System...Device Manager (Figure 7.20 to 7.22), and then under "Monitor," you'll see that a generic monitor is listed (Figure 7.23). Windows knows it's a Plug and Play monitor, but it doesn't list the exact model. This means the PC recognizes and can use your monitor, but it doesn't identify the exact model of the monitor (Figure 7.24 shows the correct monitor recognized).

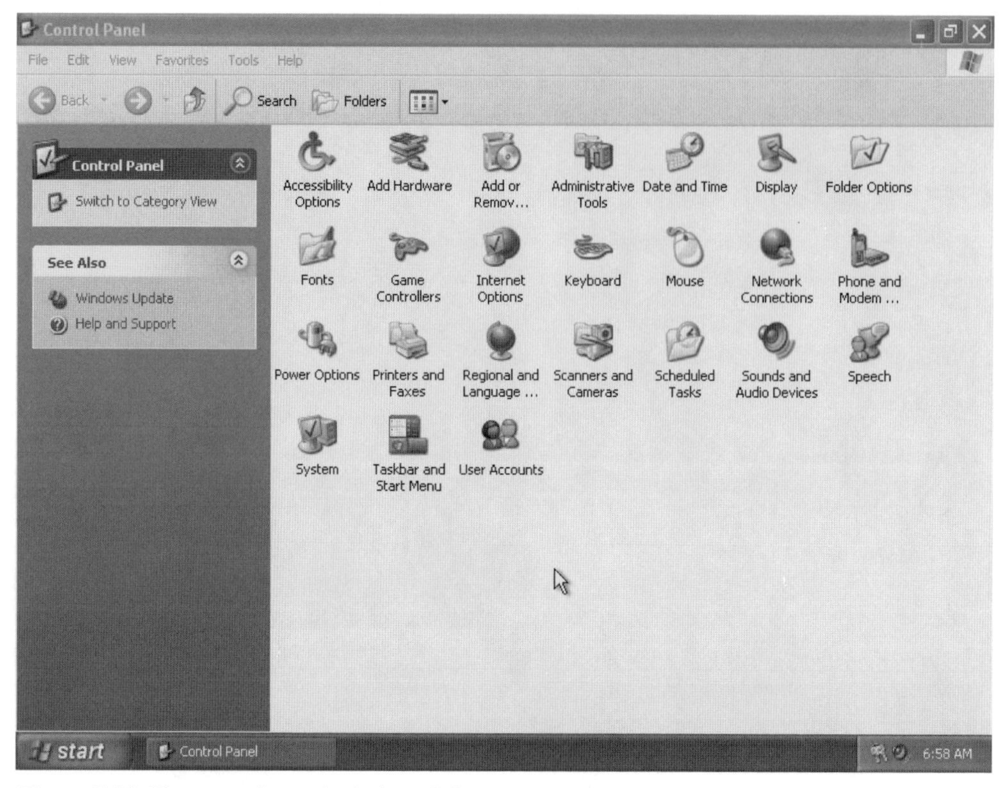

Figure 7.21. The control panel window. Select "System" to get to Device Manager.

A disk came with the Viewsonic monitor, and we'll put that in the CD drive. Autorun starts a program to install a new driver, but it fails with the message that it couldn't find a better driver. The generic plug and play driver will still be used. This could be because the CD only has a driver for Windows 98 and not XP yet. Or sometimes software just sucks! We tested the CD with Windows 98 and found it also didn't work properly. In this case, we learned the software just sucks. The lesson is that sometimes you'll do everything correctly and something just won't work. The failure isn't your fault. It's a flaw in the program. But, you must find a workaround.

We'll go to the website for viewsonic.com and look under "Download Drivers." When looking for updated drivers for a device, your first visit can be to the hardware manufacturer's website. Viewsonic.com sends us to microsoft.com to see if the A70f+ monitor is "Signed" or "Unsigned" for Windows XP. "Signed" means the monitor or other device is designed for

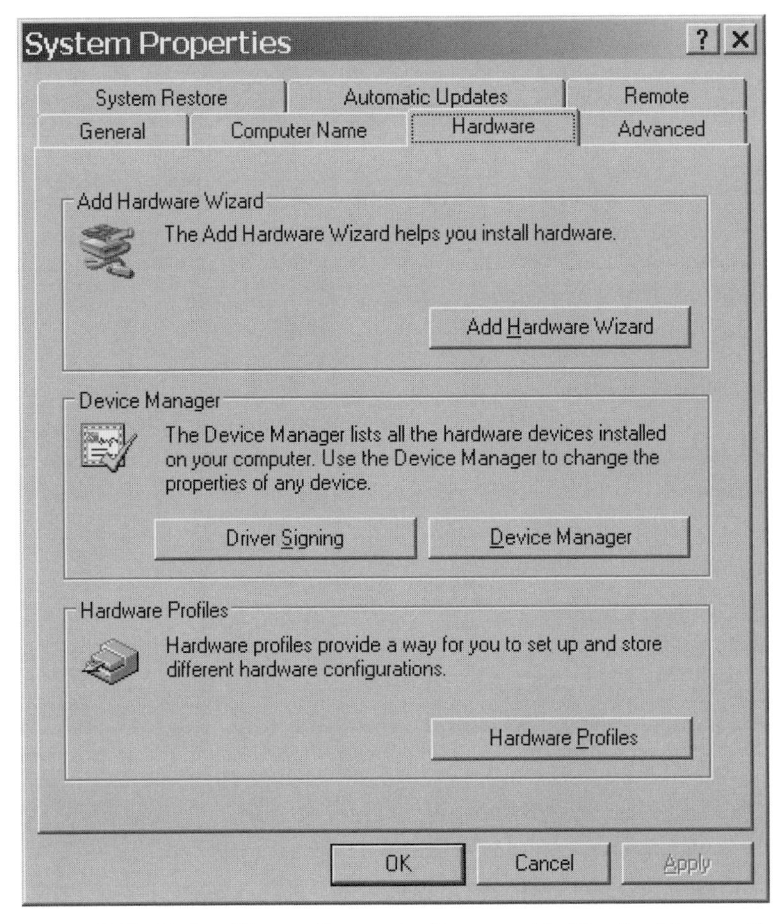

Figure 7.22. Under "System Properties," we can hit "Device Manager." This dialog box is using the "Windows Classic" look. Your dialog box might look slightly different.

Windows XP. "Signed" means "Approved." "Unsigned" means the monitor isn't designed for Windows XP. It might work, but there are no promises.

The Viewsonic A70f+ is signed for Windows XP. Going back to the viewsonic.com website, it says for all Windows XP signed monitors, we should download the file vs-winXP.exe as the driver. We download the 1.72 MB file and save it to our hard drive. Then, we double click on the vs-winXP.exe program (anything ending in .exe is an executable program) and it installs the proper monitor information.

In addition to drivers, there are also .inf files which provide information about a device. A monitor doesn't actually have drivers. Monitors are driven by the

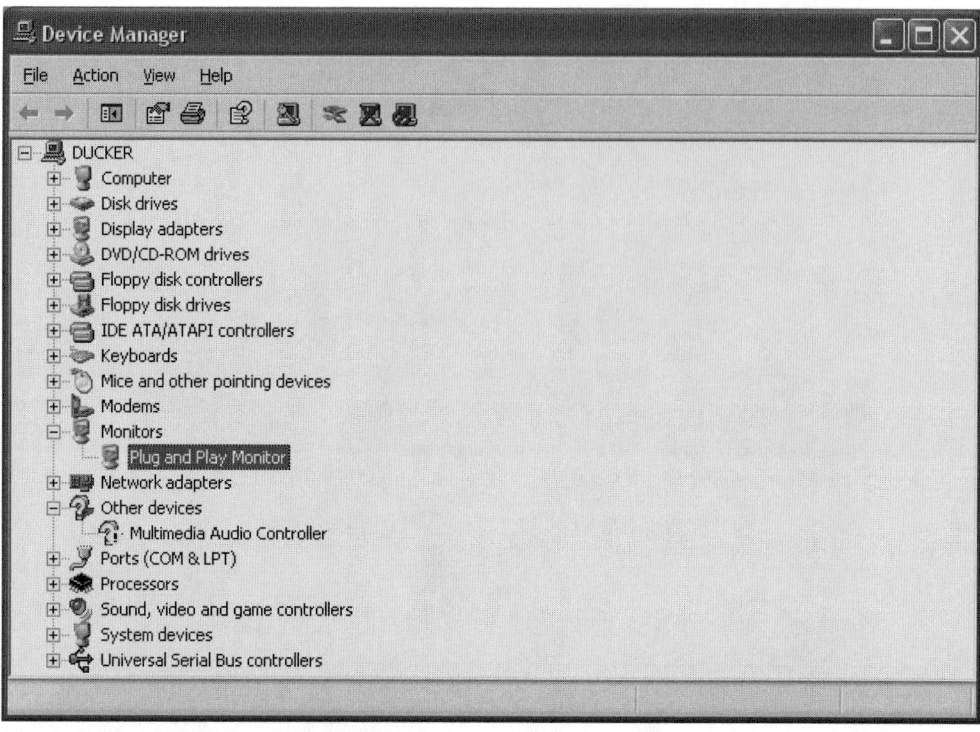

Figure 7.23. Only a plug-and-play monitor is recognized. We'll change that in a minute.

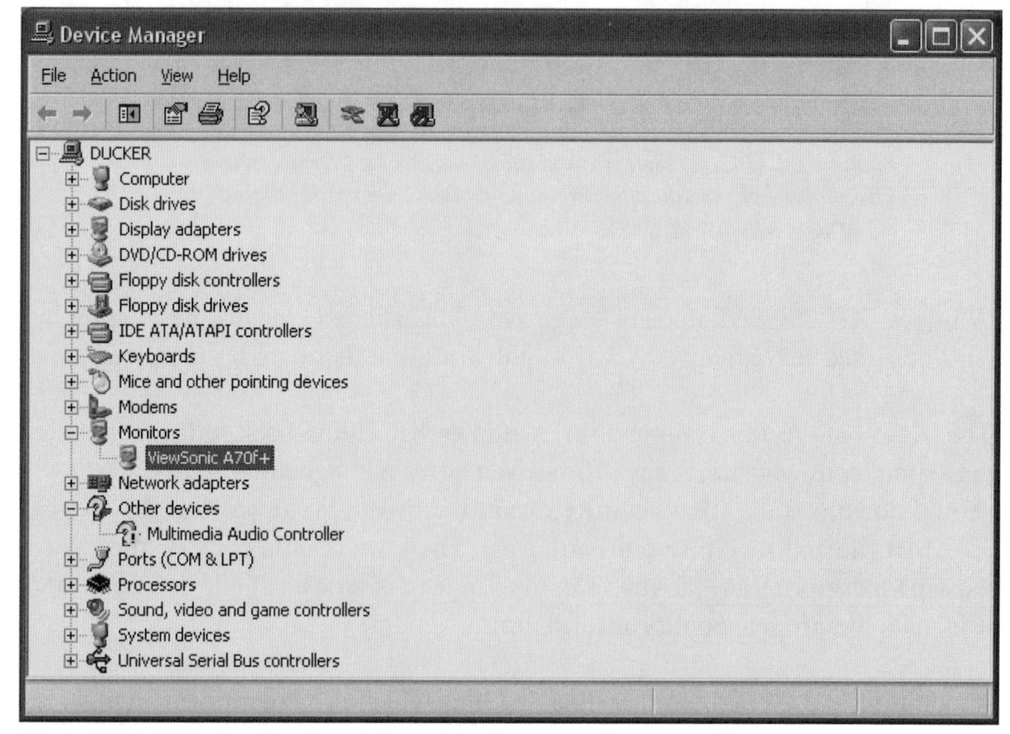

Figure 7.24. After downloading and running the proper driver installer from Viewsonic, the correct monitor is identified.

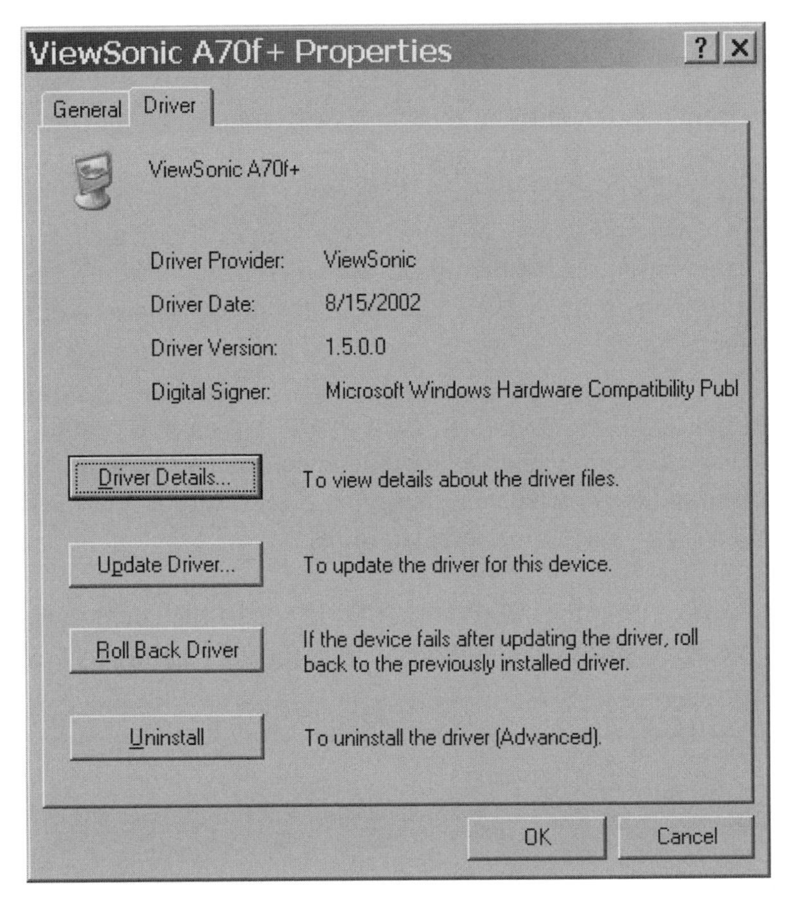

Figure 7.25. Right click on the Viewsonic monitor in the Device Manager window to bring up the monitor properties. Notice that the driver can be updated here. When in doubt, right click!

video card. So, the monitor "driver" is really just an information file telling the actual driver what settings the monitor supports.

We now examine Device Manager again and it lists the monitor as a ViewSonic A70f+ (Figure 7.24). This means the correct monitor is identified. If we right click on the monitor in Device Manager, we bring up its properties dialog box (Figure 7.25).

In general, if your device needs a device driver or an .inf file, see if a CD or disk came with the device. If it didn't or it doesn't work, see if you can find the manufacturer's website using google.com. Most manufacturers have free drivers online for their products.

It's good for the computer to know the exact model and make of your monitor before you install non-generic video drivers, because some video drivers might try to operate the monitor at a faster refresh frequency than the monitor can handle. If this happens, your screen will go very fuzzy or blurry. Prolonged time doing this can damage the monitor. A hissing sound from the monitor is especially bad. If this happens, restart the PC immediately in "Safe Mode" and temporarily disable the hyped-out video driver until the proper monitor information is provided. To start in "Safe Mode," press F8 during the boot up of Windows.

You can start the operating system in "Safe Mode" which will disable unnecessary drivers. Then, using Device Manager, you can remove the offending driver and make whatever changes are necessary to your system. Safe mode uses a very safe, generic video driver.

Installing the proper monitor information files is one of the small things that purchasing a fully assembled PC will have done for you. Trying to drive a monitor at too high a refresh rate is one of the very few things that you can mess up with software that has the potential to destroy hardware.

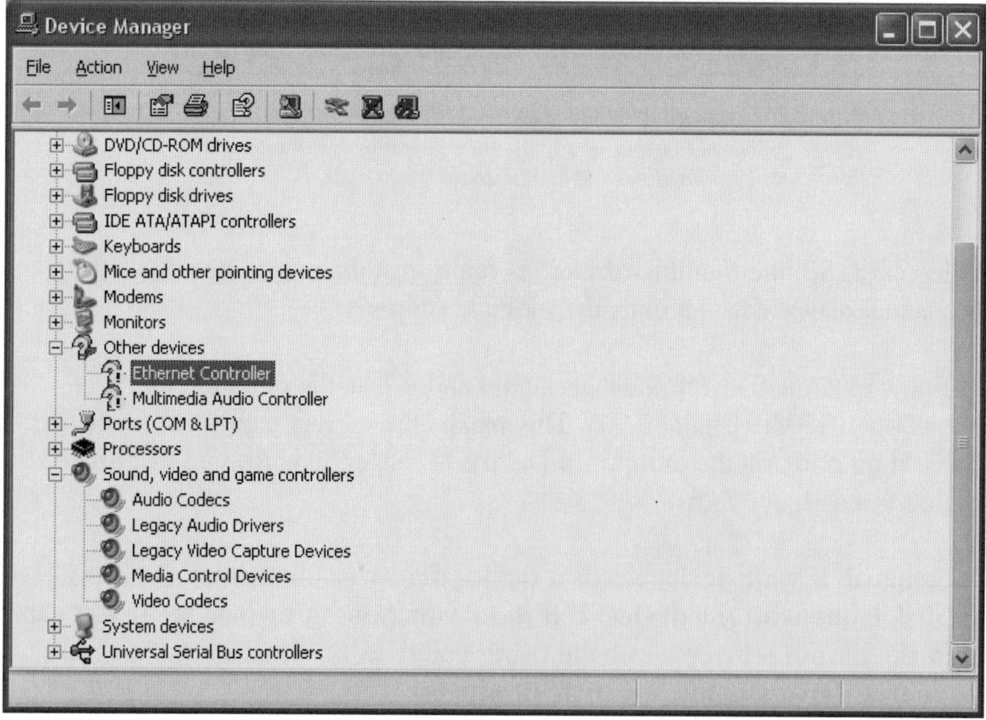

Figure 7.26. An ethernet controller isn't recognized yet. We need to install the proper driver.

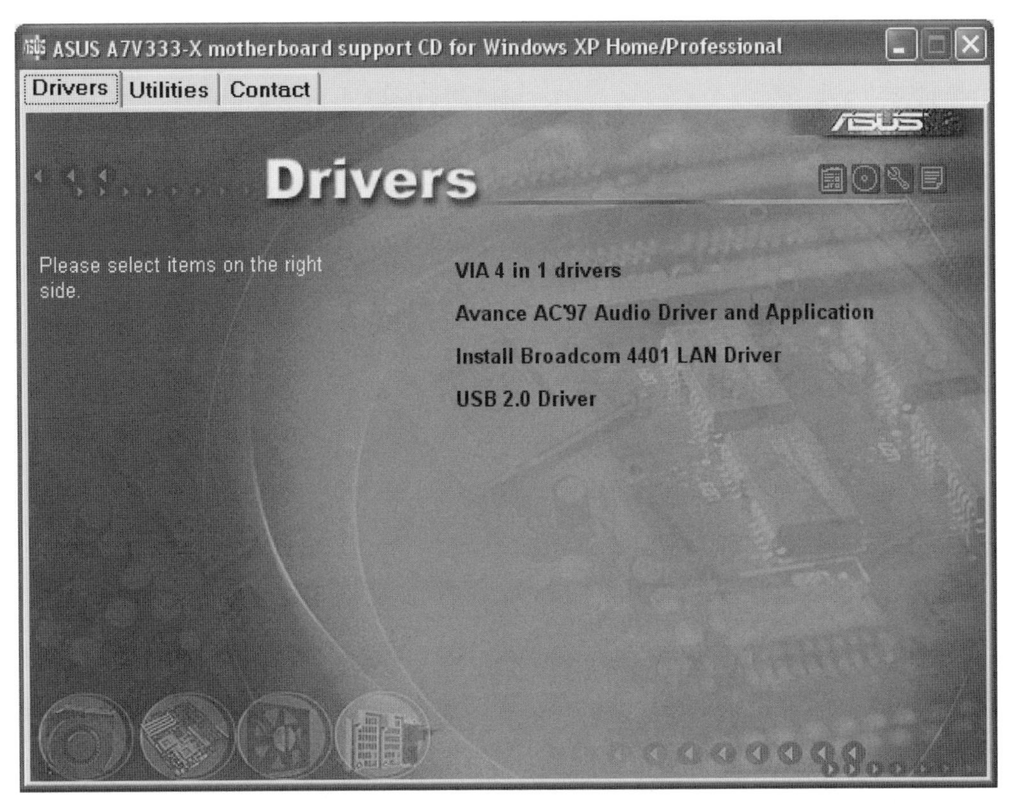

Figure 7.27. Installing network drivers from the CD that came with the mainboard. We install the LAN driver.

Proceed similarly to install drivers for your other devices, such as a sound card if you have one. Whenever a device doesn't seem to be working properly, ask if you've installed the proper device driver or if it's been done automatically. Looking for the device under Device Manager in Windows is a good way to see if the device driver is installed. We'll install a controller for the built-in networking (Figure 7.26). A question mark by Ethernet Controller in Device Manager shows that network drivers aren't yet installed.

If your mainboard has built-in sound or networking, a CD that contains drivers probably came with the mainboard. Place the CD into the CD drive and let Windows XP search for the appropriate driver.

If we place the CD that came with the mainboard into the drive and double click on the CD drive letter in Windows, the CD shows us that drivers can be installed for AC'97 sound, USB 2.0, and networking (Figure 7.27). After

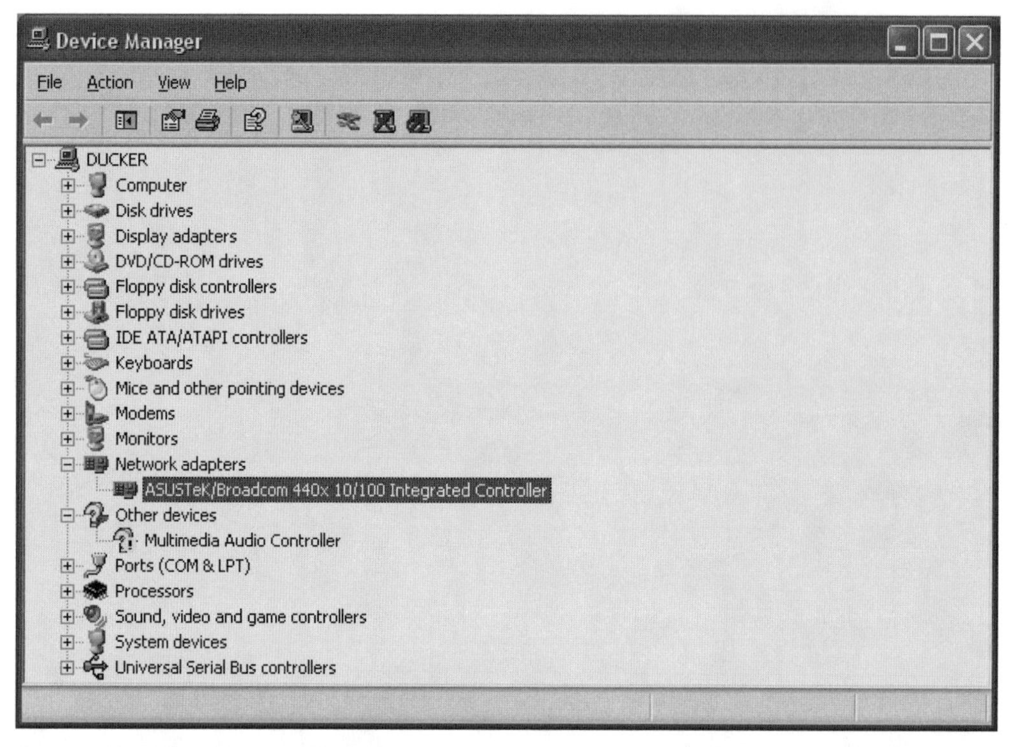

Figure 7.28. After selecting "Install Broadcom LAN driver," we inspect Device Manager to be sure the network driver is properly recognized.

installing the LAN (Local Area Networking) driver, Device Manager shows us the network driver is installed (Figure 7.28).

A missing driver is one of the first things to check for if added hardware won't work. For example, if we try to use the mainboard's built-in networking to connect to another PC in our home, it won't work. It's not that the built-in hardware for networking doesn't work. Examining Device Manager...Other Devices...Ethernet Controller (Figure 7.26), we see that no driver has been installed (Figure 7.29). The key expressions telling us something is missing are "Unknown" and "Not Available." Things should be known and available to our PC! Question marks next to devices in Device Manager aren't good either! When in doubt whether a driver is installed, right click on the device in Device Manager to see the driver information.

If we hadn't already run the CD that came with the mainboard to install all the drivers for onboard devices, we could proceed as follows to install the Ethernet driver. Hit "Update Driver" (Figure 7.29). We're taken to a

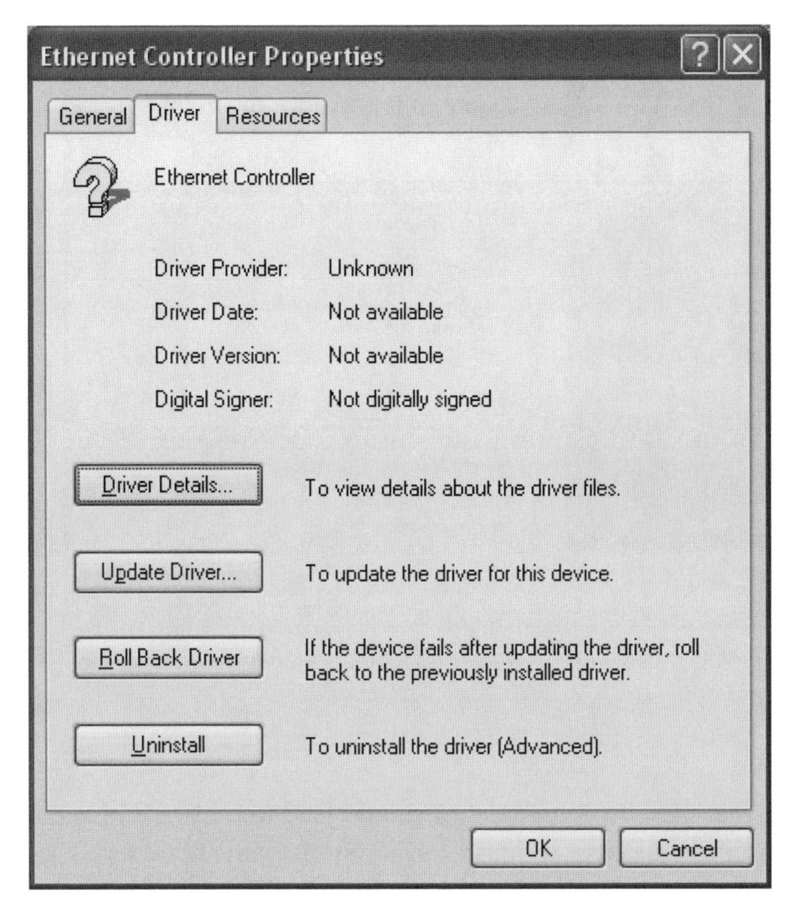

Figure 7.29. Right clicking on the Ethernet Controller in Device Manager is another way to change the network driver. If some piece of hardware isn't working, ask if the device needs a driver and see if the proper driver is installed.

"Hardware Update Wizard" screen (Figure 7.30), which allows us to install the driver software. We're told to insert the CD that came with the hardware. In this case, the network adapter is part of the mainboard, so we insert the CD that came with the mainboard.

If we insert the mainboard CD now, the system appears to hang. So, we hit Ctrl+Alt+Delete and receive a message that the Hardware Wizard program isn't responding. That confirms our hunch that the Wizard wasn't working. We close the non-responsive program.

Trying again, we select "Install from a list or specific location" (Figure 7.30). Then, we select the CD as the removable drive to search for a new driver. You

Figure 7.30. Selecting "Update Driver" brings up the hardware update wizard.

might think that these two approaches should lead to the same result, either failure to install or success. It doesn't turn out that way, however! The Wizard now runs and properly finds the driver! Examining Device Manager, we see the proper network adapter is recognized (Figure 7.28). And, if we look under "Network Connections" (Figure 7.31), we see that the Local Area Network (LAN) is enabled. And, our new system can connect to other systems in our house (We have a network hub and cables installed already).

It's important to realize that sometimes a CD with drivers won't run as desired. For example, the Viewsonic CD didn't work for us. Sometimes, double clicking on the CD drive letter will start the CD and it will run then. Sometimes, it still won't run, but, possibly, the drivers are on the CD and fully usable. Using Device Manager to find the device and then selecting its properties and using the "Update Driver" to start the Windows Hardware Update Wizard will find and successfully install the drivers from the CD.

If you have difficulty installing a driver, try the various approaches: First, just try to run the CD that came with the hardware. Insert the CD and wait. If it

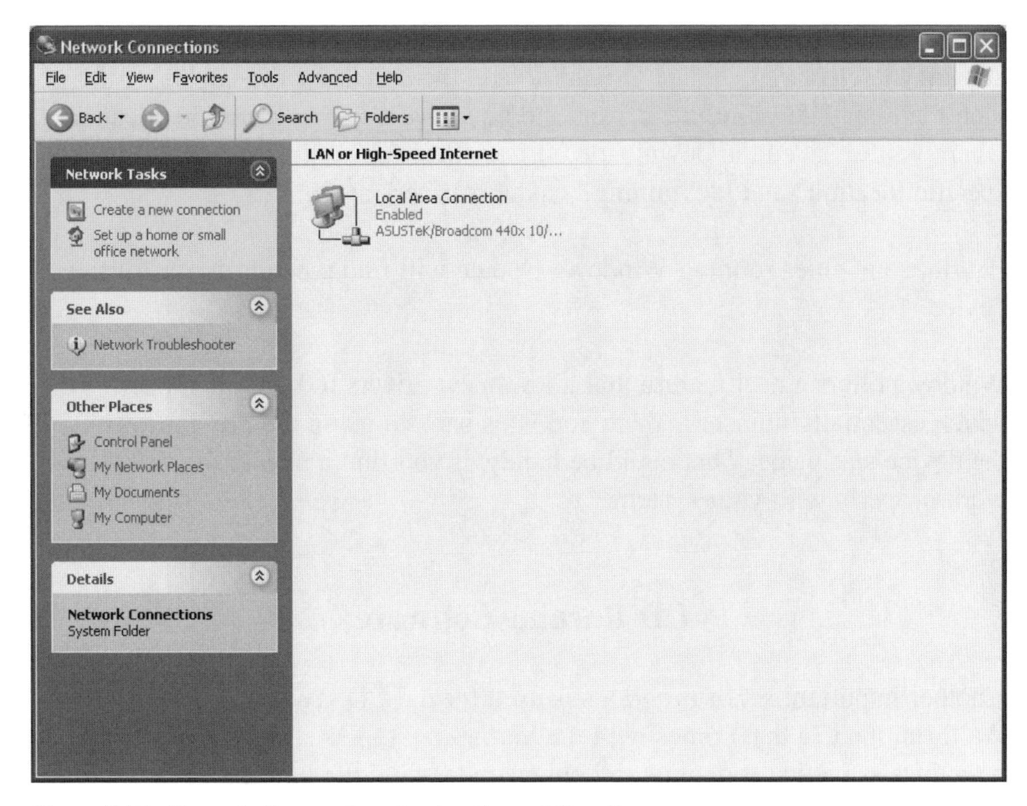

Figure 7.31. Network Connections (under Control Panel).

doesn't autorun, double click on the CD drive letter and see what happens. Maybe, it will run and install the driver.

Second, examine the manufacturer's website for a new driver and run that program instead. **Be sure to save all your downloaded driver files or updates to a CD.** Also, I think it helps to create a text file on your backup CD that describes the file and its purpose. For example, we downloaded the file vs-winXP.exe. We might add some text such as:

"vs-winXP.exe. Downloaded from viewsonic.com. This file installs the monitor information for the Viewsonic A70f+ monitor in Windows XP. Just double click on the file vs-winXP.exe and it will install the monitor information. After doing that under Device Manager... Monitor, we'll see the A70f+ is recognized."

You'll appreciate these notes to yourself if you need to repeat the same procedure several years later.

Third, find the device in Device Manager and use the Hardware Update Wizard by selecting "Update Driver" to add the driver for the device. If it won't automatically find the driver, and you have a CD or know the location where you've saved the downloaded driver files, select "Install from a list or specific location" and try running "Update Driver" again.

Fourth, sometimes running Windows Update will find a better driver for the device.

Windows offers a neat feature that allows new drivers to be "rolled back" which essentially uninstalls them and goes back to using the previous driver the device was using. That could be handy, if you find a new driver doesn't work properly with your system.

CD Burning Software

Another important set of programs is used for the CD-RW and DVD drives. We'll run the CD that comes with the Verbatim CD-RW. It installs software to burn CDs as well as a manual to help us understand the burning software.

Your CD-RW will come with its own software to burn CDs. If you purchase a CD-RW on eBay and don't get any disks, search for your CD-RW model online with google.com and see what burning software typically comes with it. Then, find the manufacturer's site and download this burning software and the drivers. You might also want to see if there are updated drivers online, even if your drive came with drivers.

After installing the InCD and Nero 5.5 software for the Verbatim CD-RW, we find that InCD works nicely, but Nero 5.5 won't burn CDs. When run, Nero 5.5 doesn't seem to recognize the Verbatim CD-RW. (Yes, I know, Nero *came* with the CD-RW. So, you might think it should work!) Reading the help that was installed with Nero, we learn that if a CD or DVD drive isn't recognized, it might be a newer drive. It's suggested we go to nero.com and update our Nero software which should recognize the newer drives.

We go to nero.com and get the update for Nero 5.5 and install it. Now the Verbatim CD-RW and Nero play nicely together. InCD and Nero are actually a wonderful software package for such a low-priced drive.

Sometimes when software isn't working properly with a new system, software updates can be found at the manufacturer's website that will correct the problem.

Backing Up Windows XP

If you've install all Windows System Tools (under Programs....Accessories) onto your PC and you're familiar with Windows 98, you might be surprised to see Windows BackUp, which is a program to back up your computer, missing.

Basically, BackUp can backup your entire C: or D: drive into a smaller compressed file. That file can then be restored if necessary using the program BackUp.

A small 2 GB logical drive will occupy less than 2 GB if you choose the compression option. Our new C: drive with Windows XP installed took 1.07 GB when backed up.

With DVD recordable drives holding 4.7 GB, you can back up your entire newly-installed Windows XP system onto a DVD. Another option is to install a second, low-cost hard drive and back up to that drive. That way if your main hard drive fails, you can restore from the secondary hard drive. And, a 40 GB hard drive might only cost $40. The probability of both hard drives failing at the same time is very small.

With Windows XP Home Edition, Microsoft wanted to stop providing a backup utility. Many people complained and mumbled "Linux." Microsoft compromised and decided to hide the backup utility on the Windows CD. You need to open the CD and look in the "ValueAdd" folder (seems it should be called the "ValueRemove" folder) to find a file called "NTBACKUP." Double click on that and it will install BackUp onto your PC.

Microsoft Professional XP comes with a more complete version of Backup. However, considering the price differential between the Professional and the Home Edition, I think most home users will do well with XP Home Edition. (A dual processor board is one of the few reasons I'd recommend XP Professional).

If you're not familiar with BackUp or backing up your system in general, I highly recommend that you begin backing up your important data regularly. You don't want to lose your crucial files.

If you're new to BackUp, try this as a simple test: Create a small test folder and place some stuff in it. Run BackUp and choose to only back up that selected folder. Save the backup file somewhere (for the test, it can be on the same hard drive). Then, delete the original file and run backup again to restore the deleted folder. You'll see your folder is safely restored. That will be a confidence builder if your system ever fails and it occurs to you that you've never actually seen BackUp restore successfully!

You can also run BackUp over a home network, backing up the C: drives of all your other PCs. For example, maybe you have another PC running Windows 98. This is helpful because your original Windows 98 CD contained a very un-updated version, whereas a complete current backup will provide all the updates to your Windows operating system. And, if your old system only has a CD-RW, but your new system has a DVD, you'll be able to back up your entire operating system.

If you only backup your personal files and the hard disk fries, you'll need to install Windows from the CD, then redo all the Windows updates, which assumes they remain available. You'll also need to reinstall all drivers and updates for your other program files.

Some programs such as Norton Ghost make duplicating the contents of a hard drive easier. These programs tend to deal with hidden files and system settings better.

Restore Points

Microsoft added a great feature with XP, by allowing users to create "Restore Points" giving you the option of reverting to a previous version of your operating system. Before you install new software, you might want to create a Restore Point. That way if the new software causes problems, you can revert to the operating system before the changes were made.

More Booty For You: Installing A Dual Boot Operating System (Linux And Windows XP)

This chapter assumes you want to install Windows XP and Red Hat Linux 9 on the same hard drive so that you can conveniently run either operating system. Installing two operating systems on one hard drive so that you can run either operating system is called dual booting. You can also do three boot systems, such as Windows XP, Windows 98, and Linux.

The first step is to install Windows XP. See the chapter for installing Windows XP. When you partition your hard drive using the XP setup program, you'll want to leave some unpartitioned space. This unpartitioned space can be used to install a Linux partition. Be sure to plan ahead how much disk space you want to allocate to Windows XP and how much for Linux.

Step 1. Install Windows XP. Be sure you leave some unpartitioned space for the Linux partition.

Step 2. Backup any valuable data from your Windows system. This isn't important if you've freshly installed Windows. But, if you've worked with Windows for awhile before deciding to dual boot, you should backup your important files. Before adding another operating system or partitioning a disk, always backup your important data.

Step 3. If your system won't boot from a CD, you might need to make a bootable Linux floppy disk to start the installation process. If you were able to boot from the Windows XP CD, this means your system will boot from a CD. You can change your system's BIOS settings to allow the system to boot from the CD instead of making a bootable floppy.

Step 4. Perform the Linux installation from its CD. It will recognize that Windows XP is already installed and offer you the option of keeping it and adding Linux also.

Let's begin.

You might find that after installing Windows onto your hard drive that if you put a bootable CD in the tray, the system will start up from the hard drive and not from the CD. This probably means that your system can boot from the CD, but the order that the computer uses to find a bootable operating system is: First, floppy drive; Second, hard drive; Third, CD drive. This information is set by the system's BIOS. Because BIOS finds a bootable operating system on the hard drive, it runs that operating system. So, it doesn't need to look at the CD at all.

We want to run Linux installer from its CD while a bootable XP system is already on the PC, so we'll enter our system's BIOS setup and change the boot order so that the system first looks for a bootable system from the CD and then from the hard drive (Figure 8.1). Or, you could just make a bootable Linux floppy and treat the install as if your system couldn't boot from a CD.

Your mainboard manual should tell you which key to press as the system starts up to enter BIOS. Remember, changes to BIOS are important and should only be made when you understand what you're doing and when the change is necessary.

Assuming your PC boots from the CD, insert CD 1 from the Red Hat Linux set into the CD drive and restart your system. A Red Hat install screen appears (Figure 8.2). Hit "Enter" to install in graphical mode.

A bunch of text will scroll by (Figure 8.3), and it might appear your system is hung. But, it's probably just working away behind the scenes. The first screen of the install process allows the single option of hitting "Next" (Figure 8.4).

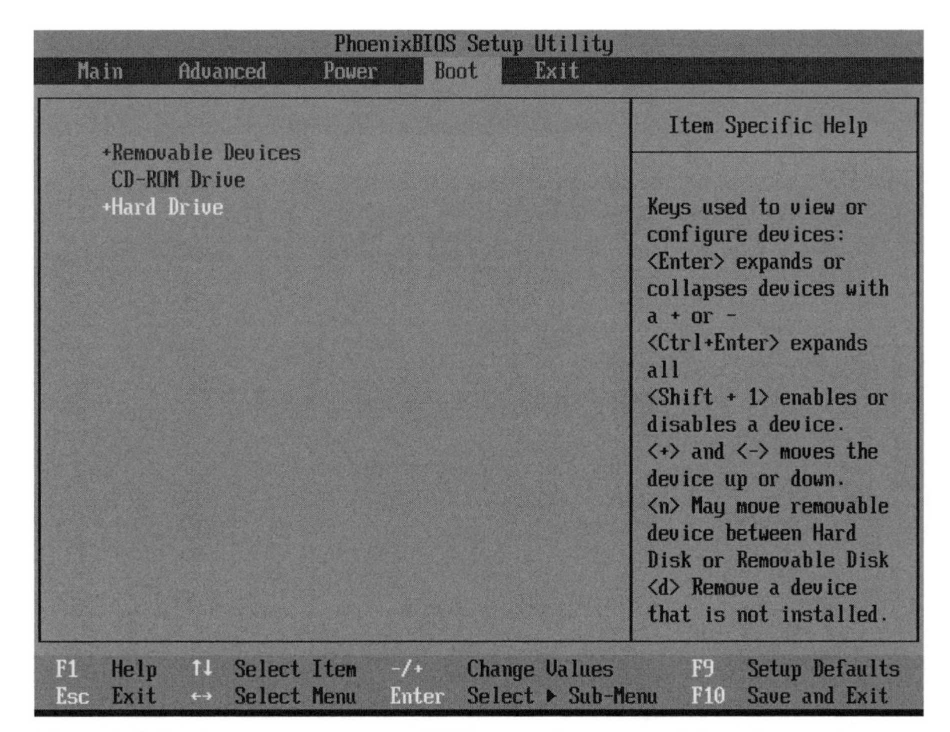

Figure 8.1. During startup, we enter BIOS setup. See your mainboard manual to determine which key brings up BIOS during startup. We moved the CD drive above the hard drive in the boot order. This means the system will first look for a bootable CD before trying to boot from the hard drive. This is important because we already have a bootable operating system on the hard drive, but we wish to boot from the CD drive. Exit and save the changes.

The next screen shows language options. Select “English” (Figure 8.5). Be sure to select “English” for the keyboard options also (Figure 8.6).

The next screen asks you to select your mouse (Figure 8.7).

Next up is the “Installation Type” screen, in which you’ll choose “Personal Desktop” (Figure 8.8). For learning Linux, a standard workstation setup is best. Later, if you want, you can set up Linux as a server or experiment with other setup options.

Now, you’ll be asked to partition your drive (Figure 8.9). You can have your system automatically partition your drive, or you can do it manually. We’ll do it automatically.

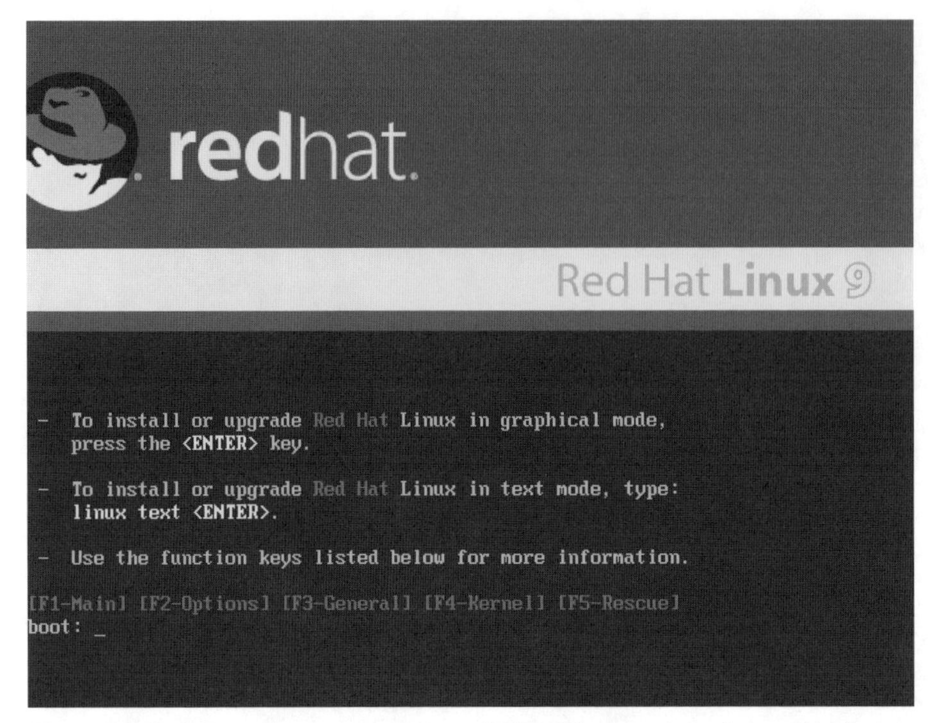

Figure 8.2. Red Hat welcome screen. Press "ENTER" to continue the graphical installation.

```
usb.c: registered new driver hid
hid-core.c: v1.8.1 Andreas Gal, Vojtech Pavlik <vojtech@suse.cz>
hid-core.c: USB HID support drivers
mice: PS/2 mouse device common for all mice
md: md driver 0.90.0 MAX_MD_DEVS=256, MD_SB_DISKS=27
md: Autodetecting RAID arrays.
md: autorun ...
md: ... autorun DONE.
NET4: Linux TCP/IP 1.0 for NET4.0
IP Protocols: ICMP, UDP, TCP
IP: routing cache hash table of 2048 buckets, 16Kbytes
TCP: Hash tables configured (established 16384 bind 32768)
NET4: Unix domain sockets 1.0/SMP for Linux NET4.0.
RAMDISK: Compressed image found at block 0
Freeing initrd memory: 2645k freed
EXT2-fs warning: checktime reached, running e2fsck is recommended
VFS: Mounted root (ext2 filesystem).
Greetings.
Red Hat install init version 9.0 starting
mounting /proc filesystem... done
mounting /dev/pts (unix98 pty) filesystem... done
checking for NFS root filesystem...no
trying to remount root filesystem read write... done
checking for writeable /tmp... yes
_
```

Figure 8.3. Whenever Linux boots or reboots, you'll see a screen of scrolling text. Sometimes, it might appear that the system has frozen. Just be patient, and it will continue. For example, it might take awhile to search for a network connection.

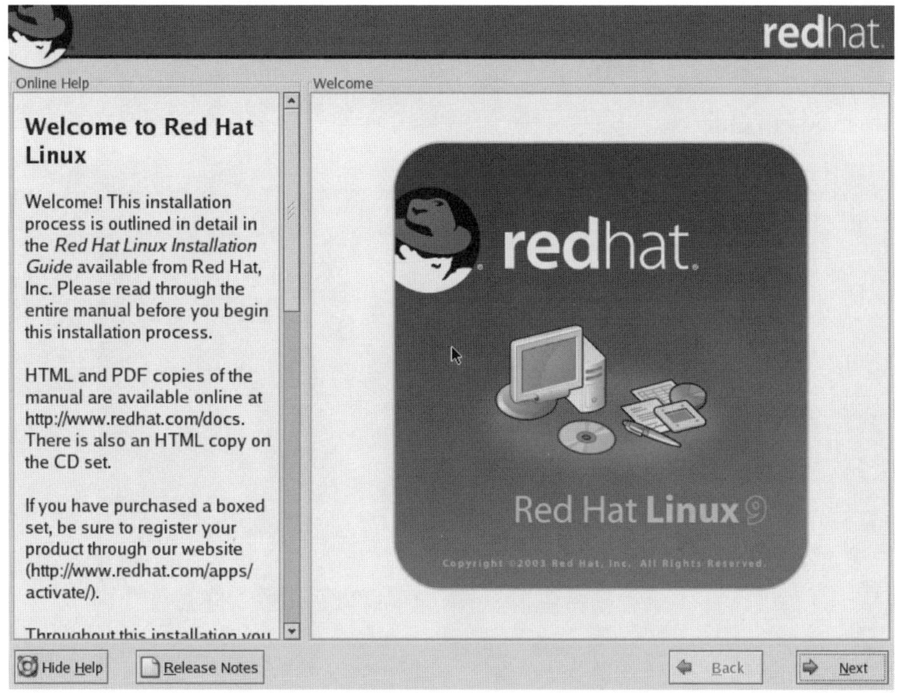

Figure 8.4. Another welcome screen. Hit 'Next."

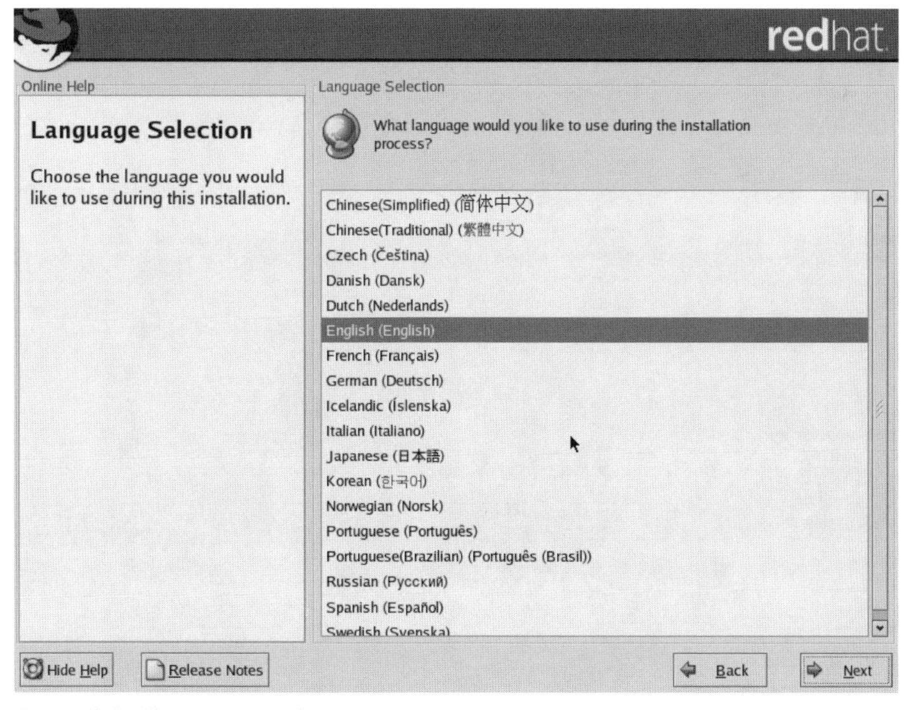

Figure 8.5. Choosing your language.

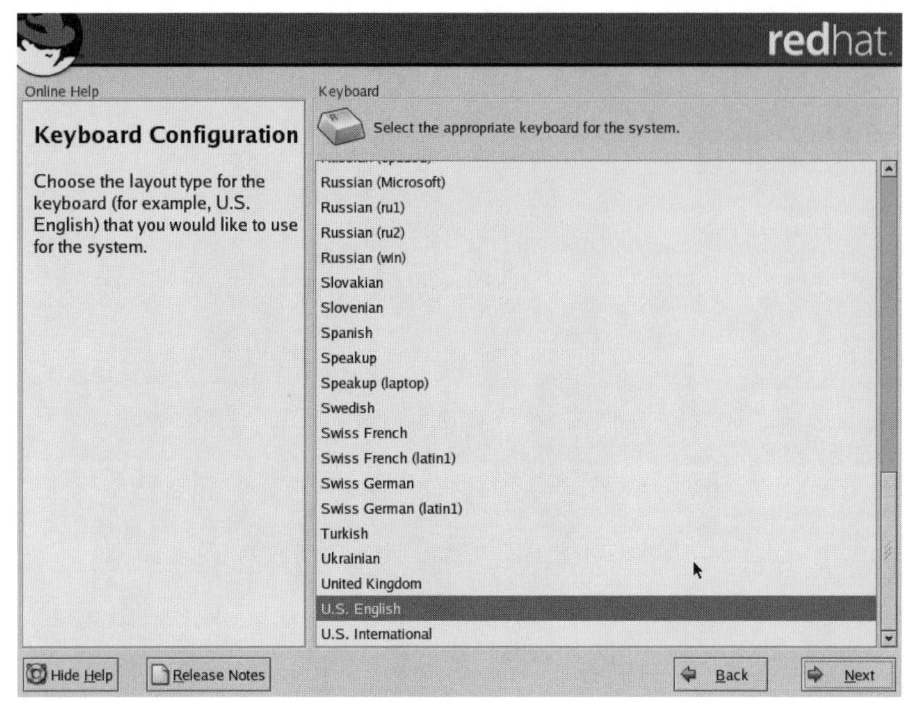

Figure 8.6. Choose U.S. keyboard and hit "Next."

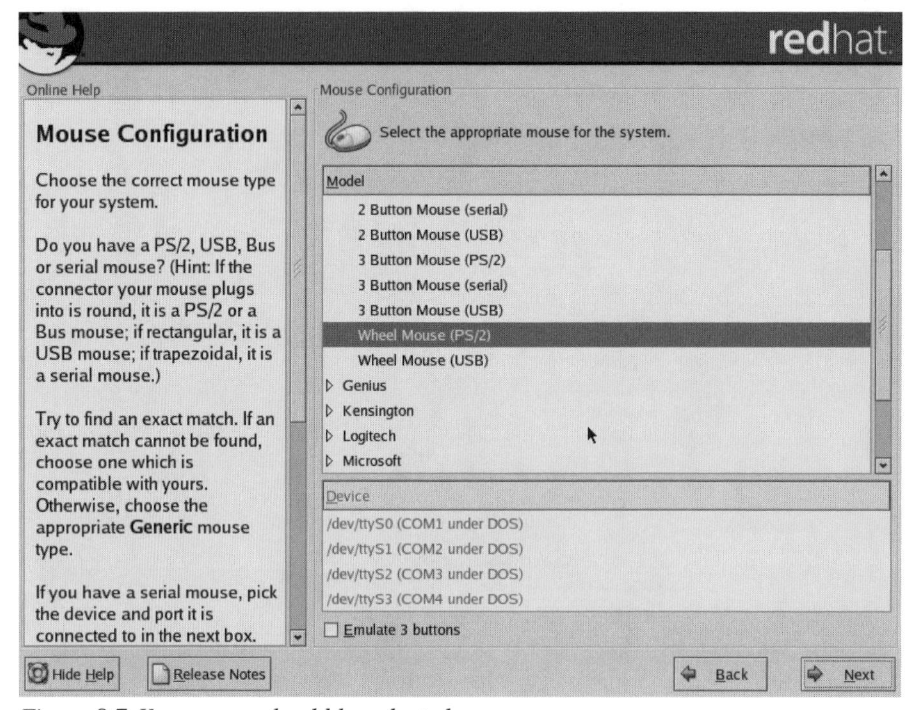

Figure 8.7. Your mouse should be selected.

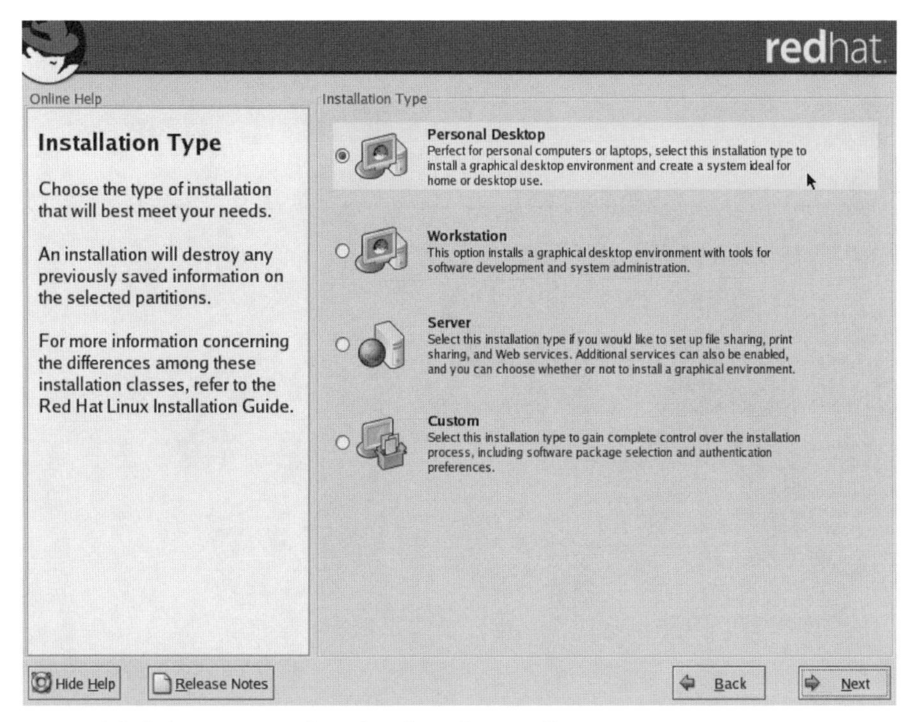

Figure 8.8. Select "Personal Desktop" as the installation type.

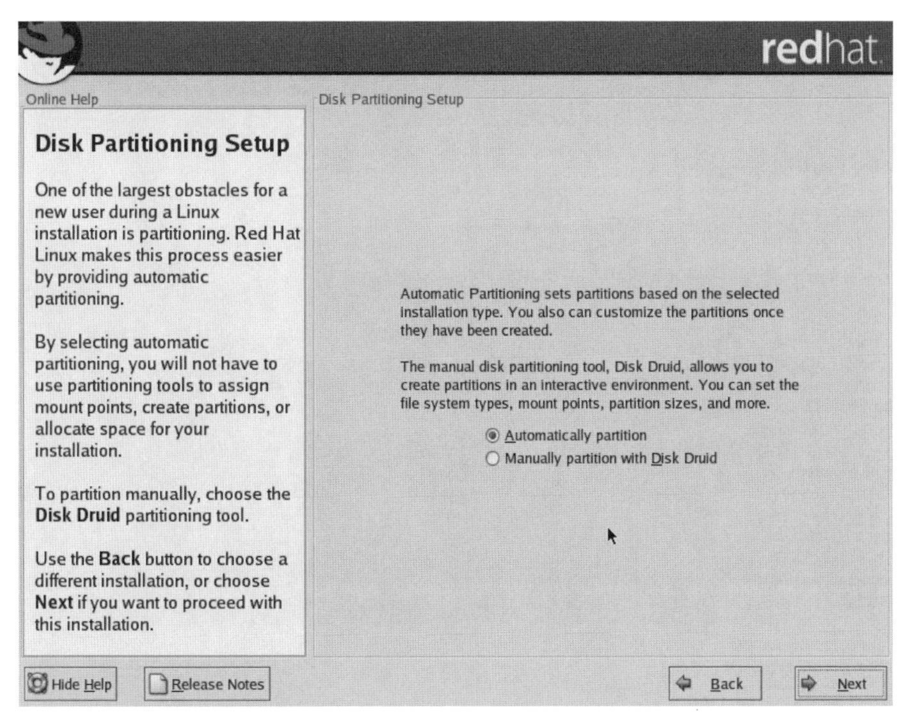

Figure 8.9. Select "Automatically Partition." Don't worry. This step won't wipe out your exisiting operating system.

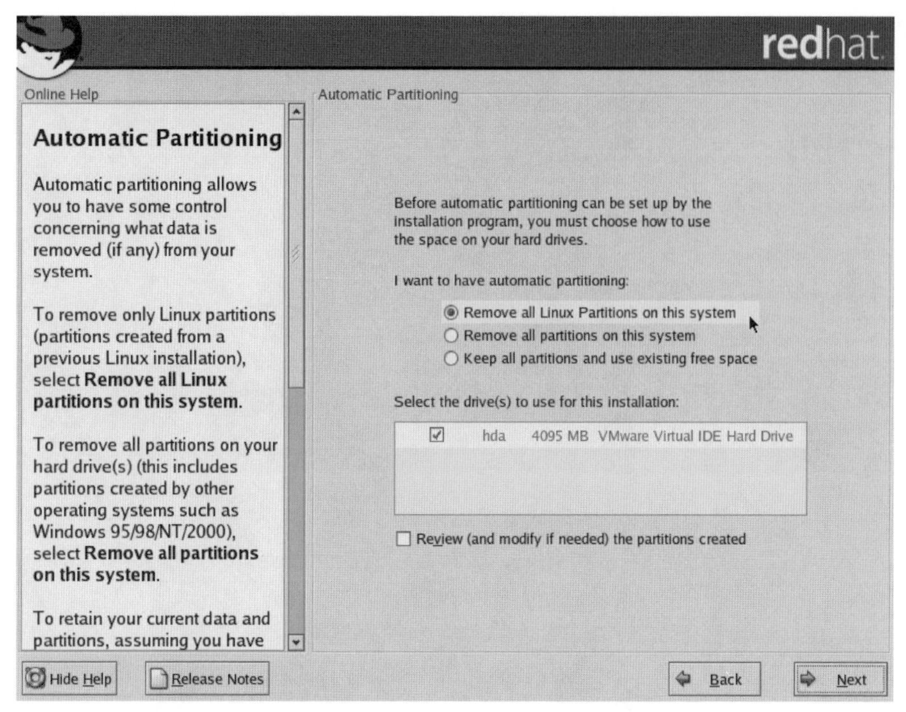

Figure 8.10. Choose to remove all Linux partitions. Don't remove non-Linux partitions, because we wish to keep Windows XP installed also.

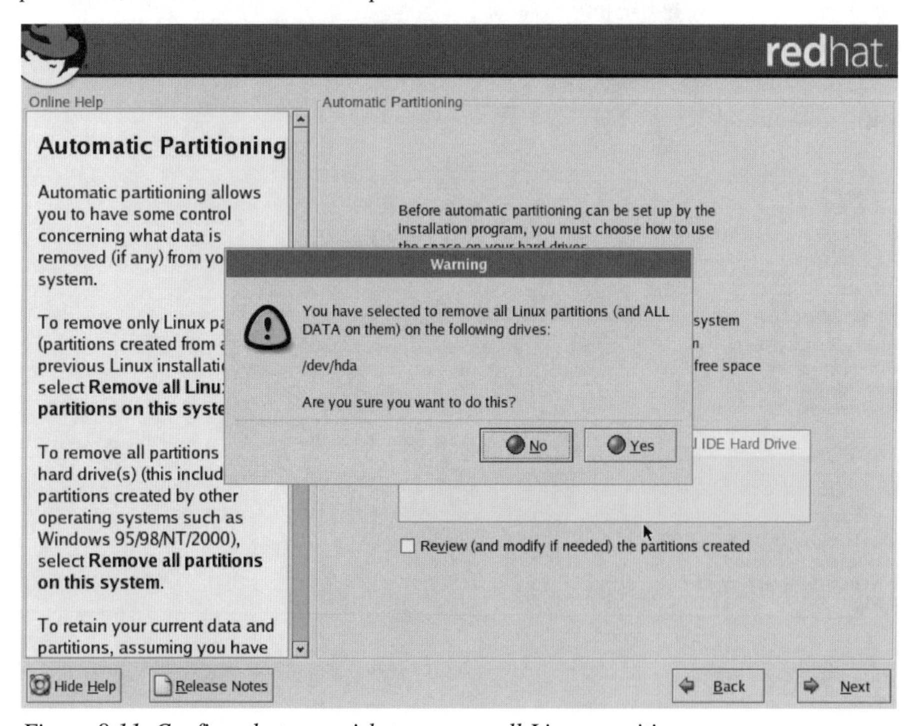

Figure 8.11. Confirm that you wish to remove all Linux partitions.

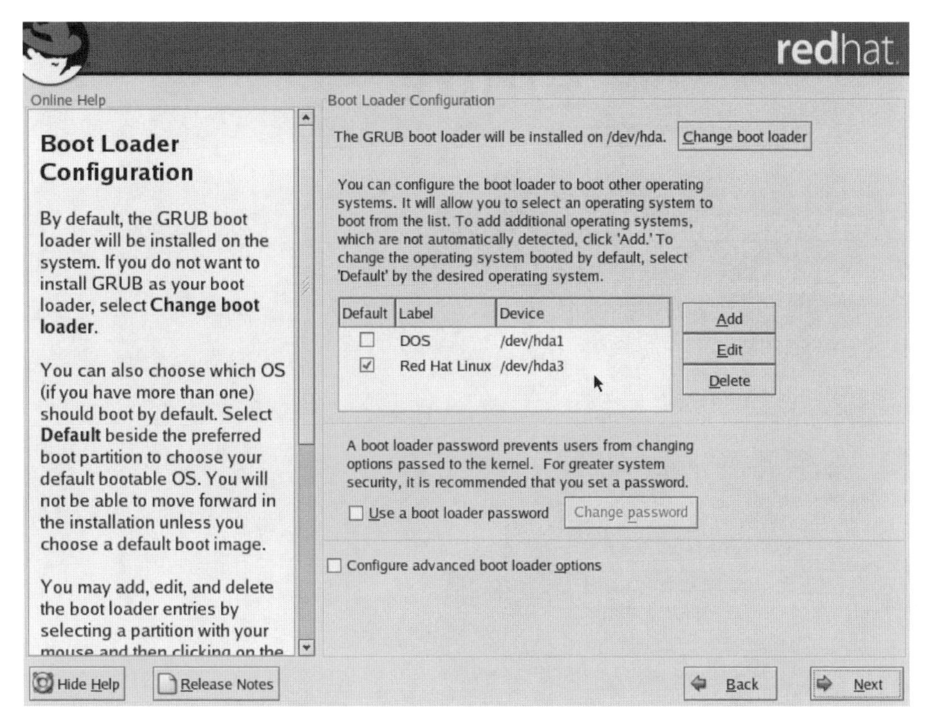

Figure 8.12. Under the default checkbox, Linux is selected. This means that when the system boots up, after a short while Linux will boot as the default operating system. If other users, who are familiar with Windows, but not Linux, will be using this PC, be sure to select DOS, which is Windows XP, as the default operating system to boot.

The next screen (Figure 8.10) shows the option of removing all Linux partitions. There are no Linux partitions on this hard drive yet. It won't find any to remove, but that's OK. Be sure not to remove all partitions. You want to keep the non-Linux partition on which Windows XP is installed. That is your NTFS formatted partition.

A popup box will ask you to confirm your decision. Click "Yes" to remove any Linux partitions (Figure 8.11).

If a warning message appears saying the boot partition /boot may not meet booting constraints, hit "OK."

The next dialog box will ask you to choose a default operating system to be loaded by the Linux boot loader (GRUB) (Figure 8.12). Select "DOS" as the default. This will mean that Windows XP will become the default operating system to boot, unless a conscious choice is made to boot to Linux instead.

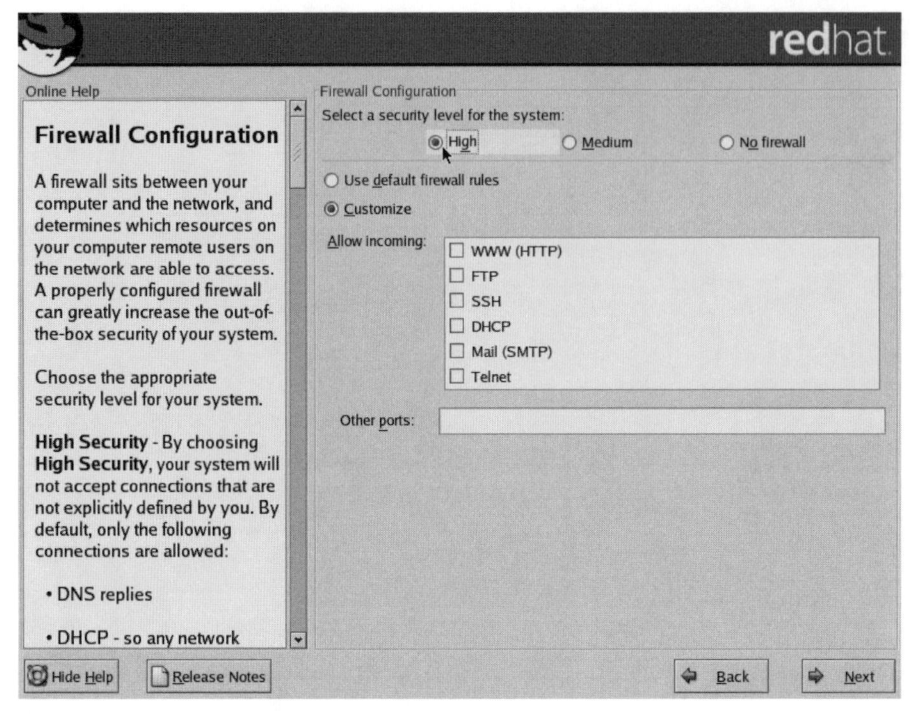

Figure 8.13. Choose "High" as firewall security.

Selecting Windows as the default usually makes sense if anybody not familiar with Linux must use your computer.

Next, is a firewall configuration dialog. Choose a high level of protection (Figure 8.13). Firewalls help prevent hackers from getting into your computer.

The next dialog box asks us to set up language options (Figure 8.14).

The dialog after that sets up your time zone information (Figure 8.15).

Next, you'll be asked to choose a password for "root" (Figure 8.16). In Linux, root is the supreme commander of the operating system. Logging in as "root" allows you to modify the operating system. As a general rule, you should only log in as the root user when it's necessary for administrating your computer. For general Linux use, log in as a normal user. That helps prevent you from inadvertently modifying your system.

redhat

Online Help

Additional Language Support

Select a language to use as the default language. The default language will be the language used on the system once installation is complete. If you choose to install other languages, it is possible to change the default language after the installation.

Red Hat Linux can install and support several languages. To use more than one language on your system, choose specific languages to be installed, or select all languages to have all available languages installed on the system.

Use the **Reset** button to cancel your selections.

Additional Language Support

Select the default language for the system: English (USA)

Select additional languages to install on the system:

English (Great Britain)
English (Hong Kong)
English (India)
English (Ireland)
English (New Zealand)
English (Philippines)
English (Singapore)
English (South Africa)
English (USA)
English (Zimbabwe)
Estonian
Faroese (Faroe Islands)
Finnish
French (Belgium)
French (Canada)
French (France)
French (Luxemburg)

Select All
Select Default Only
Reset

Hide Help
Release Notes
Back
Next

Figure 8.14. "English" should be selected as the default. Hit "Next."

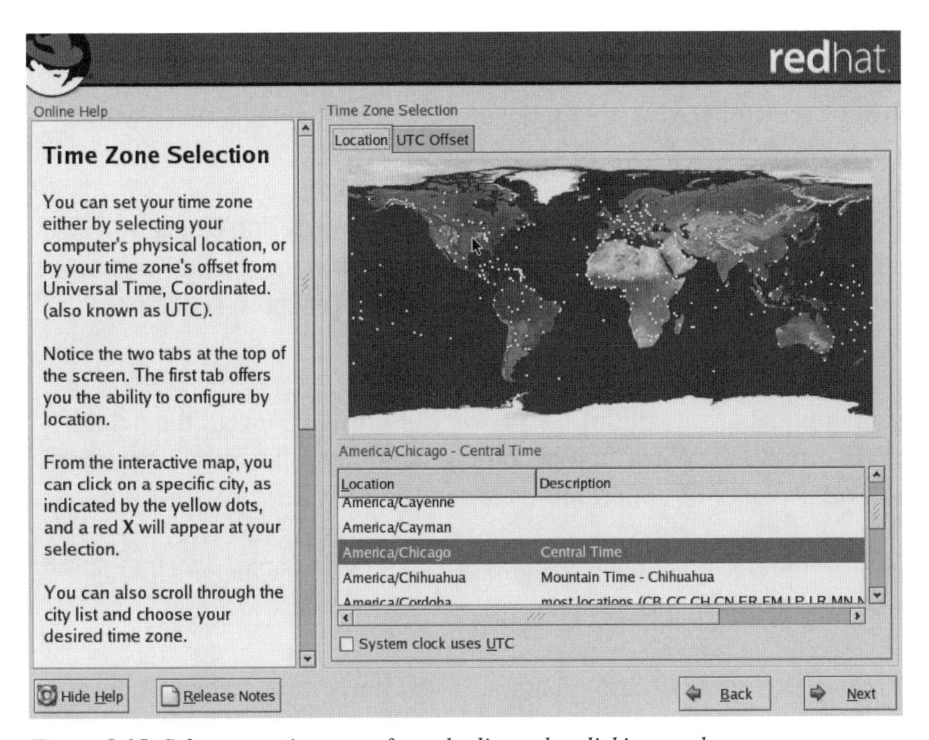

Figure 8.15. Select your time zone from the list or by clicking on the map.

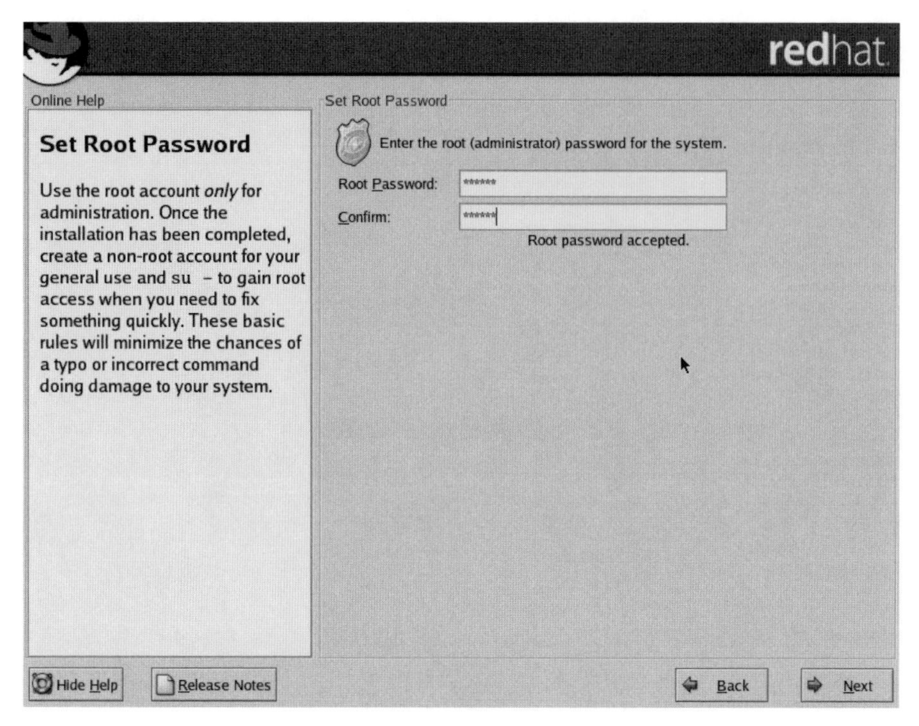

Figure 8.16. Select a password for "root." You'll login as "root" when you wish to modify your Linux operating system.

You'll have the opportunity to create regular user accounts later. Be sure to write down or remember your root password. You must enter it twice to confirm it.

As soon as you start typing, a message that the passwords don't match appears. Don't let this throw you. You haven't had a chance to enter anything into the second password box yet! Eventually, you'll get those suckers to match! Linux is case sensitive.

The next dialog gives you options for packages to install. Accept the default packages (Figure 8.17). When first becoming familiar with Linux, a standard install will offer plenty of opportunities to familiarize yourself with Linux.

Now, the install process can begin (Figure 8.18 and 8.19). Change CDs as requested. Files will be copied to your drive.

You can select "No" to boot disk creation, if you don't have an extra floppy disk handy (Figure 8.20).

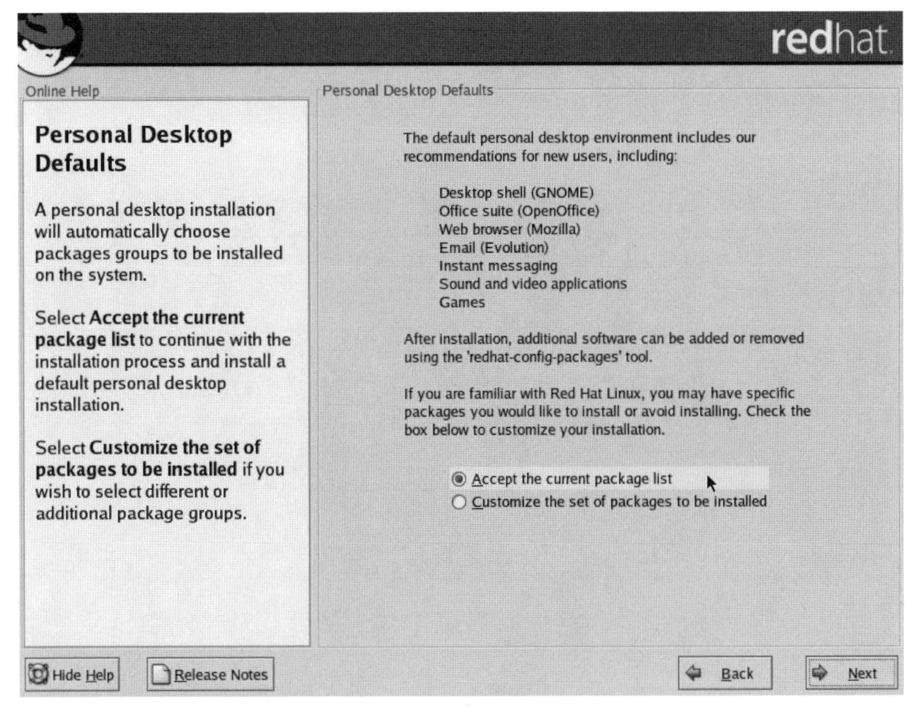

Figure 8.17. Accept the default packages. Hit "Next."

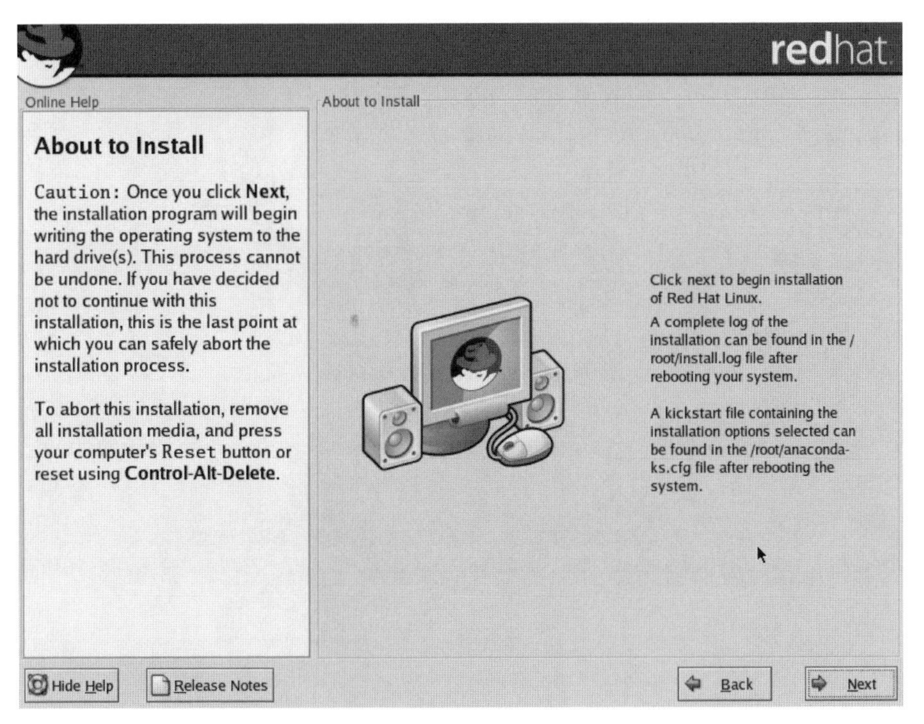

Figure 8.18. Hit "Next" when that's the only option!

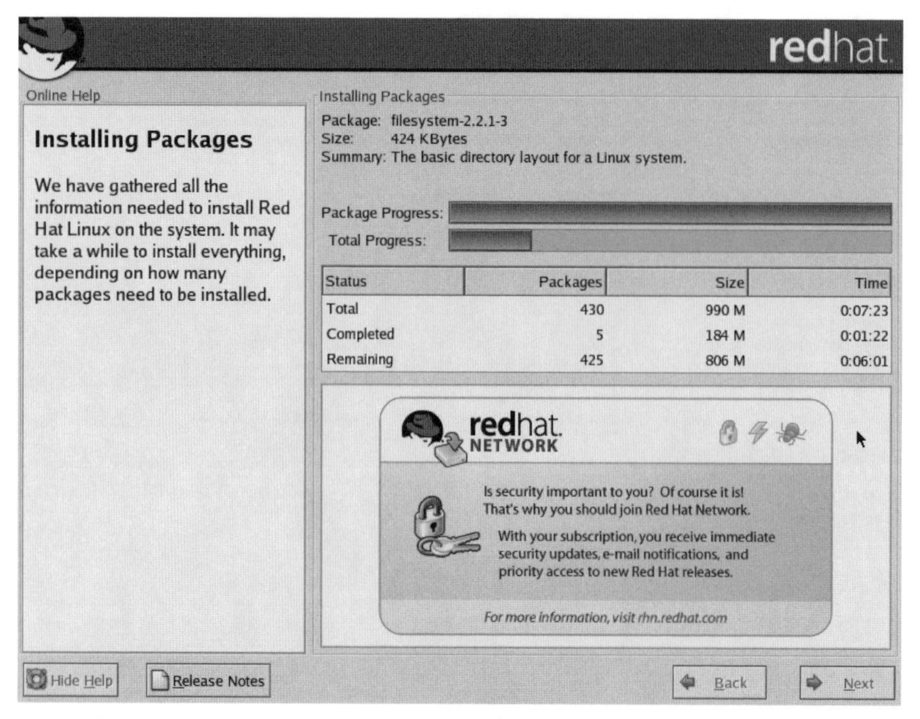

Figure 8.19. Progress bars will show the installation progress. You might want to go do something else for awhile and return later. Change CDs as requested.

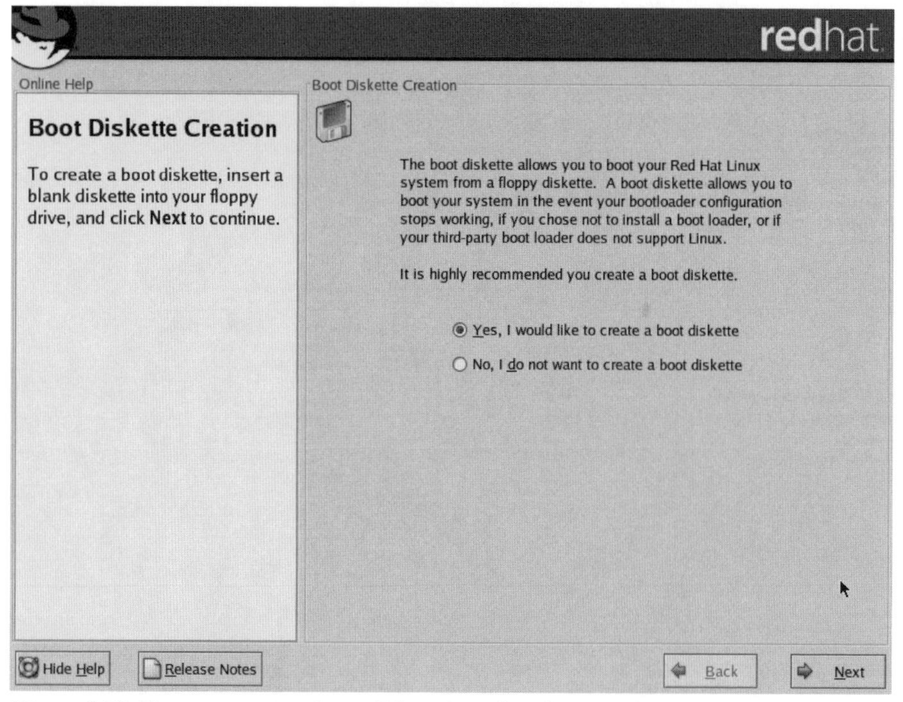

Figure 8.20. You can create a boot disk or just skip this step for now. If the installation fails, you'll probably start again from the CD, so you don't really need a boot disk now.

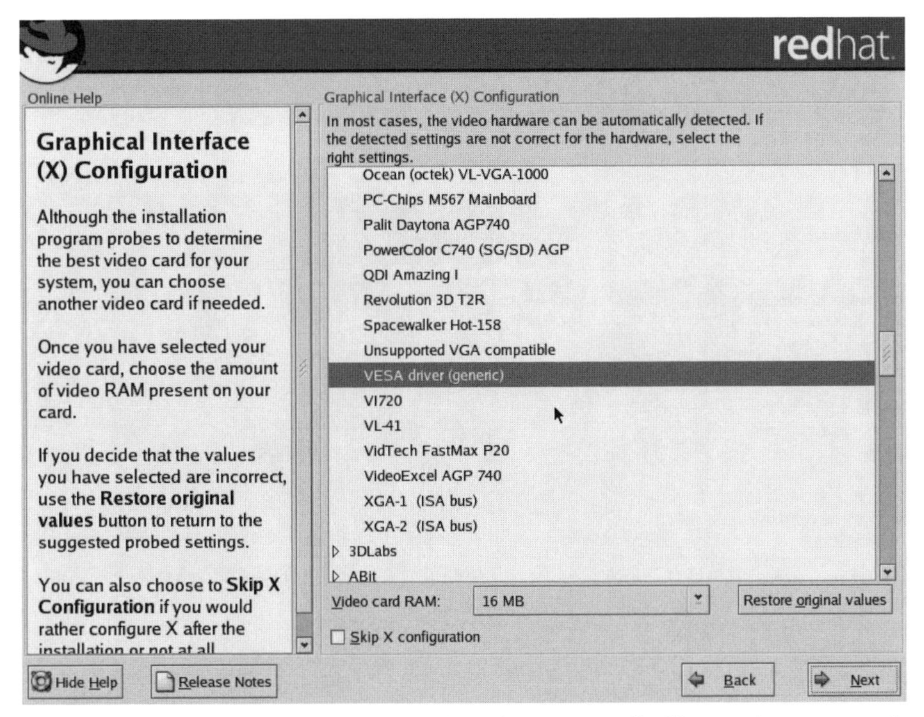

Figure 8.21. Your video card might be selected automatically. If not, select your card from the list.

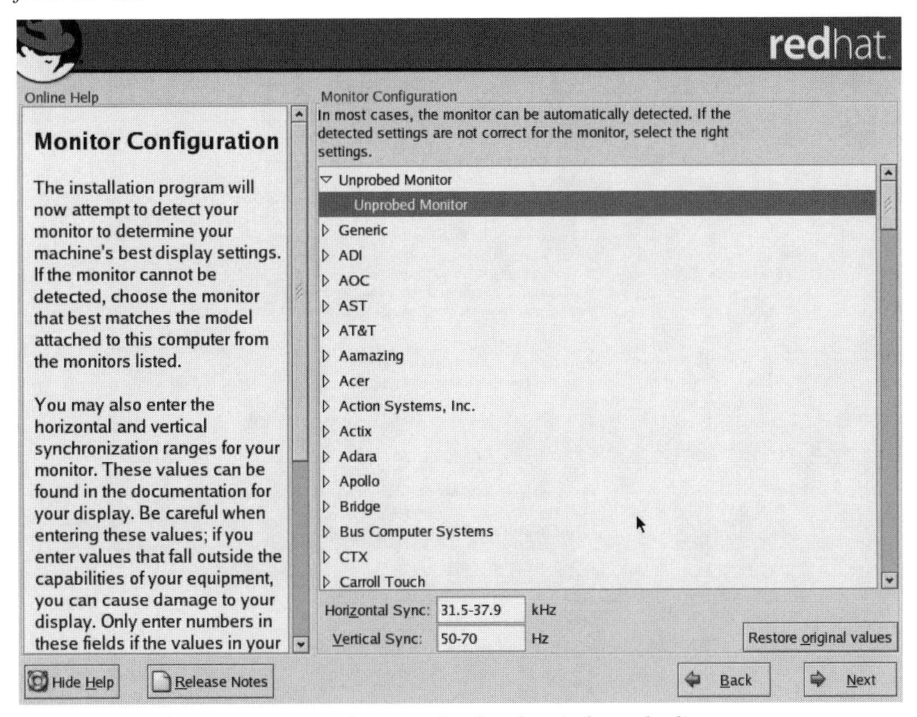

Figure 8.22. If your monitor isn't recognized, select it from the list.

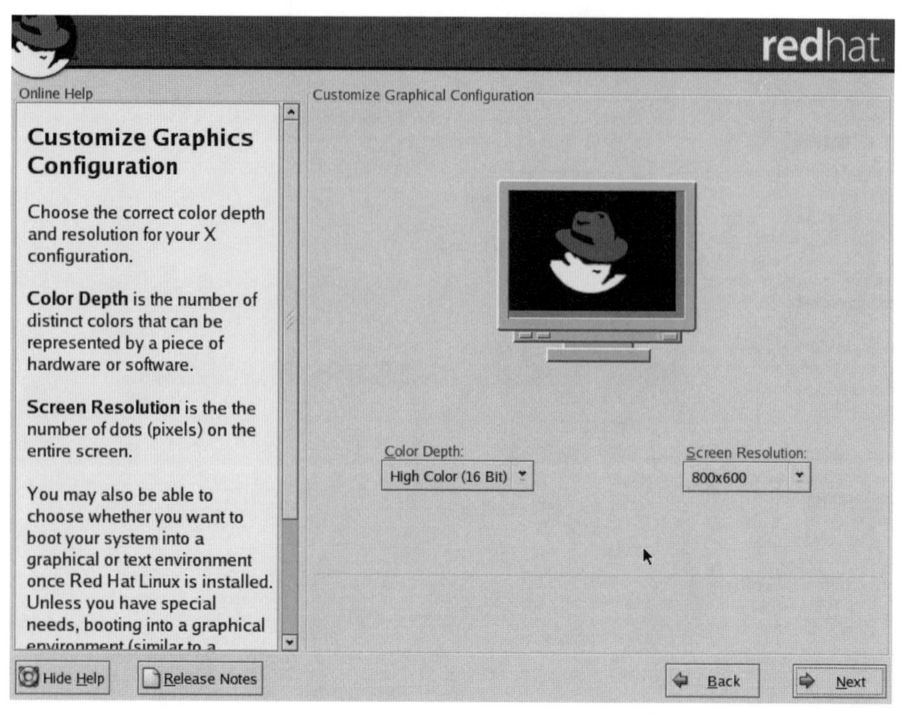

Figure 8.23. Setting the color depth and screen resolution. For most monitors today, 1024x768 pixels is a good resolution. You might want to decrease the color depth from high color.

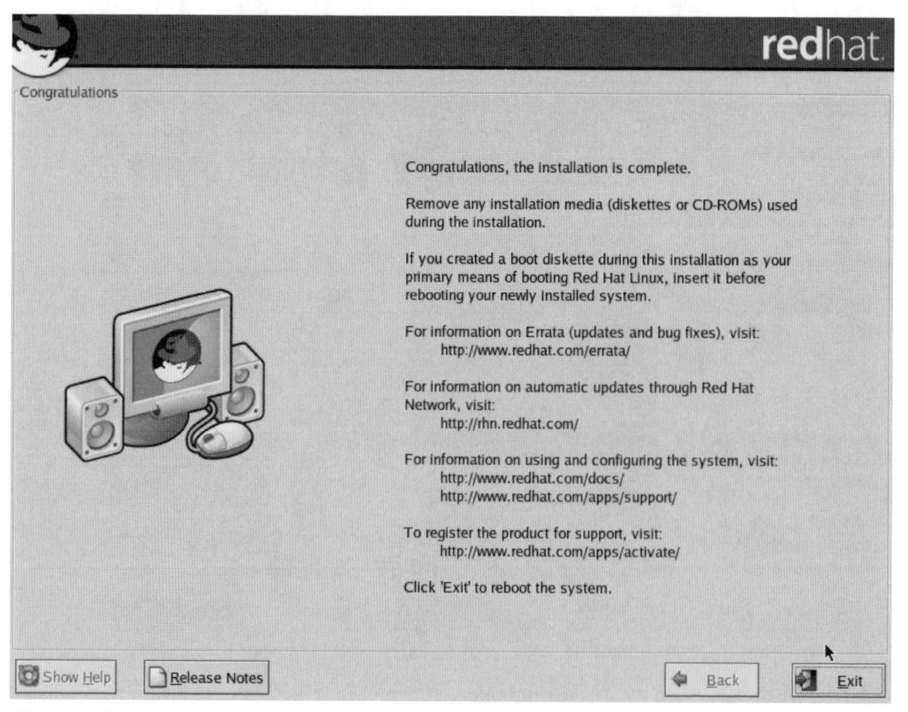

Figure 8.24. Click "Next."

A dialog asks you to select your video card (Figure 8.21). It will probably already be recognized. You'll also be asked to select your monitor (Figure 8.22), or it will be detected.

The next dialog box (Figure 8.23) will ask you to choose a screen resolution and a color depth. Color depth refers to how many colors you want your monitor to display. Resolution is how many pixels by how many pixels your monitor displays.

Now, we must restart the PC (Figure 8.24), and a dual boot screen will appear (Figure 8.25). Use the arrow keys to select "Linux" as the operating system you want to run and hit "Enter," so that Linux will have a chance to complete its installation.

After restarting Linux, the installation process continues (Figure 8.26). You'll have the chance to create a user account. Choose a name and a password for the user account (Figure 8.27).

The next dialog screen will ask you to set the date and time (Figure 8.28). A dialog will set up your sound card (detected automatically here for the onboard sound, Figure 8.29). The system is now set up and ready to use. We choose not to register (Figure 8.30), and we'll skip additional CDs (Figure 8.31).

Whenever your computer starts, you'll see the GRUB Linux bootloader, which will give you the option of choosing to boot to Windows XP or to Linux (Figure 8.25). If you wait and can't make up your mind after a reasonable time, the PC will boot to Windows, assuming you selected Windows as the default.

In summary, it's important to note that the installation of a dual boot operating system went smoothly because we installed each operating system to its own partition. And, we never deleted or removed an existing partition when we added the new operating system. We ran the Linux Installer, and it left Windows XP intact, because we chose not to remove non-Linux partitions. Then, the Grub bootloader recognizes that we have two bootable operating systems on our hard drive, and it gives us the option to boot from either.

For this dual boot installation, we installed Windows XP first. Then, the Linux bootloader recognized the existing operating system and it allowed us to

Figure 8.25. At startup, the bootloader offers you the choice between Windows XP (listed as DOS) and Red Hat Linux. The default is highlighted.

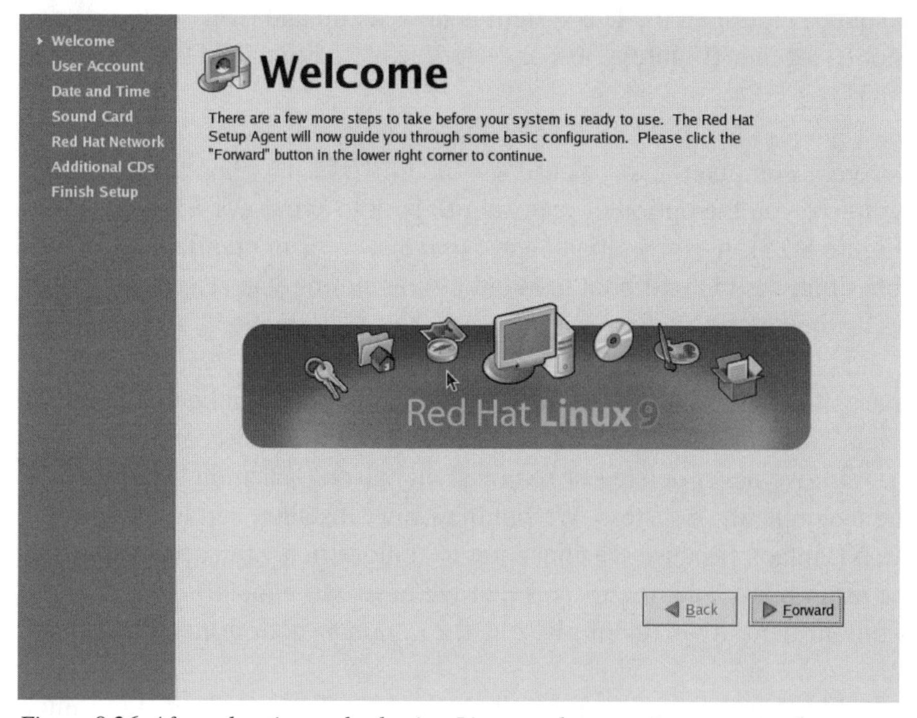

Figure 8.26. After rebooting and selecting Linux as the operating system to boot, Linux will show us some more setup screens.

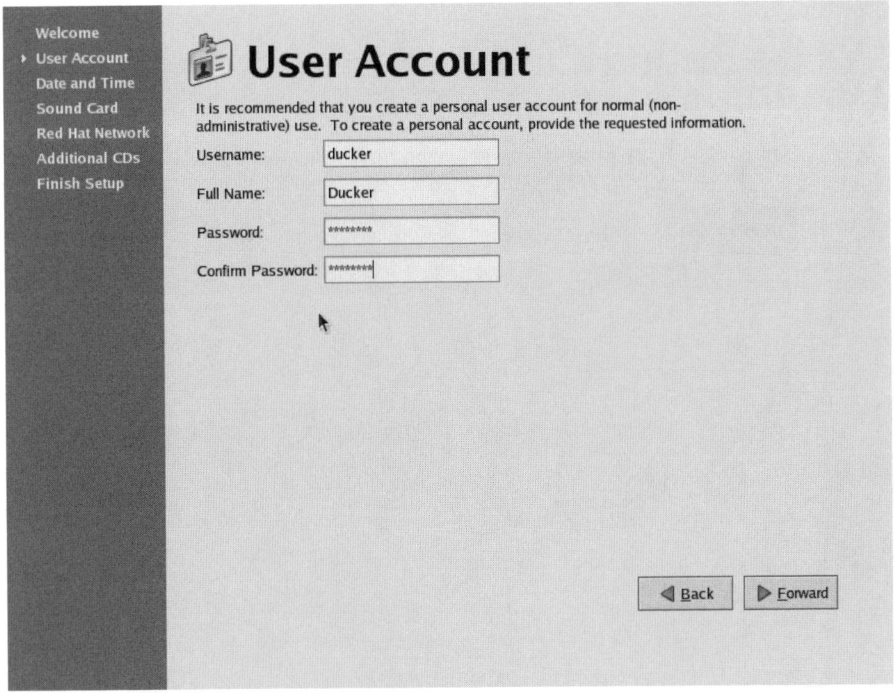

Welcome
User Account
Date and Time
Sound Card
Red Hat Network
Additional CDs
Finish Setup

User Account

It is recommended that you create a personal user account for normal (non-administrative) use. To create a personal account, provide the requested information.

Username: ducker
Full Name: Ducker
Password: ********
Confirm Password: ********

Back
Forward

Figure 8.27. Creating a user account. Type the password exactly the same in the confirm box. Passwords are case sensitive. Usernames should be lower case. Use this account (and not root) for routine work.

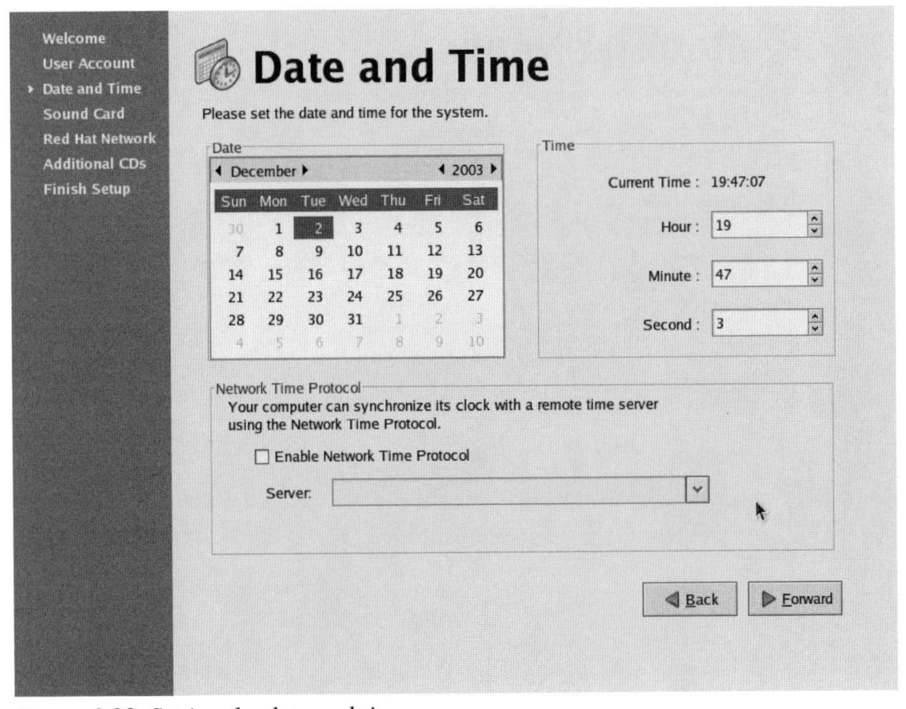

Figure 8.28. Setting the date and time.

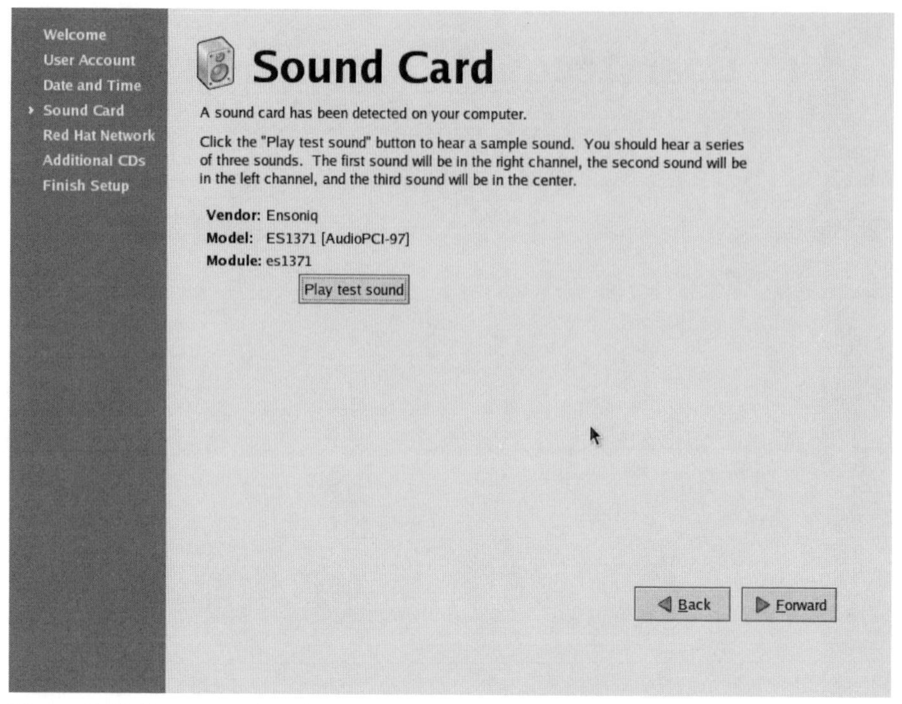

Figure 8.29. Your sound card will probably be automatically detected.

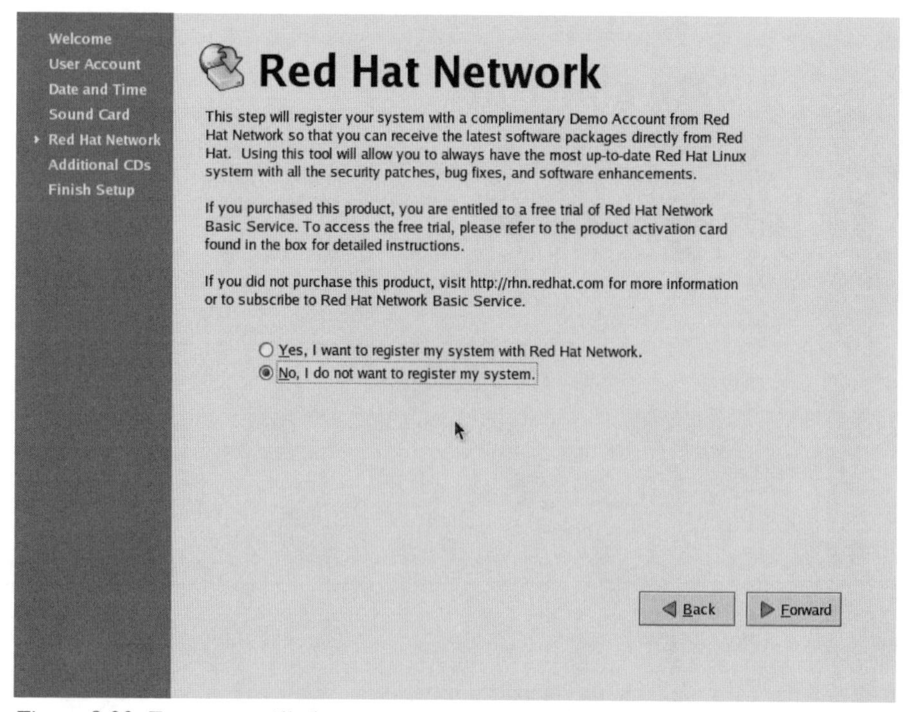

Figure 8.30. For now, we'll choose not to register Red Hat.

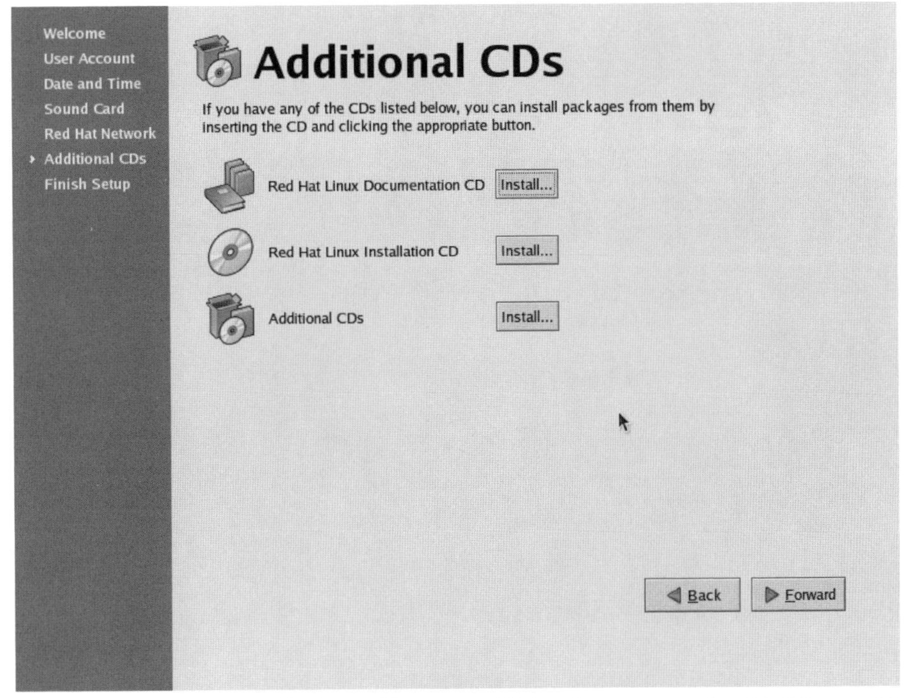

Figure 8.31. For now, we'll skip adding any additional programs. Just hit "Forward."

install the dual boot operating system. That's the purpose of a bootloader. It lets us choose between different operating systems at startup.

Windows XP also comes with its own bootloader. So, for example, if you have Windows 98 installed and then install Windows XP, the XP bootloader would allow a dual boot between Windows 98 and Windows XP. Windows 98 doesn't provide a bootloader, so you couldn't install Windows XP before Windows 98.

Congratulations! You've now installed a dual boot operating system on your new PC!

Modifying GRUB

We're going to show you how to modify the GRUB bootloader. This step is optional. First, login as root (Figure 8.32 and 8.33). In general, only login as root when you plan to make changes to your operating system. For other common uses, use a non-root account. This helps prevent you from inadvertently changing the operating system. Navigate to the simple word

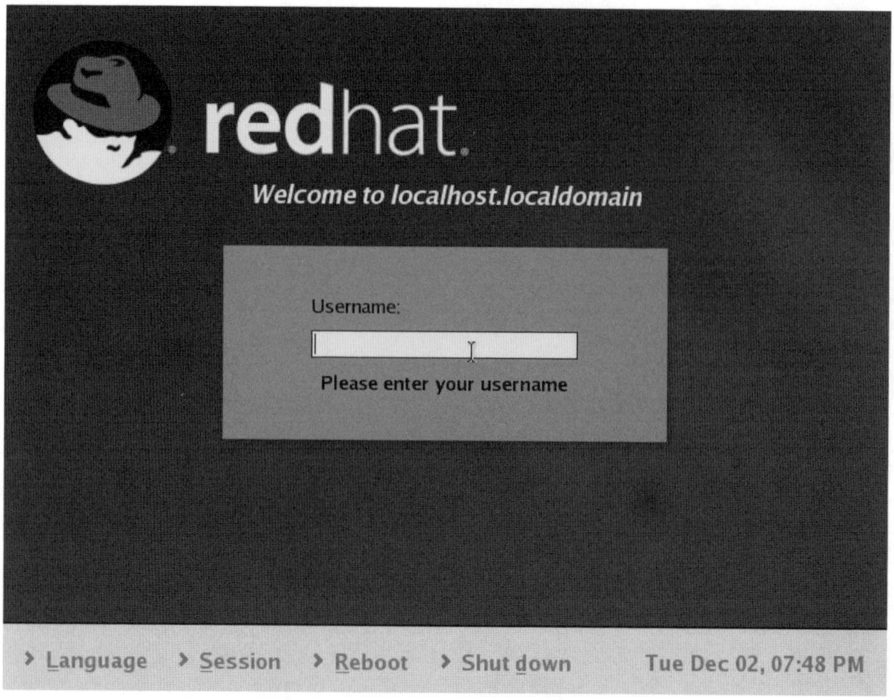

redhat.
Welcome to localhost.localdomain
Username:
Please enter your username
Language
Session
Reboot
Shut down
Tue Dec 02, 07:48 PM

Figure 8.32. After booting to Red Hat, we're asked for our username. Hit "Enter" after entering your username to go to the password screen.

redhat.
Welcome to localhost.localdomain
Password:
Language
Session
Reboot
Shut down
Tue Dec 02, 07:48 PM

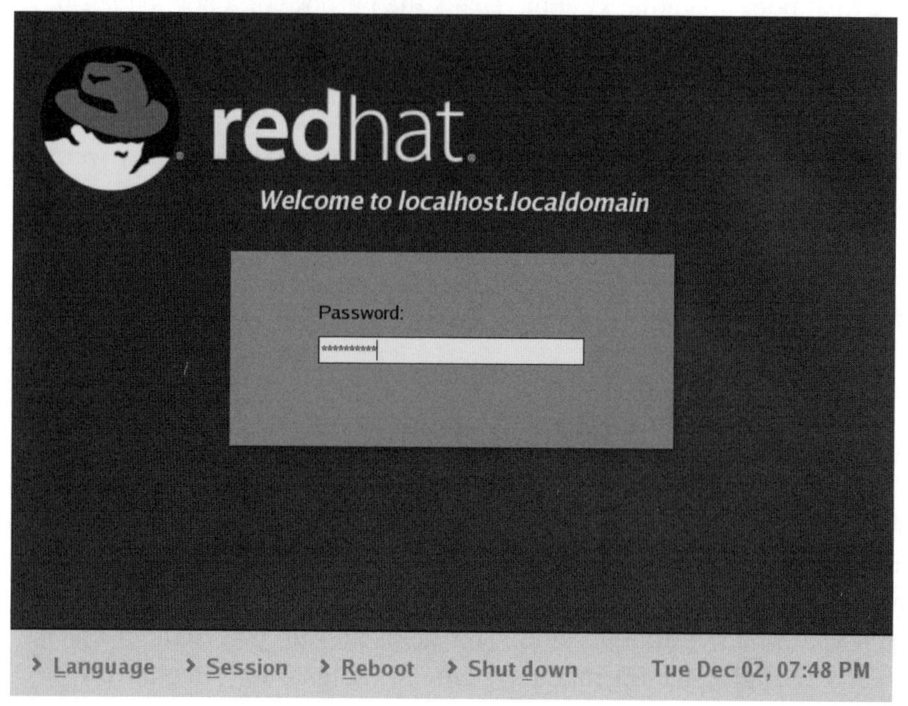

Figure 8.33. Red Hat password screen. Enter your case-sensitive password and hit "Enter."

Figure 8.34. One of many Red Hat GUIs (Graphical User Interface). Click on the red hat at the lower left corner to see the menu. Notice toward the middle of the task bar, four squares are shown with one highlighted. These correspond to individual workspaces. For example, if you open a word processor in the current workspace, click one of the other squares and open another program there, each workspace will contain its own programs. So, it's like having four monitor screens available.

processor called gedit (Figures 8.34 to 8.36). Gedit is handy for Linux shell scripting and for making changes to configuration files.

Now, go to "File...Open" on the menu (Figure 8.37) and navigate to the directory /etc. Inside the directory /etc, you'll see a file called grub.conf (Figure 8.38). This is the configuration file for the Grub bootloader. As a general rule, if you're making changes to configuration files, it's good to save a backup copy somewhere in case you want to revert. But, for the simple changes we're making, we'll just directly modify the grub configuration file.

We will change the "Timeout" value to 20 (Figure 8.39), which means that we want the default operating system to boot after 20 seconds. Before 20 seconds have elapsed, you'll see the Grub bootloader screen which will allow you to choose either operating system. If you're fast on the draw, you might need less time. We increased the time from ten seconds to twenty.

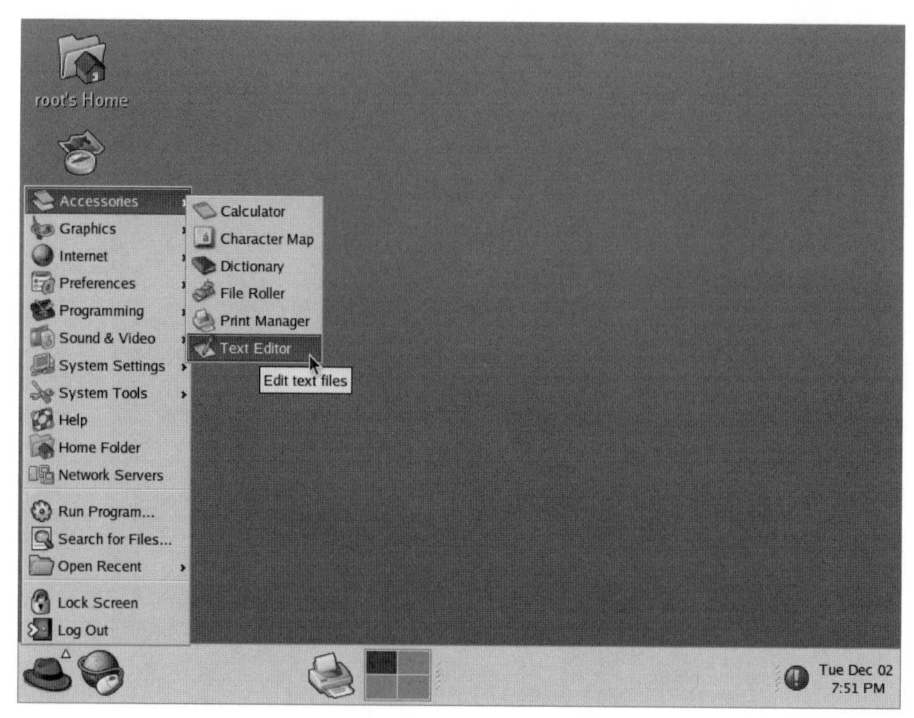

Figure 8.35. Go to Accessories...Text Editor to bring up the Text Editor.

Figure 8.36. The gedit text editor. This program can be used to modify Linux configuration files or do shell scripting.

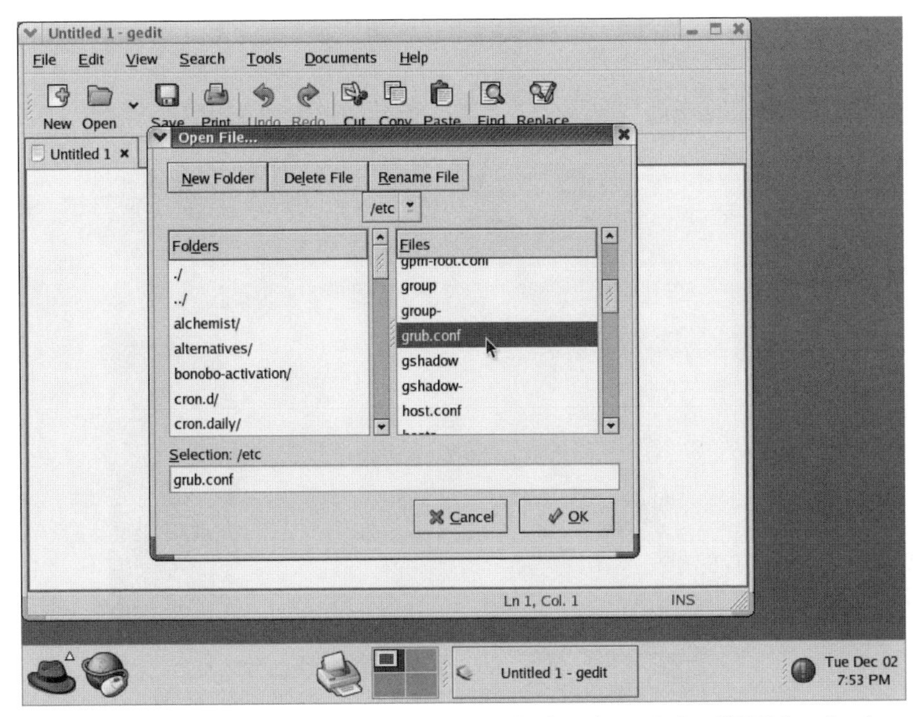

Figure 8.37. Navigate to the /etc directory and find grub.conf, the GRUB bootloader configuration file. All folders start in the root directory denoted as "/" (slash).

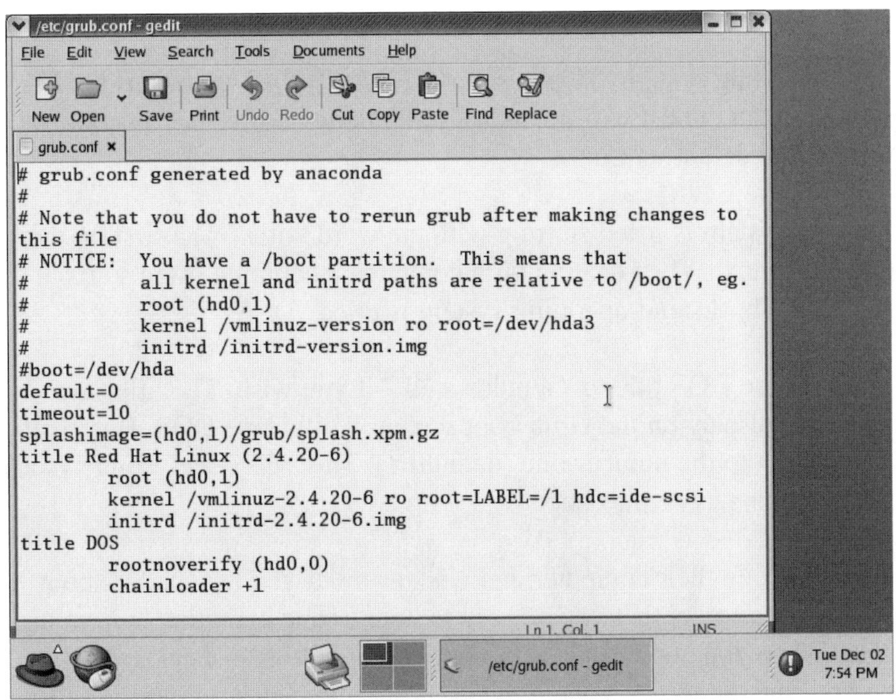

Figure 8.38. Opening grub.conf we see the multiple boot options each listed under its own "title" (See Figure 8.25). One is DOS, which we could change to "Windows XP."

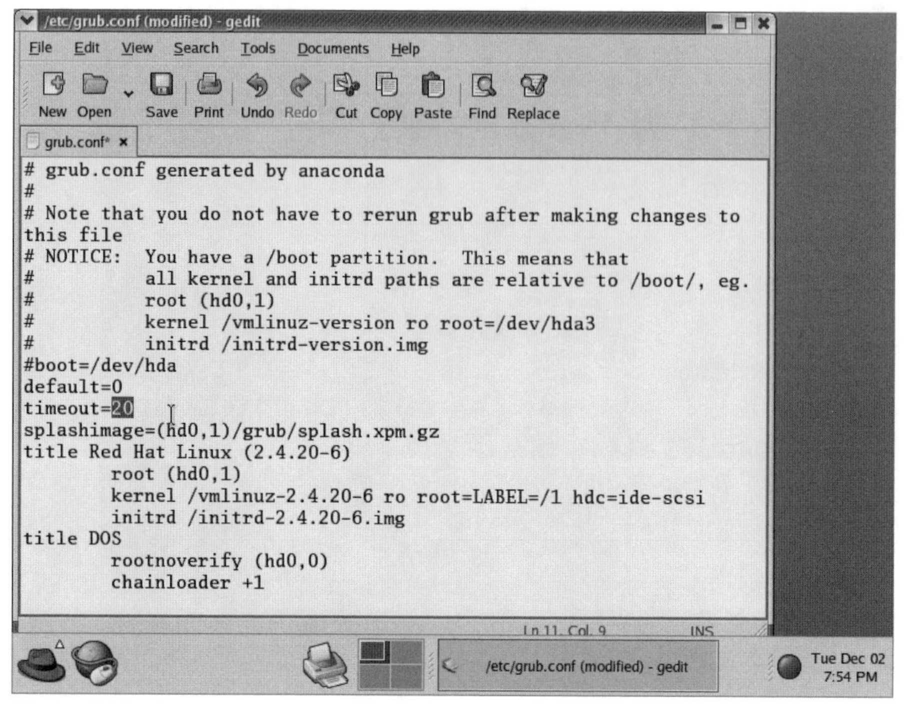

Figure 8.39. Timeout sets how long we have to select the OS to boot. After the timeout, if no other choice is made, the default OS is loaded.

The default operating system value is set at 0 (default=0). This means the first operating system on the list will be booted to by default, after the timeout has expired. Here, the default is Linux.

Each operating system is listed starting with the word "title." The first on the list is Red Hat Linux. When dealing with computers, counting often starts at 0 rather than one. The second operating system is titled "DOS."

You can change the DOS title to "Windows XP" if you wish. The title says what words will display on the Grub boot screen. We'll leave DOS. But, we'll change the default to the number one (default=1). This will select Windows as the default operating system to boot.

Many people start up their computer and walk away. If you have a dual boot system, it's easy to forget that you wanted to boot to one operating system and not another. When you come back with your cup of coffee, or Pepsi, or whatever, you find the wrong operating system has booted. And, you need to restart. So, it's best to have the operating system you use most commonly set

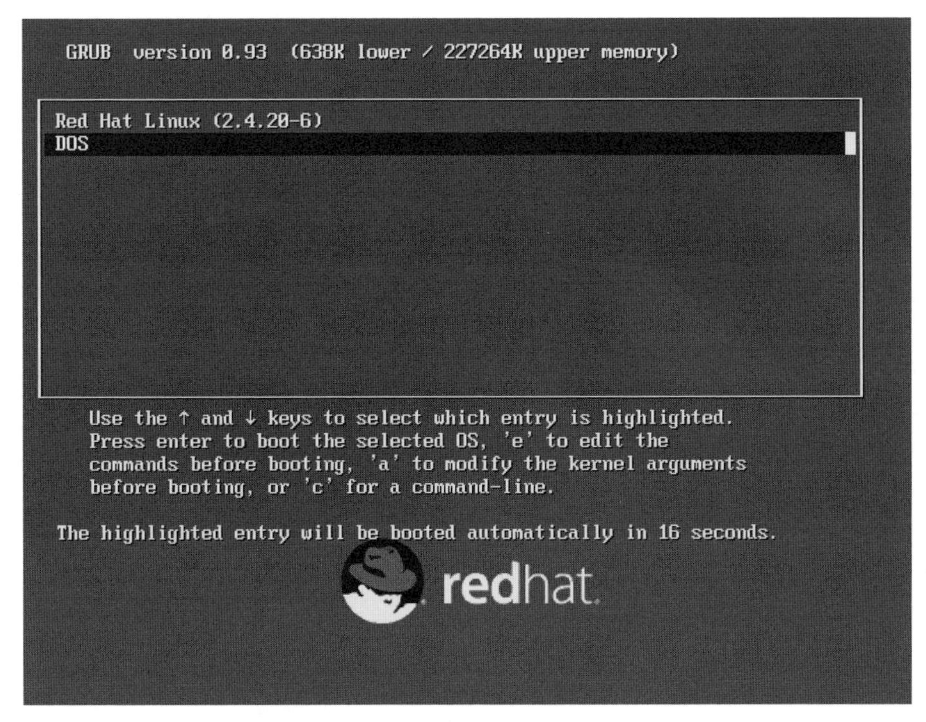

Figure 8.40. The timeout has been changed. Here we have 16 seconds left to choose our operating system before the default is selected. Notice, we have also changed the default to "DOS" (Windows XP) which is now highlighted.

as the default. We now save our changes and restart our computer to see that the second operating system on the list (DOS) is highlighted. And, we see that we have more time to make up our mind to choose an operating system. It says we have 16 seconds remaining to choose the non-default operating system (Figure 8.40).

Linux is based upon Unix which was written by computer programmers for use by computer programmers. If you think about it, suppose you had to write your own operating system. Rather than writing an operating system with a fancy GUI (Graphical User Interface, which Linux now uses), you'd probably write a basic command-line-based operating system. That would take the least amount of work, and you'd understand the operating system well, so working at the command line wouldn't bother you. Because of this origin, many things done on Unix or Linux today have a basis in a text file, such as the Grub bootloader using a text file to set the configuration settings.

Knowing how to modify or write text files so that they run as programs or as configuration files is known as Linux or Unix "shell scripting." Shell scripting is very powerful, because it can allow you to do things automatically that otherwise might take personal time. What you've just done is basic shell scripting.

More advanced shell scripts can be written. For example, suppose you're a network administrator for a company and you need to install Linux on one hundred different computers. You could go through the installation process in this chapter, using the graphical Linux installer. But, that would take a lot of time.

Another option would be to write a script that installs Linux on all one hundred computers over the network. All you'd need to do is run the script once from one computer, and you'd be done. This shows the power of shell scripting. Don't forget to call your boss and let him know you'll be working from home the next day. Yawn and tell him you had a busy night installing Linux on all one hundred computers!

There are many websites and books to help you learn more about Linux. Searching for "Linux" on google.com or at Amazon.com will bring up many resources to help you learn more.

Finally, we should note that there are other options that allow multiple boot operating systems. For example, software developers sometimes install a virtual PC, such as VMware (VMware.com) which is a software program that mimics a PC. You need a fast PC, but you can run multiple operating systems at the same time on the same computer with a virtual machine. This is a relatively expensive option.

Installing a special removable hard drive holder (also known as a hard drive rack) into one of the 5.25" drive bays is another option to achieve multiple boots. Cyberguys.com is one source of these devices. These drive racks install like any other 5.25" drive, and they hold standard 3.5" hard drives inside of a removable cassette case. You can purchase multiple cassettes to hold different hard drives. The cassette is easily and rapidly replaced from the front of the PC case when the system is off. This allows each person in a family or school to have their own cassette holding their own hard drive. Each cassette could have a different operating system installed on its hard drive.

With prices on DVD burners, video editing software, and PCI firewire cards dropping, even those on a limited budget can get into moviemaking.

So, You Want to Be The Next Steven Spielberg?

Choosing A DVD Burner

Today, DVD burners can be purchased for reasonable prices. Amazon.com offers a Sony 4x DVD±RW drive for $240. Currently, Best Buy offers a 4x +RW HP DVD300I (internal IDE) drive for $179. And, by the time you read this, prices should be even lower.

Often an "I" at the end of a drive model number means "Internal." And, an "E" at the end of the model number means "external." Internal drives are usually less expensive. So, unless you really need to move the drive between multiple PCs, you might want to purchase an internal drive and save some money. Many people purchase external drives because they aren't comfortable opening up their PC. But because you know how to build and upgrade a PC, an internal DVD IDE drive is a great choice.

Internal IDE DVD drives install just like any other IDE drive, such as your CD-RW drive or your computer's hard drive. At the back of the drive, there will be a jumper to configure the drive as master, slave, or cable select. There will be a molex power connector to power the drive. There will be an IDE ribbon cable to send and receive signals between the drive and the mainboard.

So, once you've installed a CD drive, you know everything you need to know to install DVD drives.

Put a DVD drive on the mainboard's secondary IDE interface. Try to leave the mainboard's primary IDE interface exclusively for your computer's hard drive. If you have both a DVD drive and a CD-RW drive, you probably should put both on the secondary IDE interface, before adding a second device to the primary IDE interface. This is because only one device can send and receive signals through the IDE ribbon cable at one time. You don't want your computer's main hard drive waiting for the DVD or CD drive to finish using the cable. The PC's main hard drive should have uninterrupted access to the mainboard.

In addition to internal IDE drives, there is a wide selection of external DVD burners using USB (the Universal Serial Bus) which allows the burner to be easily moved from PC to PC.

If you don't feel a need to burn DVDs, but you wish to watch DVD movies on your PC, you could purchase a DVD-ROM (Read only DVD) drive for about $30. Then, use a CD-RW drive to back up your system and make audio CDs. CD-RW disks typically hold about 650 MB of data, while DVD disks can hold 4.7 GB. So, if you don't have huge files, you might not need a DVD for backing up your important files. The CD-RW will work fine.

DVD disks holding video are referred to as DVD-Video disks. DVD-Video disks should play on any DVD-ROM, either in a DVD PC drive or in a stand-alone DVD player.

As with CD-RW speeds, DVD drive speeds are measured with a multiplier. For example, 1x DVD transfers data at about 1.3 MB/Sec. A 4x drive could transfer data at four times that speed or about 5.2 MB/Sec. Compare this to the 0.15 MB/Sec data transfer for a 1x CD-RW and you'll see DVD drives are much faster. Almost ten times faster.

All DVD videos play at 1x speed. And, because DVDs are extremely fast relative to CDs, you probably won't need a very fast DVD burner. A 4x speed is more than enough horsepower.

DVD burners will also write to CDs and read from CDs, so you won't really need a CD-RW drive, if you have a DVD burner. However, it's common to see both a CD-RW and a DVD-ROM drive on one PC. A PC with both a CD-RW and a DVD burner is also common.

When selecting a DVD burner, you'll want to consider the format that the drive can write and the software that's bundled with the drive. To date, there is no standard format for creating your own DVDs.

Today, there are two competing standards for the DVD format. They are known as the "Plus" and the "Minus" formats. DVD+R and DVD+RW are one format. They are called the "plus" format because of the plus sign. The other format is DVD-R and DVD-RW. These are the "minus" format.

DVD+R and DVD-R are the write-one-time versions of each format. DVD+RW and DVD-RW are the write and be-able-to-rewrite (RW stands for re-write) versions of each format. DVD+RW and DVD-RW can be written to about a thousand times. This situation is similar to CDs which have +R disks and +RW disks. +R disks can only be written to once at any disk location. +RW can be written to, erased, and rewritten to the same location.

To confuse things more, DVD-R format actually has two subformats, DVD-R(A) and DVD-R(G) where A stands for "Authoring" and G stands for "General."

Dual format drives can be purchased which can write to either format, plus or minus. These drives are referred to as DVD+-RW drives (or sometimes the ugly DVD+R/+RW/-R/-RW). The advantage to purchasing a dual format drive is that regardless of which format emerges as the standard, you'll be covered, because your drive won't wind up writing to an obsolete format.

However, with DVD drive prices dropping, I wouldn't worry too much about being left with the wrong format, if you can get a great price on a single-format DVD burner. For example, the HP DVD300I is only a plus format drive, but it's $60 less than the dual format Sony 4x DVD±RW. Is the dual format worth the extra $60? Only you can decide.

Currently, it looks like the plus format will win. It's supported by Hewlett Packard and Sony. And, many of the minus format companies are now making dual format drives.

Be sure you purchase the matching format DVD disks for your burner, either plus or minus format. You need to use DVD+R disks for the plus format drive. You need to use DVD-R disks for the minus format drive.

Either format can be used for creating videos, and either format can be used for backing up data. It's generally believed the DVD+ format is slightly better for data backup, while DVD- format might be slightly better for creating videos.

There is also another format called DVD-RAM which is considered the best-of-all for backing up data. DVD-RAM disks are usually inside cartridges that hold 4.7 GB per side. Each disk can be written to hundreds of thousands of times. DVD-RAM disks have an estimated life of 100 years. But, DVD-RAM disks will only read in drives that are specially designed for that format. And, these drives tend to be more expensive. The average home user is probably better off with the DVD plus or minus formats.

Technically, DVDs work a lot like CDs. Data is recorded via pits. DVDs use a shorter length laser which allows the pits to be spaced closer together. This allows more data to be recorded on the disk.

For more information about DVDs, check out http://www.dvddemystified.com/dvdfaq.html

DVD Software

After choosing a format, it's important to look at the software that comes with the DVD drive. For example, Digital Research has an Internal DVD+RW drive that comes with Pinnacle Instant CD, Pinnacle Studio 8, and WinDVD. Pinnacle Studio 8 is a superior program for digital video editing. You might pay quite a bit for a stand alone version of Studio 8. So, if your goal is to produce videos, you might want to select a DVD burner that comes with quality video production software. That can save you some money.

The HP DVD300I comes with ArcSoft ShowBiz DVD, Veritas RecordNow and DLA and Simple Backup. That bundle of software probably isn't as great.

Verbatim DVD burners come with Nero Express, Vision Express, InCD, Sonic MyDVD, and WinDVD.

Typically, the software included with a DVD burner will include software for watching DVD movies (WinDVD), software for creating and editing videos (Studio 8 or ArcSoft), and software for using your DVD burner as a backup device (InCD or Nero Express). Windows Media Player will also play DVD movies.

FireWire 1394 Versus USB 2.0

Now, to get video into your computer, you'll need an input bus with a fast data transfer rate. The two basic choices are FireWire 1394 (which transfers data at up to 50 MB/Sec) and USB 2.0. Many people believe USB 2.0 will eventually replace FireWire. Either one should work great. (For $50 you can purchase PCI expansion cards that add both FireWire and USB ports to your PC.)

Your video camera can determine whether you use USB or FireWire. Some video cameras have FireWire output while others have USB output capability. Incidentally, if you wish to convert your personal VHS tapes to DVD, you'd also need a video camera which supports an analog input. Then, you could record your VHS into the digital video camera and out onto your computer with FireWire or USB.

If your DVD burner didn't come with good video editing software, purchasing an expansion card for FireWire or USB gives you a second chance to get a good deal. For example, if you want professional level editing software, Pyro Professional bundles a FireWire card with the full version of Adobe Premier for under $500. Premier is a top-notch program for video editing. You'll pay as much purchasing the stand-alone version of Premier as you pay for the full version bundled with the FireWire card.

For more information about getting started in DVD video creation, I recommend http://www.videoguys.com/started.html. VideoGuys.com also has great reviews of other card/software options for up-and-coming video producers.

As with your DVD burner, always examine the software that's bundled with your video input card. You'll usually want the full version, not a watered down program.

If you already have a FireWire card and if you're a student, another option is to purchase student software. Student software is typically fully equivalent to the full retail version. But, the software companies often charge students much less for it. For example, Adobe typically offers student versions of its main programs (PhotoShop, Premier, etc.) for under half of the cost of the retail version.

So, if you're a struggling film student following in the footsteps of Robert Rodriguez, you'll need to sell fewer pints of blood to shoot your films by taking advantage of student software discounts! It's interesting to note that computer video production systems that would have cost many tens of thousands of dollars only a few years ago can be purchased or built today for under a thousand dollars. That's the general rule of computers. As time goes by, prices come down and PCs become more powerful. You get more, and you pay less. That works for me.

What's Next? Careers In PC Repair

While this book provides all the information you need to successfully build your own PC, if you wish to learn more about computers and PC repair, I recommend the following more advanced books: *PC Hardware in a Nutshell* by Robert and Barbara Thompson; and *Upgrading and Repairing PCs* by Scott Mueller.

If you really enjoy fiddling with PCs and if you're looking for a computer-related career, one way to build your resume is to add PC repair skills. To certify PC repair technicians, CompTIA (http://www.comptia.org) offers A+ certification.

A+ Certification involves taking two multiple choice tests to demonstrate your knowledge of PC repair. One test is about hardware. The other test is about operating systems. If you successfully pass both tests, you become A+ certified. Each test costs about $200. To help you study for the A+ exam, many good books exist, including *A+ Certification All-in-One Exam Guide* by Michael Meyers.

Many people earn extra money by offering PC upgrading and repair services. When he was a college student studying biology, Michael Dell decided to earn extra money by building PCs in his dorm room and selling them through mail order ads. His business became successful. And, he dropped out of college to devote full time to building Dell Computer. Today, Michael Dell is a billionaire, and Dell is a respected name in personal computers. Rumor has it that Michael's mom still wants him to return to college and finish his degree, just so he has something to fall back on. Moms are like that!

If you're interested in learning more about starting a business in the PC repair field, I recommend *Start Your Own Computer Business: Building a Successful PC Repair and Service Business by Supporting Customers and Managing Money* by Morris Rosenthal.

Even if you don't aspire to work in the PC repair field, knowing how to build and repair your own computers is a valuable skill. You'll be able to save some money, and you'll be confident when you perform future PC upgrades, whether at home or on-the-job. Plus, you'll understand far more about how software interacts with hardware, understanding concepts such as software drivers. If you found this book useful, I hope you'll visit amazon.com and post a positive review. We appreciate your support! Congratulations on learning how to build your own PC! Charlie and Ducker.

Recommended Reading And Other Resources

For those who want to learn more about PCs, I recommend these resources:

Books

Build Your Own PC, Third Edition by Morris Rosenthal. This book is a photo-intensive guide to building your own PC. It's aimed at the beginner to intermediate-level builder.

Building a PC for Dummies by Mark L. Chambers. Covers satellite Internet and some things not covered in other books.

PC Hardware in a Nutshell, 2nd Edition by Robert Bruce Thompson and Barbara Fritchman Thompson. A more advanced book (an 800-page nutshell!) for those who want to understand hardware selection at a deeper level. (The authors also have a companion website, hardwareguys.com, which gives their current hardware recommendations.)

Upgrading and Repairing PCs by Scott Mueller. This is a huge book. You might only want to read the parts of it that interest you at the time. This book is a standard text in many computer repair classes and has sold over two million copies. Scott Mueller is to PC repair what Michael Jordan is to basketball. For the intermediate to advanced builder. The companion website is UpgradingAndRepairingPCs.com

Upgrading and Repairing Networks (3rd Edition) by Terry Ogletree.

Internet Sites

http://www.tech-report.com
(http://www.tech-report.com/reviews/) has many mainboard reviews.

google.com. Once you find a mainboard that interests you, search google.com for reviews of that particular mainboard by entering the name of the mainboard. For example, if you contemplate purchasing an Abit Is7 mainboard, type "Abit Is7" into google.com and look for reviews of it. In fact, google.com is probably one of your best resources to obtain information about nearly anything. Try searching on various keyword combinations about the topic.

http://www.pcguide.com This website is highly recommended. It provides a wealth of information about how computers work. A good place to start is with the "Introduction to the PC" at http://www.pcguide.com/intro/index.htm

http://www.pcworld.com

TomsHardware.com. Another great site. It also includes a complete guide to building a PC. A good place to start is with "Tom's Guides."

http://www.anantech.com

http://www.computing.net

http://www.buildeasypc.com

http://www.pcmech.com (Information about building PCs)

http://www.amd.com (AMD has information about building a PC with their Athlon processors, including a complete pdf booklet which discusses proper airflow, cooling, and more.)

Index